TIME TOWARD HOME

Other Books by RICHARD JOHN NEUHAUS

Theology and the Kingdom of God (Editor)
Movement and Revolution (with Peter L. Berger)
In Defense of People

Richard John Neuhaus

TIME TOWARD HOME

The American Experiment
as Revelation

A Crossroad Book

THE SEABURY PRESS, NEW YORK

for

Abraham Joshua Heschel, 1907–1972

Arthur Carl Piepkorn, 1907–1973

fathers in God

The Seabury Press
815 Second Avenue
New York, N.Y. 10017

Library of Congress Cataloging in Publication Data

Newhaus, Richard John.
    Time toward home.

    "A Crossroad books."
    Includes index.
    1. United States—Religion—1945-   2. United
States—Civilization—1945-   I. Title.
BR526.N42   200'.973   75-5714
ISBN 0-8164-0272-8

Contents

Debts

Rabbi Abraham Joshua Heschel and Father Arthur Carl Piepkorn were scholars of two quite different traditions, the one of Hasidic Judaism and the other of classical Lutheranism, yet both helped me understand our common hope for the home we hail from afar. The dedication of this book to their memory is slight measure of the debt owed them.

Once again, my thanks to the people and pastors of the Church of St. John the Evangelist, Brooklyn, New York. On them I continue to count for what is home so far from home.

Peter and Brigitte Berger persist in transcending the trials of friendship. Robert and Carol Wilken are supportive even in their exile from the prolepsis of the New Jerusalem that may be New York City. Thomas and Betty Edge provide welcome respite from duties, especially from the self-imposed ones. William Purdy and Michael Kerrine have contributed to this book in ways beyond their understanding, and mine. The people at *Worldview* magazine, especially James Finn, Susan Woolfson and Florence Norton, have been more than patient. For his editorial suggestions I am grateful to Justus George Lawler of Seabury Press.

In various ways and degrees, they are all responsible for the views and whatever may be the strengths and weaknesses of this book.

A Word to the Prospective Reader

This is a book of theology, cultural criticism, politics, philosophy and ethics, among other things. Whether the result is a reckless careening across interdisciplinary lines or a synthesis of usually diverse angles of vision is for the reader to judge. It is one way of trying to view the American experiment with religious seriousness.

The theological heart of the argument, and the heart of the book, is chapter 7. Chapters 1 through 5 deal with contemporary culture and its sense of the future, or lack thereof. Chapters 10 through 13 treat more explicitly the philosophical and religious components in our understanding of time and its promise. The ethical implications are spelled out in chapters 14 through 18, and the argument concludes with two chapters on "public piety" and some practical steps for reviving the vision of the commonweal to which the American experiment must be redirected.

The author believes in the sovereignty of politics in the making of history. It is not, of course, an absolute sovereignty; politics is checked by many forces, from the economic to the biological; but politics is the chief enterprise to which we must attend in bringing about the changes we desire. A further bias is that politics is a function of culture. That is, the culture proposes or excludes the possibilities which are the subject of political decision. And at the heart of culture is religion—the ways we give meaning to reality and the values by which we would live.

In America today there is little vision, and the people perish because we have become repressive and tongue-tied about the religious meanings that motor our social experiment. The answer is not to "return to religion." It is rather to become more honest and articulate about the religious dynamics that do in fact shape our public life. Such honesty leads not to a return but to heightened anticipation of what America may yet be. In a time of widespread pessimism, it might be tempting to write an upbeat book about America. I hope that temptation has been successfully resisted. I do believe, however, that within history, including the history we call America, there is a destiny, although at present it is far from manifest. This book is about that destiny which brings our past and present under judgment and directs us in time toward home.

R.J.N.

Brooklyn, New York
The Day of St. John the Evangelist,
December 27, 1974

1

A Sense of Journey's End

America's bicentennial celebration promises to be more requiem than revival. "A sense of an ending," one critic has suggested, "is the distinctive literary image of the time."[1] The mood is not confined to literature, but pervades every field of reflection. We are sated by the apocalyptic. In sociology, history, political science and economics, few words are more frequently encountered than the word *post*. That there is a future we are not certain; that the past is finished there is no doubt. The intuitions of what will be are hinged upon the termination of what has been. Whatever else may be said of our time, it is, in Peter Drucker's phrase, the "age of discontinuity."[2]

Examples abound. Economist Ralf Dahrendorf declares that we are living in a *postcapitalist society* in which class warfare has been replaced by the tension between governmental elites and the rest of us. George Lichtheim describes our time as *postbourgeois*. "There cannot be a bourgeoisie without a proletariat, and if the one is fading out, so is the other, and for the same reason: Modern industrial society does not require either for its operation." Amitai Etzioni begins the argument of his *The Active Society* with the assurance that we are in a *postmodern era*. Sam Beer *(British Politics in the Collectivist Age)* describes contemporary politics as *postcollectivist*. The Preacher of Ecclesiastes notwithstanding ("Of making many books there is no end"), Marshall McLuhan has convinced many that ours is a *postliterature culture*. Reaching yet further, Kenneth Boulding asserts this is the *postcivilized era*. But they will all have to go some to reach the more ultimate heights achieved by sociologist S. N. Eisenstadt with his *posttraditional society*, not to mention Roderick Seidenberg's entry, *posthistoric man*. Compared with these more adventuresome souls, Daniel Bell seems excessively modest in announcing merely *the coming of postindustrial society*.

Nor can religious thinkers be accused of withholding their benedictions from the rites of ending. I resist the temptation to cite the most obvious, the sundry madnesses that paraded under the Dionysiac banners proclaiming the death of God around the Year of Our Lord 1963. Sufficient to the point is the sober judgment of historian Sydney Ahlstrom in his distinguished *A Religious History of the American People* that our period is

1

"a time of calamities. As the American people moved toward the bicentennial of the nation's independence, they could see few living signs of the self-confidence and optimism that had marked the centennial observances of 1876, and even less of the revolutionary generation's bold assurance. . . . The nation's organic connections with the sources of its idealism and hope were withered."[3] Our situation, he writes elsewhere, is *post-Puritan, post-Protestant* and *post-Christian.*[4] So pervasive is the sense of ending that any more sanguine conclusion would certainly have been faulted for failing to come to grips with the crises of our times, or for ignoring the revolutionary impact of changes occurring with unprecedented rapidity, or for holding out false hopes in a day of hopelessness or for some other high crime against the intellectual consensus.[5]

The "theology of hope" that emerged in the late 1960s would, from the sound of it, appear to be an antidote to the moods of dejection. And in fact it was frequently and, I think, superficially criticized for being optimistic, even Pollyannaish. In its intellectually serious and more lasting forms—as presented by Jürgen Moltmann and, most particularly, by Wolfhart Pannenberg—it did indeed provide "a reason for the hope that is within you" (1 Peter 3:15). But in its more facilely politicized forms, as with James Cone and, more particularly Gustavo Gutierrez, the theology of hope was little more than the baptismal sprinkling of various revolutionary ideologies that licensed extravagant apocalypticism in the face of the irredeemable evil of past and present.[6] Thus refugee radicalisms from the 1960s found a home in religious thought.

The interdependence, indeed symbiosis, of hope and despair is frequently manifest. In "the Movement" of the 1960s many half-believers in the revolution thought their radical words and actions not really all that threatening, since the much-detested liberal establishment could be counted upon to pull things out of the fire.[7] Similarly, the white, upper-middle-class celebrants of Charles Reich's *The Greening of America* took it for granted that the lesser, Consciousness II, types would do the necessary work to keep the system going.[8] It is not so clear what is the basis for hope among those who now greet with unrestrained glee the prospect of economic disaster set forth in the Club of Rome's *Limits to Growth* and similar literature predicting ecotastrophe. One suspects the glee will be short-lived if or when the consequences of collapse begin to impinge too directly upon the conveniences to which we have grown accustomed.

People who want to change *everything* usually assume that the things that really matter to them will somehow be exempted. As Peter Berger has observed, the only revolutionary who can be trusted is the sad revolutionary.[9] In its politically bowdlerized forms which omitted the indelicate dimensions of historical modesty, the theology of hope posited the certain coming of a "Kingdom of God" that was indistinguishable from the fulfillment of whatever radical projects engaged our loyalties now, the chief radical project being the condemnation of all that is and has been. Thus, far from being an antidote to despair, the theology of hope was seen as an invitation to despair's wholehearted, even orgiastic, indulgence.

Whether in melancholia, in panic or in religious-revolutionary ecstasy, many experience our time as a sense of ending. It is sensed most particularly as an *American* ending. To be sure, many environmental prophets envision an ending that encompasses the whole of Spaceship Earth, at least. The more political see the end of America with all its pomps and all its ways, overcome by the revolutionary rage of the Third World. Other critics, of a more cultural bent, look hopefully beyond the end of America to the wisdom of the East that will reconstitute our social and spiritual reality. The more exotic the alternative, the more hopeful it is. The more unknown, the more it is devoutly accepted by faith. It is the known that is intolerable. The one inadmissible alternative is that there should be an American future.

The mood is caught in the title of Peter Schrag's *The End of the American Future.* [10] It is a generic title; the brand-name versions are to be discovered by the hundreds in any respectable bookstore. In calling it a mood I do not suggest it can be dismissed by an act of will or that it has no basis in fact. Moods too have their reasons. Although intellectuals are notoriously prone to fashion, and although their perceptions reinforce one another, no conspiracy of writers, publishers and media people contrived one day to declare this the decade of despair for America.

While it is true that we live in the world not as it is but as we describe it to be, our descriptions are in response to real events. They may not always be rational responses, of course. My dissatisfaction with a friend may have nothing to do with the friend and everything to do with my having a headache. But the headache is real. As are Vietnam and inflation and slums and Vietnam and Watergate and unemployment and racism and Vietnam. Whether declaring the end of the American future, whatever that may mean, is the rational response to these real events is another matter. My acceptance of the end may simply guarantee that others will be in charge of the future.

Elisabeth Kübler-Ross has skillfully analyzed approaches to death and dying. [11] The first stage, she writes, is denial and isolation, the second is anger, the third, bargaining, and the fourth and fifth are depression and acceptance. Beyond that, it is to be hoped, is hope. My argument may be placed somewhere between denial, anger and bargaining. Which means this book refuses to face reality. Unless, of course, the reality is that America is not dead or dying. In which case, we have arrived, somewhat ahead of schedule, at hope.

2

Looking Homeward

If there is one place where the prefix *post* would seem unquestionably appropriate in describing our time, it is in saying that this time is post-Vietnam. By the beginning of the seventies America's misbegotten war in Indochina was not over, of course, in the real world of events. But in the world as we describe it, in the world of consciousness and of moods, we were living post-Vietnam.

Because, contrary to what many seem to believe, America has not dismantled the "Vietnam wars policy" that invites further such conflicts, it is necessary to keep in mind the tension between the world of external events and the world of public moods. We should be wary of the element of wishful thinking that goes into speaking about this time as post-Vietnam. That which is intolerable we tend to deny. Already in 1968 people, myself included, were writing about "America after Vietnam." It was intolerable to think that the war should continue, and reach even more destructive heights, through another five years. In the one year after the conclusion of "peace" in Indochina, more Vietnamese were killed than there were Americans killed in the previous ten years of the struggle. The web that tied of the fate of America to that of the dictatorships of the world's Saigons is strained but far from broken. So it is with severe reservations that we speak of our time being post-Vietnam.

The mood is post-Vietnam. Exercising the skills of selective perception, excluding inconvenient evidence, we have persuaded ourselves that we have put Vietnam behind us. If four or seven years from now we are again embroiled, directly and massively, in such wars, we will give that period a new name. We will not perceive it as the continuation of the Vietnam war, which it most certainly will be. Such observations may seem excessively pessimistic, for, after all, have we not "learned the lessons" of Vietnam? Hegel, Marx and a host of others are credited with the observation that the only thing we learn from history is that we never learn from history. Too cynical perhaps, but closer to the truth than the sanguine confidence that America's disastrous defeat in Vietnam will preclude similar ventures in the future.

4

One reason for pessimism on this score is that we have put Vietnam behind us, so to speak, without any national effort to understand what it was all about. To be sure, we are inundated by books and commentaries on the "lessons" of Vietnam, but these are of interest chiefly to a dwindling circle that has about it the faint scent of being left over from the dissent and protest of the tumultuous sixties. By national effort I mean that which is done through the institutions that provide social and political legitimacy. And, bitter truth to tell, the national response to Vietnam was accurately articulated in the election and reelection of Richard Nixon. What he was selling, and what the American people bought, was a way to end the pain without examining the disease. He promised a shortcut to the post-Vietnam era, bypassing self-examination, confession, repentance and redemption. Of course, societies do not repent. Individuals repent. But there can be social approximations of repentance, quasi-religious rituals whereby wrongs are acknowledged and there is a corporate resolve to begin anew. That touches on the field of civil religion, as it is called, to which we shall return shortly. The point here is that Nixon offered the alternative of evading the acknowledgment of wrong, and the American people chose that alternative. And of course Mr. Ford was operating by the Nixon mandate also, as his friends on the right of the Republican Party constantly tried to remind him.

The carefully orchestrated return of the prisoners of war in early 1973 was the supreme ritual of evasion. "Peace with honor" had been achieved by refusing to examine the meaning of either peace or honor. The "post-Vietnam era" came into being by presidential fiat, to which a war-wearied American populace sighed its amen. The question of amnesty for prisoners and exiles who had in various ways resisted the war could not be entertained. Later, under President Ford, there was a program of "earned reentry," an offer that, with few exceptions, resisters understandably declined. A real amnesty raised painful uncertainties about the meaning of the war and, yet more intolerable, about the meaning of honor. These are precisely the questions Nixon promised to help us forget. Vietnam is past. It is so because we say it is so. And because he was able for so long to command the institutions and symbols of legitimacy, Nixon succeeded in imposing, also upon his opponents, the post-Vietnam mood. In truth, the deception was as welcomed by his opponents as by his supporters, for all sides were tired of the tedious debate over a war that refused to end and was therefore simply declared no longer to exist. Only the Vietnamese, victimized by the bombs and terror of continuing war, were denied the sweet relief of the dawning of the post-Vietnam era.

But, the more hopeful reading of recent history might ask, does not

Watergate and the public reaction to it represent a repudiation of the dismal deceits described above? Perhaps so, at least in part. We can leave aside for the moment whether the whole cluster of events called Watergate tells us more about the strengths or weaknesses of our social order. That is, are we more impressed by the disease exposed or by the fact that it was exposed and remedies were sought? The same question arises in connection with racism, poverty and a host of other social ills. Whether one is more struck by the problem, and is therefore depressed, or by the response to the problem, and therefore hopeful, is no doubt largely a matter of temperament. And maybe of distancing. Foreigners regularly express amazement at the way we Americans air our problems with an apparently inexhaustible supply of shock and indignation. Here at home we take small comfort in such admiration and are convinced of the need to battle an endless succession of insufferable "crises." Perhaps that is just as well, for surely there would be little prospect for needed change were we Americans to "grow up," as especially our European cousins say we ought, and, muting our outrage, resign ourselves to the intolerable. We will later return to the question of whether American "moralism," which some thinkers, both foreign and domestic, deem so dangerously immature is not in fact a saving dynamic in the American experience.

The unhappy fact about the outrage over Watergate is that, far from being a repudiation of the deceit that brought Richard Nixon to power, it may compound the climate of mendacity which is the chief environmental problem in our public life. Watergate was not so much a moment of truth, revealing the horrible truths of the past decade or more, as an emetic. Nixon was selling a lie and, if the polls are to be believed, most of the people, even many who supported him, knew it was a lie. But it was thought to be a necessary lie, a pretense which, formally declared the truth, could put behind us what we lacked the courage to try to understand. As it turned out, we got more than we bargained for.

The lie about Vietnam and what that war did to us and said about us turned out to be a huge chunk of rancid meat that we simply could not digest. Watergate was the emetic by which we threw it up, and with it all the filth the lie was intended to cover. Since, understandably, few people have the stomach to sift through the filth, we may never as a people examine the lessons of Vietnam. Those who insist upon such an examination will be viewed as morbid or as afflicted by a sick preoccupation with the excrement of a passing period of national aberration. Most Americans will feel we are at least two steps removed from Vietnam and all that. The first step was the lie we bought, the second the purgation called Watergate. It is the succession of events stemming from Watergate that will be remembered, enabling us to dismiss all that led up to that ritual of revulsion.

Even before Watergate there were efforts to minimize what the decade of war in Indochina might reveal about the American character at this moment in history. Some of the most seering indictments of American policy, such as David Halberstam's *The Best and the Brightest,* were largely content to lay the blame upon the country's patrician elites.[1] Other more ideological interpreters viewed the war as but one instance of the inevitably predatory ways of late capitalism in imperial decline. Yet others would stifle political and moral explanations of America's response to the war under various sociological theories. Daniel Patrick Moynihan, for example, asserts with his accustomed confidence that the domestic protest to the war resulted from curious demographic factors, population changes that have never happened before and will never happen again. Had there been no war at all, the sixties would not have been much different.[2] It is obviously a waste of time to try and discover large truths about the American experience in events that emerged merely from unprecedented and unrepeatable demographic quirks. One may, I hope without being unkind, note that some people have more of a stake than others in discouraging too vigorous an effort to locate responsibility for our policy disasters and for the lies by which, it was hoped, they could be removed from public consciousness.

Whether because it gets lost in the purgation of Watergate, or because we want to be persuaded by sophisticated rationalizations of the last ten years as a freakish period without lasting significance, the Vietnam war and its domestic consequences will, I suspect, be downplayed or dismissed in examinations of the state of the American soul. Deposited in an Orwellian memory hole, they never really happened. They were dropped into a psychic disposal unit during the cleanup following Watergate.

Thus two moods arrive at an awkward meeting. One, the end of the American future, the other, the "unusability" of our immediate past.[3] For purposes of defining the American reality, we find the present unacceptable, the immediate past unrepresentative and the future foreclosed. One way out of this awkwardness is to revert to some more usable past. Bypassing the inconvenient evidence of more recent history, we seize upon some moment in the past that seems more worthy of us and declare that to be the *real* America.

This stratagem is marvelously exemplified in the *New York Times* editorial "Ten Years Later," published on the tenth anniversary of the death of John F. Kennedy. We are reminded of the high idealism of the early 1960s, of the youthful vision in which promise outweighed peril, of Kennedy's call for "a grand and global alliance" in the "struggle against the common enemies of man: tyranny, poverty, disease and war itself." Somewhat sobered by the past ten years, the editors write, "The nation's mood now calls for a more limited goal—a return to its basic principles.

There are special grounds for thanksgiving today in the fact that the search for the road back has at least begun.''

The search for the road back. The experiment undertaken as a city upon a hill, as a light to the nations, as the harbinger of universal liberty, is now searching for the road back. The American David has encountered the Goliath that is history, and now returns, whimpering and frightened, to the house of Jesse. There are no more heroic illusions, no more pretensions to singularity. We tell ourselves that we are growing up and that the mark of growing up is to go back home. The mood of post-Vietnam America is one of going home again. If only we could remember where home was.

3

Returning to Where
We Have Never Been

There is no lack of guides on our homeward way. As at the holy places in Old Jerusalem, they importune the traveler at every step, plucking at his sleeve, whispering their secret knowledge, disparaging their competitors. As we approach the bicentennial, their number is fast multiplying. It is hard to know which guide to choose.

In our search for the sacred site that is "the real America," we are aided by extremely literate guides. Lowell D. Streiker and Gerald Strober work as a team. Their entry is *Religion and the New Majority*. [1] Although Michael Novak has the disconcerting habit of issuing regular and often contradictory revisions, the basic directions are clear enough in his *The Rise of the Unmeltable Ethnics*. [2] Especially popular among those who thought it a mistake to leave home in the first place is Dean Kelley's *Why Conservative Churches Are Growing*. [3] Finally, the Ur-text for all these manuals (although not always acknowledged as such), written by the real pioneers of the homeward trek, Richard M. Scammon and Ben J. Wattenberg, is *The Real Majority*. [4]

These books have in common an effort to make virtue of necessity. Increasing numbers of Americans who consider themselves liberal or radical have come to believe that the struggles of the 1960s for change and justice didn't "work." Although, as we have said, they have different ideas about where "home" might be found, each is sure that its discovery requires calling off the revolution and getting back to the way things were before everything started coming apart.

In their version of "return to normalcy," Streiker and Strober affirm Billy Graham as the man who can "catch the falling flag" and serve as the conscience for an essentially religious America in the years ahead. Dean Kelley has consulted the charts and computers and concluded that the market research favors the Southern Baptists, Missouri Lutherans, Mormons and other "conservatives." The sharp peddler of pieties will, according to Kelley, abandon the social-change field and return to the real business of religion which is religion (all of which, he admits, leaves him in an awkward position as a social-ministry officer of the National Council of Churches). Novak would have us abandon the habit of searching for rationality and universals—a search imposed upon "us" by the WASP imperialists—and return to thinking with the blood of our Italian, Greek, Hungarian, Slavic or whatever cultural-genetic heritage.[5] And of course everyone is familiar with Scammon and Wattenberg's housewife in a Dayton suburb—married to a machinist and possessing very rigid views on what they call "the social issue" (drugs, crime, busing, etc.). She is the archetype of the Real Majority whose hearts and minds (or at least hearts) must be won by anyone in search of a mass market, political, religious or other. (Never mind that a Cleveland newspaper discovered the woman who fitted perfectly the prescription. Her one son was a long-haired conscientious objector against the military draft, and she supported Eugene McCarthy in 1968.)

No one doubts that there is abroad in the country a widespread dissatisfaction with things as they are—more than usual dissatisfaction, or at least more universally articulated than usual. Whether one describes himself as alienated or as just fed up, he is with that majority of Americans who, according to the polls, believes all the major institutions of the country are failing, our problems will probably get worse before they get better, and nobody who is offering solutions, from the President on up, can really be trusted. The guides mentioned here all see themselves as addressing this pervasive dissatisfaction. In a way that they possibly do not see, they are also exploiting dissatisfaction.

Each is, almost by definition, an intellectual, yet each assumes a posture of rebellion against "the intellectuals." Without getting embroiled in the tedious debate about who is and who is not an intellectual, I would suggest that intellectuals are, broadly understood, those people who mint and market the metaphors by which a society understands itself. The reader of these four guidebooks might readily get the impression that the intellectual is a convenient scapegoat.

For Novak, "they" are the WASPs, a category that would seem to include everybody who does not consciously celebrate a genetic history stemming from the regions of the Mediterranean or Eastern Europe. (In subsequent revisions, Novak usually prefers "British-American" to "WASP," and the definition of "ethnic" has demonstrated wondrous plasticity, at one point accommodating George McGovern as the country's leading ethnic politician. But we will stay with the basic guidebook definition suggested above.) For Streiker-Strober-Kelley, "they" are the liberal churchmen, especially if they have a social-action bent. For Scammon and Wattenberg, "they" are the radical-liberals who insist on confusing bread-and-butter politics with "the social issue." Intellectual, then, comes to mean anyone and everyone who throws into question the

American reality in which the majority of Americans desperately want to believe. The common theme takes shape: During the 1960s we lost our way, in large part because the intellectuals were misleading us. We will only find our way home again if we defiantly resist the influence of those who presume to be smarter than we.

This is, of course, a perennially popular theme with honorable precedent especially in American populism. Be there a man with soul so dead who never to himself has said, "Crap!" when reading *Commentary, The New York Review of Books* or even *Worldview.* [6] We all know how parochial, presumptuous and finally precious is so much of the analysis offered by those who presume to understand. When, before his inglorious fall, Spiro Agnew excoriated the "effete snobs," it was not only the illiterate protofascists who rejoiced to hear their resentments vented. The more elegant analysis of such attacks upon intellectuals refers to the late Richard Hofstadter's description of the abiding anti-intellectualism in American life. [7] The less respectable, but I suspect more perceptive, suggestion is that there is an intellectually sound reason for what Hofstadter termed anti-intellectualism. Writers such as Hofstadter, Daniel Bell and others have argued that anti-intellectualism is rooted in paranoia. They fail to take into account that paranoiacs can be persecuted too. There is a kind of persecution felt by many ordinary Americans in the thinly veiled disdain with which they are viewed by many intellectuals. Novak's protest against the disdain with which many intellectuals view the manners and opinions of blue-collar workers is both warranted and necessary. The way in which intellectuals of the left, in search of someone to play the part of "the worker" in their revolutionary scenarios, romanticize those same manners and opinions is the other side of the problem.

Resentment against the intellectuals should not be pushed too far, however. It does not explain every social movement endorsed by the scrubbed masses and abhorred by the unwashed elite. It is highly questionable, for example, to explain popular enthusiasm for Joseph McCarthy in the 1950s as the masses' way of getting back at the intellectuals who have excluded the lesser types from their charmed circle. Such an explanation suggests a measure of paranoia among intellectuals, or at least an inflated notion of how attractive their company must seem to others.

In any case, one should not be surprised that guides denigrate their competition. The taint of distrust is so pervasive today that politicians present themselves as "nonpoliticians," intellectuals dissociate themselves from intellectuals, and guides assure you they are not guides at all. There are yet other self-serving elements in the arguments of those who would lead us home again.

Michael Novak, for example, was deeply impressed (and distressed) by Kevin Phillips's case for creating a Republican majority through a shrewd manipulation of ethnic and regional prejudices.[8] Being a good Democrat, Novak wanted to insist that "there is no need to concede the ethnic voter to the conservative movement . . . [This need not happen] if the professional elite tries to follow rather than to lead, tries to be inclusive rather than exclusive, tries to hear voices and accents against which for too long it has closed its ears." He recommends to others his own role as "an intellectual who tries to give voice to their [the ethnics'] instincts" rather than to lecture them. To which Garry Wills responded in a perhaps unkind review: "So quickly does listening to one's blood become a matter of sniffing around after loose votes."[9] Scammon and Wattenberg are even more candid about the political intent of their cultural analysis. Listened to by Nixon and embraced by Hubert Humphrey, erstwhile presidential candidate, they insist that he who would win must avoid like poison any association with "the social issues" posed by the dissidents of an unruly time. Likewise, Kelley is clearly interested in shoring up what he views as the failing ecclesiastical enterprise of which he is part.

Streiker and Strober, on the other hand, seem to be serving only their deeply felt conviction that "Billy Graham, who could be at home with Dwight Eisenhower of Kansas, Lyndon Johnson of Texas, Richard Nixon of California—is the man for this season, this trying time. For Graham, by combining religious assurance with the basic moderateness of traditional American concepts of morality and action, has put it all together." The reader who believes that the polarities of America's tortured consciousness are represented by Eisenhower, Johnson and Nixon; or that the conflicts that beset us arise from a regional contest between Kansas, Texas and California, that reader will perhaps be able to share Streiker and Strober's faith in the messianic mission of Billy Graham.

As I mentioned earlier, the themes in these guidebooks echo some aspects of "populism." American populism has had its ups and downs over the years, but is now very much alive. Populism can be either of the right or of the left. Whether espoused by George McGovern or George Wallace, whether it cultivates the label *new* populism or unashamedly identifies with the populism of eighty years ago, populism is a rebellion of the common man against the intellectuals, of "the people" against every elite that restricts, instructs or strangles the popular impulse for a better society. (Populism has been much maligned by writers such as Hofstadter and Oscar Handlin who have too often written about it in precisely that "paranoid style" which they attribute to their more vulgar opponents.) Novak, Wattenberg, Kelley et al. may be seen as representing some sort of populist renaissance, speaking out for that great majority of Americans who have not been, to use Charles Reich's term, greened. That majority is presumably confident there is nothing wrong with America that a large dose of Americanism would not cure, if only Americanism were not in such short supply.

If these guides are populists, however, their position must be termed perverse populism. Unlike the populism of the late nineteenth century, they urge retreat rather than advance; the message is not that we are moving too slowly but that we are moving too quickly. Theirs is not a struggle for change but for cohesion (even Novak's radical ethnic pluralism is an invitation to revive and indeed to exaggerate the group identities that can only reinforce the former cohesion built on abiding injustices). Their populism is not marked by radical minority movement but by conservative majority nostalgia. Only those who see no difference between Nixon's "law and order," on the one hand, and Tom Watson's or William Jennings Bryan's campaign against the banking and industrial interests, on the other, could believe that this literature and the mood it reflects represent a renascent populism. It may be that most every American feels like a homeless waif, but the genuinely populist way home is not to the bosom of the existing majority but to the adventure of a new community.

In the first part of the 1970s there was a widespread feeling that things had gotten out of hand, that the country was being fragmented in unpredictable and probably undesirable ways. Things were not falling apart quickly enough to meet the revolutionary scenario that many had fashionably advocated in the 1960s, but as things really did begin to fall apart, it became apparent how very few were really serious about revolution. The 1970s, it was said, must be the decade of putting things together again. Where were we, it was asked, before all this started? Where were we before the redemptive nonviolence of the civil rights movement was transformed into the bullying assertion of minority power? Where were we before the "defense of freedom" was mocked by innumerable Mylais? Where were we before the best and the brightest of our young people vomited their countercultural revulsion all over the sacred values, advantages and opportunities of the American Way of Life? The guidebooks under discussion here are part of a wave of social commentary urging us to *return* home, as though we once had been there.

In opposition to all this, there is another stream of American consciousness that insists our society is a lively experiment and adventure, that the American home is in a future realization of America's formative vision. There is no doubt that much of the radicalism of the past decade committed a great strategic error, and even a great evil, in rejecting also this stream of American consciousness. That is, not only was the existent America repudiated by its radical critics but, along with it, the symbols that anticipated a future fulfillment of the American experiment. An Illinois-based group of evangelical Christian radicals publishes a newspaper called *The Post-American.* A more historically and strategically keen analysis would suggest the title "The Pre-American." Historically better, because the American experiment is closely tied to the metaphors of covenant and pilgrimage, the metaphors of testing and experiment. Strategically more effective, because no people can be asked to join an adventure if they are deprived of the symbols of continuity and hope, if they are deprived of the myths which identify the community. Without such symbols of identity and hope, no people can travel with confidence.

Some years ago at St. John's Church in Brooklyn, New York, we held one of the first draft card turn-ins. More than five hundred radical young people gathered in a "Service of Conscience and Hope," and more than two hundred draft cards were gathered to be returned to Selective Service. At the end of the service I suggested to the other leaders that we should ask the group to sing "America the Beautiful." They were scandalized, much as though someone were to suggest to Bob Hope and Billy Graham at Honor America Day that the crowd should join in singing the "Internationale." Nonetheless, I went ahead, pointing out that "America the Beautiful" was not a description of the present America we knew but a song of hope for the America which, by actions such as the conscientious resistance of that day, would one day be realized. That night the network TV news carried the lustiest and most heartfelt rendition of "America the Beautiful" I had ever heard. Unfortunately, that alliance of radical hope and American piety was and is all too rare among those who press for change. The belief that our present situation is unworthy of America is, in some circles, outvoted by the dismal confidence that there is no evil not endemic to American life.

Already in 1966 among peace activists there was disagreement as to whether the Indochina war was a mistake or a deliberate and essential part of the American imperialist design. In later years that debate continued, notably between Arthur Schlesinger and Noam Chomsky in the pages of *The New York Review,* Schlesinger arguing for the mistake thesis and Chomsky for the endemic evil. On the stated terms of the debate, one may wish to side with Schlesinger. Unfortunately, he does not take seriously enough the extent to which such mistakes are built into the present systems of decision making. Even more seriously, Schlesinger's argument is flawed because he can offer few resources for correction, having ruled out of court the so-called ideological resources that are formative to the American social experiment.[10]

Schlesinger is in this respect like Scammon and Wattenberg, Novak, Kelley et al. One analyst returns to majority indifference and ignorance as the rock upon which a new American can be constructed, another returns to the ethnic passions and prejudices of contrived nostalgia, yet another returns to the revivalist fundamentalism of Billy Graham. Schlesinger returns to tinkering with the machinery of New Deal liberalism that somehow got out of whack during the rough ride through the 1960s. If these are the only alternatives, the revolutionary negative to the American experiment would win by default. There is yet another alternative, and I believe it is to be discovered in the American public symbols of hope. (This "symbol system" is sometimes termed the American civil religion. We will later examine in detail the appropriateness of calling public piety a civil *religion.*) In a sense, we must indeed return in order to reappropriate these symbols, but the return results in a forward movement, for it is the very genius of symbols of hope, no matter how ancient, that they propel us toward the future.

Notions of destiny, whether manifest or hidden, have in times past impelled individuals and societies toward new ventures, sometimes noble, sometimes destructive, often just foolish. This is perhaps true of all peoples, but it is particularly true of the American people. Because of its peculiar immigrant history, American "peoplehood" cannot be taken for granted. In an especially urgent way, Americans are a people on purpose and a people by purpose. Talk about national purpose has extremely unpleasant overtones for many of us. "National purpose" became a code word of the supposedly pragmatic anti-ideologists of the cold war and is today a notion appealed to mainly by the most regressive forces in our society, to whom the symbols of patriotism have gravitated by default. It is in resistance to these unhappy developments, and in resistance to those who would lead us backward to home, that we must project a new definition of national purpose capable of enlisting American consciousness and conscience in the continuing trek toward the new community for which this "Almost chosen people," to use Lincoln's happy phrase, was ordained. Ordained, if not by God, at least by people prepared to gamble in hope upon divine intentions within history.

I have said that we *should not* follow the course advocated by the guides under discussion. I am also saying it simply will not work in America. On the obvious level of electoral politics it has not worked. Witness the dismal failure of the Republicans' 1970 congressional campaign strategy, starring Spiro Agnew and following precisely the prescription offered by Scammon, Wattenberg, Phillips and others. Witness the collapse of Edmund Muskie's presidential effort, dependent as it was on the ethnic renaissance and the assumption that the people wanted nothing more than to be reassured that things are basically all right. Witness the similar collapse of the Humphrey strategy, which had appropriated the remnants of the Muskie effort, together with large parts of the anticommunist fear tactics left over from an earlier Richard Nixon. In the religious sphere one notes the less than spectacular success of "Key 73," the year-long effort aimed at bringing right-thinking people together to win the continent for Christ.

I do not suggest that it may not happen again, as it has happened before, that politicians succeed by exploiting the fear that seeks a return to a supposedly more secure past. But, as a general rule, successful American politics is the politics of adventure, politics in harmony with the public piety that envisions an America of new beginnings, an America both capable and worthy of better than its present state. This is the note struck by both John and Robert Kennedy Put quite simply, it is, "We can do better than this." Similarly George McGovern's plea, "Come home, America," was a call to resume the pilgrimage toward the fulfillment of America's destiny as "a good and decent land." The return he advocated was always to the task, the challenge, the dream of America's potential, never to a past point of achievement. In this sense, far from representing a radical break, McGovern echoed the almost fundamentalist appeal of the essential American tradition. That his bid was turned back because it seemed to represent radical discontinuity is another of the ironies of American history.[11]

The politics of adventure is temporarily in disrepute. Vietnam gave Camelot a bad name, and McGovern's defeat is interpreted as a repudiation of idealism (although subsequent experience with Nixon has forced hasty revisions of that interpretation). The politics of adventure, the quest for the realization of the American promise, can indeed be dangerous. But I cannot agree with those pundits who insist that America should grow up and resign itself to being a nation like unto every other nation. To be sure, our singularity is not so pronounced as we have sometimes believed. But the adventure and the quest are inherent in the American experience. Were they ever expunged, the idea and reality of America would be dramatically changed. The likely alternatives would, I suspect, be healthy neither for justice nor for freedom.

As for the church and the role of religion, one cannot help but be impressed by the arguments offered by Kelley and others, that the social activism of the sixties lost the support of much of its churchgoing constituency. The alarm was earlier and clearly raised by Jeffrey Hadden in his *The Gathering Storm in the Churches,* published in 1969.[12] We will be turning again to some of the changes in tactics, strategy and goals that we must make if those of us who are committed to the social witness of the churches are to be more effective in the future. It is sufficient to say now, in response to Hadden, that it is neither necessary nor attractive to despair of the churches' role as an agent in the quest for social justice.

In response to Kelley, we need not acquiesce to the social indifference of those so-called conservative churches that seem more statistically successful. Religious statistics are notoriously unreliable and deserving of our strongest skepticism. Kelley does not take as seriously as he ought some small and very "conservative" church bodies of the sect type that have *not* experienced the supposedly strong growth patterns of Southern Baptists, Missouri Lutherans and others. Even as to the growth of conservative bodies, Glock and Stark, in *American Piety,*[13] raise the most serious questions. They suggest that, instead of strong and steady growth, the conservative bodies simply experience more in-and-out action, more comings-and-goings of membership. Most of the goings are to the more moderate mainline bodies, with very few people moving back from, say, the Episcopal church to the Southern Baptists.

The accuracy of statistical data aside, the more mainline churches have always benefited from the revivalism generated by the sects. This has been true in the past and it seems likely to hold for the future. The kind of social activism scored by Kelley and Hadden has never been a major agency of recruitment for church membership, although it was sometimes touted as such. I doubt if many people have joined churches because the church's witness was "relevant" or "with it" with regard to race, war or urban justice. In the churches, as in the larger society, commitment to social change is a minority vocation. In a very real sense, those so committed live off the religious resources and organization sustained by people who are church members for different, and usually quite privatized, reasons.

In this respect I am sympathetic to Streiker and Strober's admiration for Billy Graham, although for somewhat different reasons. I am generally pleased when I see the crowds at his rallies coming forward to "accept Jesus Christ as [their] personal savior." Pleased because, in most cases, I imagine the decision gives them a framework for their daily life more personally adequate than the other frameworks being peddled in our culture; pleased because there are, as a consequence of that decision, more people to whom one can appeal for commitment to change in the name of Christian discipleship; pleased because, even if they don't respond to such an appeal, they are strengthening the network of Christian fellowship in which others can respond. So one can wish Billy Graham and Oral Roberts and the several evangelism boards great success. As friends and brothers, one can urge them to be more forceful and articulate about the social imperatives of the gospel, although that effort will probably continue to meet with only moderate success.

What we must *not* do, however—and this is the essential disagreement with Kelley's thesis—is conform our understanding of the Christian mission to the dictates of market research. The Christian community is a marvelously variegated phenomenon. St. Paul said it: "And his gifts were that some should be apostles, some prophets, and some evangelists, some pastors and teachers, for the equipment of the saints, for the work of ministry, for building up the body of Christ" (Eph. 4:11-12).

During the 1960s some feared that the totality of the church's mission was being preempted by the devotees of social action. And it is true that, if the avant-garde of social activism had gained control of organized religious life in the country, they would soon have run out of troops. In fact they never came close to gaining such control. They did provoke enough concern to stimulate the present recruitment campaigns for the old-time religion. Now it may be their turn again to be the anxious ones, as they were during the religious boom of the 1950s, reminding American religion that recruitment was made for mission and not mission for recruitment.

If we are committed to America's lively experiment and to the church's mission for the duration, we should not and need not surrender to the dismal arguments of the Wattenbergs and Haddens. I realize that many people despair of revitalizing the American symbols of hope. Yet I also suspect that we are facing a perhaps unique moment of opportunity. The distinguished historian Sydney Ahlstrom believes that the severe break in American political piety dates from the depression of the 1930s. If he is right, and he is not alone in this opinion, that is really not a very long time as one reads the histories of nations. Since that time we have tried to muddle through, shoring up our corporate consciousness with a combination of war-induced solidarity, secular-technological pragmatism and a strong dose of cold-war panic. As a consequence of the tumultuous sixties all these contrived solutions now seem discredited and impotent for the task of restoring American confidence.

The responses to the delegitimation of our past ways are various. In addition to the guidance of those who would take us home again, there is a serious and influential flirtation with a variety of economic determinisms, usually more or less Marxist. Perhaps equally influential are the ideologists of the environmental movement who would have us abandon history in favor of nature and give up on the political task itself.[14] Their ecological determinism has become more plausible to many as the public consciousness is more and more impressed by various energy and resource crises, real or contrived. For a variety of reasons I do not think these solutions are likely to "take" in America's way of thinking of itself. If they did, I suspect their consequences would be disastrous both for our domestic life and for the influence of America in the world.

In discussing alternative models for reconstructing the American reality I do not wish to seem more certain than our experience with history would warrant. Nor do I mean to suggest that there are various deposits of metaphors among which we may pick and choose and then quite mechanistically conform American consciousness to those we have selected. For, to be sure, it often seems that Huxley's Ford (Henry, not

Gerald) was right when he said that history is just one damn thing after another. We are all acted upon at least as much as we are actors. Nonetheless, unless we are ready to resign ourselves passively to the fates, we do decide and we do act. Knowing that decision and action are a gamble, the most promising gamble, I believe, is the interplay between explicit biblical religion and the American tradition of public piety. Both require careful nurture and constant reexamination. They exist in a symbiotic relationship, each supporting and, to some extent, checking the other. Explicit biblical religion is not coterminous with American public piety, nor is the public piety, left to itself, in consistent harmony with biblical imperatives.

Of the various themes in that public piety or "civil religion" the single theme that seems to me most compelling in our time is that of covenant. It is firmly rooted in the most hallowed statements of American purpose and consciousness. It is emphatically historical in character, keeping present reality in tension with future contingency. It comprehends the experience of judgment, of betrayal and healing, of repentance and forgiveness. After the Indochina horror, the divisiveness of myriad racisms, the corporate death wish indulged by assassinations and the emetic of Watergate, the American people long for judgment.

I do not think the vast majority thinks of itself as totally innocent, as being perfectly all right if only it were not for "them"—for the blacks, the unruly young, the corrupt politicians and other troublemakers. No, there is, I believe, a widespread feeling of unworthiness, of having fallen short of a noble calling, of being in need of judgment. But most Americans will, quite understandably, not accept the word of judgment from those who seem to be bent on their destruction; and among the tragedies of the sixties is that the most pointed social and moral criticisms seemed to be more aimed at humiliating and destroying the American reality than at healing and reconstituting that reality. One can only hear the judgment of the law when it is accompanied by the healing of the gospel, and one can only hear the gospel when it is accompanied by the law. It may be an impossible dream, but I believe we should work to create a climate within which a Lincoln might arise, a climate prepared for such a great theologian of the public piety who can turn confusion and remorse into the paths of healing.

At present those who see the horror of what America has become seem to believe not at all in what American might have been and might yet be. Those who most loudly proclaim their confidence in America, on the other hand, are exposed as fraudulent because they refuse to acknowledge the horror. So long as this situation prevails, most Americans will continue to lie to themselves in order to keep from hating themselves and will hate themselves because they have to lie. As difficult as it may seem, as much against the trend of the moment as it may seem, those who have a broader vision of social ethics must more persuasively tell the story of human failing and redemption in a way peculiarly attuned to American experience and sensibilities. We are, after all, story tellers, people who develop a frame of reference within which, in a particular moment of history, we may choose between good and evil. The title and theme of the American story is "covenant."

To say that explicit Judeo-Christian religion and the public piety are symbiotic means that they live together in intimate association and interdependence. It does not mean they are always complementary or mutually supportive, nor does it suggest that the degree of dependence is equal. (I can readily imagine a vital church surviving the death or reversal of America's public piety, but it is hard to envision the opposite.) One cause of crisis in public morality is that many of those Christians most concerned about society lost their confidence in the explicit traditions that gave religious pertinence and plausibility to their witness. To put it another way, they became so enamored with the secular order, forgetting its dependence upon moral assumptions and *their* sources, that they cut themselves off from the tree's roots in order to fondle, celebrate and affirm the grace of its leaves and branches. In short, American religion has yet to get over the severe blow dealt by Harvey Cox's *The Secular City* in 1966. (I mention that particular book not because it caused the loss of confidence, but because it so accurately represented and *legitimated* that loss.)

Many spokesmen for biblical religion have lost the nerve required to establish an independent ideological base from which to address, in criticism and hope, the public piety. Of course there is nothing new about this. It was true of the false prophets condemned by Jeremiah; it was true of the religious leadership that toadied to the establishments in order to advance the religious expansionisms of the 1950s; it is true of those who are now fawning for the favor of the counterculture and diverse radicalisms, just as it is true of those who panted for a preaching date at the White House. Whether one's goal is to be "in" with the avant-garde or "in" with the White House, the consequence is equally debilitating for credible Christian witness.

There is no easy formula for restoring confidence in biblical religion so that it can, in turn, help to restore confidence in the American experiment. But nothing very creative will happen without a major theological reconstruction. The doldrums of the American church are not caused by a lack of skill or of relevance to what is happening or of inadequate structure. Those who compulsively concentrate on practical skill, on relevance and on structure are, as one wit noted in another connection, simply rearranging the deck chairs on the *Titanic*. What we must again focus upon are the truth claims implicit in the biblical story and what they mean for individual and social life.

Nowhere have the blows to Christian confidence seemed so severe as in the Roman Catholic church. In this connection, I think Andrew Greeley's studies[15] illustrate the point I would make. The reasons commonly given for the departure of so many priests and the drastic drop in new recruits have to do with sexuality, the restrictions of church authorities, the absence of significant job challenge and so forth. If Greeley is to be believed, and on this point I tend to believe him, his extensive researches indicate that most priests are better off, and even more content, than their nonpriestly counterparts on most of these scores. The chief reason for disillusionment with the priesthood is that men are no longer very sure what it means to be a priest. If one's work is legitimated by the social change it produces, perhaps there are other jobs equal to, or better than, being a priest. If the liturgy and sacraments are simply mechanisms by which people "experience community" or get turned on to their supposedly authentic selves, no doubt there are more potent mechanisms. If there is finally no distinction between sacred and secular, between religious and worldly, then why hold a position that poses such awkward differentiations? In short, without a theology of the priesthood, there is little sense in being a priest. The dialectic that made sense of priesthood is then lost.

Dialectic is central to the relationship between biblical religion and public piety. We will be examining that dialectic more closely in later chapters. It turns around the notion of the Kingdom of God as the goal of universal history, and of the church as the community which signals, anticipates, celebrates and supports that oncoming Kingdom. Within such a dialectic, people concerned for shaping the church's social witness have a new opportunity. For there is a meeting point between that hope for the Kingdom and America's constituting vision.

The effort to bring together these themes of hope can be distracted in many ways. One distraction is proposed by those who, weary of the past decade's confusion, would lead us home again to the "real majority." Our vocation, however, is a minority vocation exercised for, and indeed often it will seem against, that majority. Indeed, we should be going home again, but our home is ahead of us. If we take seriously both biblical religion and the American vision at their best, we know that we've never been home—not yet.

4

Ideological Convergences
on the Way

The desire to go home again is not, of course, a recent cultural phenomenon created in response to the last few years of America's tumultuous history. Nor is it a peculiarly American phenomenon. As much as anything can be properly called universal, the idea of renewal through return, of going home again, is universal. It is deeply rooted and explicitly celebrated in the religious myths of primitive man; it is as deeply rooted although more obliquely stated in the world views of those who consider themselves modern and even postmodern. On the face of it, the idea of return seems conservative, but it is often more pronounced in the belief systems we usually call radical. It is present and seductively powerful in elements of the American civil piety, especially in the seventeenth-century Puritan language about America as New Israel or as New Eden. At least the language is susceptible to being interpreted as renewal through regression or through the recapitulation of a past and presumably better time. And indeed the biblical literature itself—from which the Puritan and Enlightenment fathers drew so heavily in giving shape to America's piety—offers some comfort to those who join the trek backward toward home. All these factors must be taken into account in arguing that home is still ahead of us.

In *The Homeless Mind* Peter Berger and associates described the experience of what was a few years ago called the counter-culture, or as Lionel Trilling termed it, the "adversary culture."[1] The feeling of homelessness was, Berger wrote, created by the modern world of functional rationality, that is, "the imposition of rational controls over the material universe, over social relations and finally over the self." The counter-culture "is in rebellion against all three forms. The engineering mentality, which rationally apprehends and manipulates both material and social reality, is denigrated as a perversion that deprives human beings of a 'natural' relationship to the world."[2] The rebellion against the engineering mentality of the modern world Berger calls "demodernization." All functional definitions of roles must be repudiated as "alienating" or

22

"dehumanizing." Demodernization contained also a strong "time" thrust, encouraging the notion that the "true self" could be discovered only in some premodern social form, such as "the tribe" or "the family."

Every kind of social differentiation was to be condemned as falsifying. The enormous popularity of Herman Hesse's works helped sustain the belief that "All is One." You are me. I am you. Liberation is dissolution into the All. An assault was launched upon the elementary distinction between private and public existence. Thus the determination to make public, even "political," the acts of defecation and copulation were more than an effort to shock conventional sensibilities. They were revolutionary political actions aimed at overthrowing the falsifying distinctions that separate self from self. In a "repressive" society captive to such distinctions, R. D. Laing and others argued, schizoid "madness" was in fact the mark of personal sanity. Demodernization was one way of going home. As the Charles Manson and other murders illustrated, returning to the premodern tribe was not without its moral ambiguities. As many young people have now found out for themselves, there were also severe economic and social limitations in trying to take the "greening of America" all the way. What remains today of the celebrated counter-culture seems less bizarre and certainly less culturally and politically potent. It would be a mistake to think, however, that the dynamics of demodernization have been exhausted.

The theme of renewal through return reappears perennially whenever discontents with things as they are become intolerable. The use of the prefix *post,* as, for example, in Daniel Bell's "postindustrial society," sometimes suggests a moving on to the genuinely new, a launching out into uncharted waters. Just as often, however, perhaps more often, *post* is synonymous with *pre.* As noted earlier, much of the writing about postmodern man or postcivilization society suggests that we have so botched the job of history that our only hope is in return to some prior state. Thus, in classically circular fashion, the condemnation implicit in *post* is joined to an invitation implicit in *pre.* While talk about the good old days and about how the modern world is going to hell in a handbasket is associated with certain varieties of disgruntled conservatism, the underlying theme of return through renewal is at least as characteristic of attitudes and movements deemed to be radical or liberal. As I have argued at length elsewhere, one of the most curious examples of this is the success of old-fashioned conservationism in selling itself as a movement of the left.[3]

The point here, however, is the twist by which a program for the privileged can be presented as radically progressive and accepted as a movement of the left. As *post* can become interchangeable with *pre,* so there is a sense in which the essentially conservative impulse to return

to the past can become radical. If one advocates a return to the world of
fifty years ago, he is rather generally thought to be a conservative. A
return to the world of three hundred years ago, however, is correctly seen
as being radical in its implications; it is a challenge to the modern world
at its roots.

Whether renewal through return is viewed as radical or conservative
depends, then, upon how far back one wishes to return. This ambiguity
has plagued the last century or so of socialist thought in various countries.
For some, socialism was a matter of directing and humanizing the process
of industrialization, while for others it was a protest against the modern
world and in favor of reviving what was thought to have been the human
solidarity of an economy based upon the crafts and guilds of a semifeudal
past.

In America today we experience a similar confusion in shifting definitions of what constitutes conservatism, liberalism and radicalism. These
changes are pertinent to our understanding of the political options facing
the American experiment. The shift may turn out to be as major as that
which distinguishes the nineteenth-century laissez-faire Manchester liberalism from the twentieth-century statist New Deal liberalism. Among
conservative groups in this country, such as Young Americans for Freedom, there is a clear conflict between the Law and Order Party and the
Libertarian Party. The former more neatly fit the TV newscasters' notion
of conservatism, but the latter are more conservatively consistent in their
opposition to governmental programs conventionally espoused by liberals
and some radicals. Similarly, during the dying years of "the Movement"
of the 1960s, it became apparent that much of the liberationist rhetoric
was in tone and substance as repressive, even fascist, as the repression
it condemned. The parallels between youth-cult radicalism of the American sixties and youth-cult radicalism of the German thirties were apparent enough to those who wished to see them.

On numerous policy choices before us today, we are at a loss to say
what is conservative and what radical. Christopher Jencks and Milton
Friedman both advocate a dismantling of the present public school
system in favor of a greater pluralism based upon some kind of voucher
payments that would empower parents and smaller communities. Jencks
is celebrated as a radical, while Friedman is thought to be in the front line
of American conservatism. On questions of Third World development,
Peter Berger and Ivan Illich both challenge the liberal development-
planning establishment and both advocate quite similar alternative models
of development. Berger calls himself a conservative, while Illich's creden-
tials as a radical are almost never challenged.[4] One could expand for
many pages upon similar examples of shifting identifications among
political viewpoints.

In times of such confusion, it is tempting to suggest that we should forget about labels altogether. Why fret about what is right and what is left, what is reactionary and what is radical? There is a strong strain in American political life, much celebrated among liberals until recently, that is emphatically pragmatic. The genius of American politics, it was said, is that ideological questions are always subordinated to the question of what will work. In this view, the ideologist—or the idealist, as he was often called—was a compulsive raiser of unnecessary and divisive questions and must therefore be kept outside the mainstream of decision making. While it is true that ideology must, in this captious world, be tempered by practicality, the notion of liberal, mainstream, nonideological politics has been deservedly challenged from many quarters. Policies turned out to be neither so liberalizing nor so enlightened as they promised. The boundaries of the mainstream were so drawn as to exclude most Americans. And, most important, those who celebrated "the end of ideology" were found to be concealing a host of ideological assumptions about human nature, history, freedom, equality and just about every other concept of public importance.[5] The illusion of a society in which everybody rules may mean that nobody rules. It more often means the society is ruled by those with the most brute force. So also the pragmatic proponents of anti-ideology, who would have us forget about labels and get on with the business at hand, are likely engaged in a cryptic but real ideological contest.

In debates over public policy there is no getting around the unsatisfactory business of digging into presuppositions—historical, anthropological, moral and religious—and affixing labels. We might fondly wish this were not the case. It would be welcome relief not to have to fret about political alignments or categories of thought. We are always tempted to leap over the particular in order to arrive at the universal, to have done with the partisan in order to affirm the commonweal. In a fragmented world of alienating differentiations we hunger for the Whole, for belief in that which "puts it all together."

The most fundamental Christian affirmation—overwhelmingly confirmed by the evidence of everyday existence—is that history has not yet got itself together. Only the coming of the Kingdom of God, of God's rule in its fullness, will resolve the dialectics and contradictions of historical existence. Every other resolution proffered is premature, false and, if we submit to it, finally idolatrous. From Rousseau's General Will to John Gardner's Common Cause, every attempt to escape from drawing ideological lines is illusory. Some illusions are less dangerous than others. Common Cause is a relatively harmless illusion. It may even have a benign influence, but that is precisely because it is not in power but is defined by its opposition to prevailing procedures and powers, and thus is anything but a *common* cause. Rousseau's General Will, on the other hand, or the claim of the Soviet Communist Party to embody the universal thrust of history has been the source of unspeakable tyranny. In public affairs every attempted escape from particularity and provisionality must, if it gains power, become tyrannical. That is, every party that denies it is partisan must, in order to be consistent, drive toward absolutizing itself. In addition to the Soviet Union and China, the most grotesque instance of this in the twentieth century is Hitler's Third Reich.

If the American experiment can be viewed as radical—and I believe it must—it is important to understand what we mean by radical. I hold no hope for any radicalism that is not hinged upon a fulfillment of promise that is still in the future. That promise is in biblical language called the Kingdom of God. The only radical who is to be trusted is the radical who is painfully aware of the "not yetness" of history, who has no illusions about the provisionality of our moment in the still unfolding drama. This is what distinguishes the radicalism affirmed here from the various radicalisms that from time to time capture the fears and hopes of American public life.

It is not enough for a proposal or a vision to "feel" radical. Many of the radicalisms of the sixties were more affective than substantive. That is, there was an inordinate concern with the fashions and feelings of being radical—with the "life-styles" of radicalism, as they were called—while the questions of effectiveness were often disdained. The effective and affective were commonly set in opposition. Concern about being effective was "mere reformism," while adopting a radical life-style in clear distinction from the "system" was seen as revolutionary. And, indeed, there is a kind of logical consistency in this viewpoint. If the American experience is entirely corrupted, any successful effort to reform it can only prolong its life and thereby delay the hour of revolutionary judgment. By radicalism, however, I mean precisely radical reform. Successful reform can have revolutionary consequences while failed revolutions only compound the identity crises of disillusioned ex-radicals.

In addition to focusing on the effective rather than the affective, the radical perspective from which I would evaluate the American experience differs from other radicalisms in yet another major way. It follows the fault lines of the society rather than the discontents of the successful. That means it differs dramatically from the radicalism advocated in, for examples, Charles Reich's *The Greening of America* or Theodore Roszak's *The Making of A Counter-Culture.* Their radicalism took its clues from the discontents of usually upper-middle-class youth who "had it made" in American life and found their privileged positions utterly wanting. Thus a student could in 1967 sue Columbia University for failing to provide him with a "satisfying life experience," and many people thought the complaint quite reasonable. Thus also it was commonly said that only those who lived in Scarsdale could really know how oppressive the American system is, and many students fashioned themselves "the niggers of America."

The most obvious problem with a radicalism that emerges from the discontents of the successful is that it shifts attention from the very real sufferings of the unsuccessful, from the complaints of the objectively poor. I may find little personal fulfillment in the career track promised by a Harvard education and I may be sickened by the surfeit of things surrounding me in a consumption-crazed society. But that complaint is quite different from the complaint of the man who lives out his years in brutish labor with no hope of reward other than the possibility of something to eat from day to day. The difference between these complaints seems so elementary as to require no elaboration. Much that now passes as radicalism, however, obscures or denies that elementary difference. Orwell predicted a world in which war would be described as peace. We have already arrived at a time in which success is failure, wealth is poverty, and the powerful deem themselves the most oppressed.

Again, great unhappiness can coexist with, even result from, having it made as our society—or any other society—defines making it. Growing up is a process of arrivals without the satisfaction of having arrived. To transfer such discontents into the realm of politics, however, leads to a false and dangerous radicalism. Radicalism that takes its cues from the dissatisfactions of the privileged often greatly overestimates the province of the political process.

It is fashionable to say that all of life is politics and politics is all of life. But it is not true. There is a necessary line between the personal and the political, between the private and the public, although, to be sure, these spheres are interdependent and act upon one another in a multitude of ways, some of which are seldom noticed. There is, in short, a definite limit to public policy. Loneliness is not amenable to political solution, just as we cannot legislate sexual attractiveness. Yet there is a species of radicalism that insists upon defying the limits of public policy. It envisions a totalist society in which, as in a medieval monastery, the entirety of one's life would be collectively ordered, thus indeed making all of life politics and politics all of life. The result is indeed radical in the sense of having revolutionary consequences, as, for example, in contemporary China. Totalist politics are totalitarian in consequence.

A totalitarian society with greater justice may seem preferable to a less just society with greater individual freedom. But these are seldom, if ever, the alternatives posited by history. Totalist societies have more often than not diminished both justice and freedom. Even more important, the Christian acknowledges the limits of public policy and repudiates every form of totalism because he knows that ours is a partial and provisional moment in history. The totalist impulse betrays unfaith, a refusal to live now by the promise of what is to be. While the power of the coming Kingdom is indeed present in our labors for a better world, the Kingdom is not established by our labors. Were it otherwise, it would be the Kingdom of Man, not the Kingdom of God. Our propensity for mistaking the former for the latter has been the source of infinite grief through the centuries.

The radicalism affirmed here, then, is effective rather than affective, focused upon the sufferings of the poor rather than upon the discontents of the rich, and, most important, contingent upon a promised New Order that, in its final fulfillment, may yet be millennia distant. The last is the hardest point to accept. As St. Augustine and others have contended, pride is the root of all sin. Not just personal pride but what we might call historical pride; the illusion that our moment on the stage is utterly singular, that the best of all possible worlds is available now, if only we have the courage to will it into being. Those who bid us "wait upon the Lord" are pilloried as escapist peddlers of pie in the sky. And, of course, talk about waiting on the Lord has often been used to evade the tasks at hand that can be done. As often, however, those who refuse to wait upon the Lord have, in their success, imposed even greater suffering upon humankind, or, in their failure, retreated into a paralyzing and bitter disillusionment. Historical modesty is an essential ingredient in the radical- ism that is capable of sustained address to the tasks of liberation and healing, the radicalism that is contingent not upon present success but upon future promise.

At its best, America is, as Sidney Mead argues, a "lively experiment." It is contingent upon future promise.[6] The word *experiment* accentuates the contingent. Experiments are designed to demonstrate the truth or falsity of a proposition. Experiments can turn out badly or well. This kind of historical modesty is deeply rooted in American public piety. Just as deeply rooted is the weed of historical pride, and at times it has seemed to triumph altogether. Contingent, provisional, experimental—these are the words appropriate to history and to the part of history that is the American experience. Too often the American experience has been viewed as definitive, absolute and final. But surely, it might be objected, this prideful view of ourselves is not something of which radicals are guilty. In truth the loss of the sense of the experimental is found as frequently on the left as on the right. This is revealed in the way in which the theme of renewal through return is touted by radical and reactionary alike. The conservative impulse is to call off the experiment in order to keep things as they are, or, sometimes, to return to a prior and presum- ably better time. The radical impulse is to dismantle or replace the experiment, confident that it has definitively failed. *Neither looks for the future vindication of the continuing experiment.* In one sense, the radical version of renewal through return is more infiltrated by historical pride than is the conservative. The conservative is, for the most part, resigned to the unsatisfactoriness of what he calls the human condition. His impulse is to make the best possible settlement with what he knows to be far from the best of all possible worlds. The radical, on the other hand, is not about to settle for things as they are. The biblical invitation to seek first the Kingdom of God is an invitation to radicalism. But there is radicalism and there is radicalism.

One radicalism looks to the future. "We have here no lasting city, but we seek the city which is to come" (Heb. 13). Another radicalism seeks not just renewal but revolution through return. One radicalism groans with a creation in travail, knowing we are not yet what we are to be (Rom. 8). Another radicalism believes that we are what we are meant to be and are hindered only by falsifying structures and institutions that keep us from our true selves and which must therefore be destroyed. One radicalism is marked by historical modesty, the other by historical pride. The radical experiment that is America is torn between the two.

5

Taking Out Insurance
Against the Future

The American experience and the public piety that surrounds that experience cannot be explained without reference to their religious roots. At least they cannot be explained adequately without such reference, although a host of "revisionist historians" has at times come close to establishing as historical orthodoxy a "nonsectarian" version of the American story. The religious roots are varied and often contradictory. At the risk of a too broad generalization, one may accept the distinction between the seventeenth- and the eighteenth-century origins of American public piety. The seventeenth-century understanding of the American experience is Puritan and explicitly biblical. The eighteenth-century understanding, which dominated the political thought of the revolutionary period, reflected the deism and the devotion to natural order of the Enlightenment.

From the seventeenth century we learn that the American people is the New Israel acting out the sacred history of God's chosen race. From the eighteenth century, that America is, according to the back side of our one dollar bill, *Novus Ordo Seculorum,* the new order of the ages revealing the universal truths that will one day be realized among the whole of the human race. Within both streams of piety there is an ambiguity about the connections between past, present and future. The explicitly biblical stream establishes the magnetic poles of Eden and the New Jerusalem, drawing hope either backward or forward. The Enlightenment stream posits eternal and universal truths which, when rationally perceived and applied, are essentially timeless. "We hold these truths to be self-evident, that all men are created equal, that they are endowed by their Creator. . . ." Yet even here the self-evidence was not absolute. There was an element of contingency built into the expectation that these "self-evident" truths would one day be recognized and acted upon by all. Thus, although in a limited sense, even these truths are vulnerable to history. In the biblical hope of the New Jerusalem and in the Enlightenment expectation of universal confirmation, there remained the possibility that the American experience could be either vindicated or repudiated by historical change. The metaphor of America as "lively experiment" was never entirely lost.

In the Puritan view it often seems the magnetic pole of Eden is stronger than that of the New Jerusalem. Or, to be more precise, the New Jerusalem was to be reached by returning to Eden, or at least to the sacred history of ancient Israel. The Puritan view was also emphatically English. It emerged from the Protestant theology of the early seventeenth century, a theology which "gave God his glory, man his place, events their meaning—and England its due."[1] As later American revolutionists fought, they said, to "exercise the rights of Englishmen," so the earlier Puritans understood themselves to be preserving in America the true English Protestant Reformation against the corruptions of the Established Church at home. The identification with past sacred history was reinforced by this English connection. The Anglican William Crashaw declared, "The God of Israel is . . . the God of England."[2] And, of course, the Reformation itself reinforced this theme of renewal through return. Both in England and on the Continent, popular understandings of the sixteenth-century religious reformations vibrated to ideas about returning to the Bible, casting off the corrupting accretions of Rome and restoring the purity of the early church.

Later conflicts and ambiguities are implicitly anticipated in the thoughts of Gov. John Winthrop aboard the *Arbella* before the landing in 1630: "We shall find that the God of Israel is among us. . . . For we must consider that we shall be as a city upon a hill, the eyes of all people are upon us."[3] A new beginning through identification with the past, an experiment testing truths of universal validity and even something of the notion Martin Marty has termed "righteous empire"—all were present in the beginning.[4] Historical pride and historical modesty were intermixed. Perhaps they are even symbiotically related, one reinforcing the other. Only those convinced they have been chosen for such a great task can fully estimate the seriousness of the judgment that would accompany their failure. In individuals, seeming arrogance and true humility are often conjoined. Only those with a high estimate of themselves can feel keenly how far they have fallen short of the mark. So also the apparent pretensions of the American experiment both invite and are tempered by the ominous prospect of the experiment's failure.

The desire to escape from the prospect of failure and its judgment is perfectly understandable. If we have made a promise that we failed to keep, and now see no chance of keeping it, we might, rather than admit our failure, deny that we ever made the promise in the first place. At the present moment in the American experience there is a rush to dissociate ourselves from the promises of our beginning. We will not recognize the right of the fathers to obligate the children. Their commitments are not our commitments, nor their covenant our covenant.

In the last few years a number of widely acclaimed histories have been devoted to debunking the "illusions" of Puritan and Revolutionary fathers that there was something distinctively promising about America. Similarly, publications occasioned by the bicentennial; the last year or so has witnessed the appearance of at least three major studies aimed at rehabilitating the popular image of the loyalists who supported England during the American Revolution, and at least one biography of George III showing that this kind, wise and just ruler was cruelly misunderstood by the hotheads in the American colonies. Outside chauvinist circles on the right, such as the Daughters of the American Revolution or the clutch of patriotic organizations that all seem to have their mailing addresses at Valley Forge, bicentennial writing seems to be dominated by the debunkers. We are not answerable for what we disown. We cannot be held accountable for the covenant we do not acknowledge. The failure of the American experiment is not our failure. Thus would we neutralize the power of the future to bring us to judgment.

To debunk means to take the bunk out of history. There is certainly enough bunk in the standard telling of American history to keep debunking squads busy at their typewriters for many years to come. But one wonders about the obsessive and sickly rejoicing in the exposure of illusions and shattering of pretensions. It is not with sadness but with a kind of glee that many American intellectuals display their discoveries of new evidence of America's incorrigible hypocrisy. Those who display America's sins see no reason in them for *them* to repent. In a very profound way they do not feel themselves part of the American experience that is found guilty. The victims of America are romanticized, be they the Indians, the blacks, the ethnic immigrants or anybody else who has little chance of ever speaking or looking like a first cousin of John Winthrop eight times removed. Indeed so many groups are deemed to be the victims of the American experience that, added up, they almost total the American experience itself. The forlorn exception is the WASP male (WASP women presumably being among the victims of a sexist society). There is a vigorous competition to identify with the victim role.[5] As in the de-Nazification period following World War II good Germans hastened to find some small evidence that they were against Hitler all along, so there are those who, anticipating the judgment to come, put it on record that they are not really part of the American experience.

It is risky to speculate about the motives that inform the varieties of doomsaying in contemporary American thought. But several distinctions can be made.[6] There is what might be called tactical or political doomsaying. This is often heightened rhetoric on the part of people who do not mean to be taken literally. It is the if-you-don't school of doomsaying. A problem or injustice is located, followed by a solution offered, reinforced by an if-you-don't. If you don't . . . the blacks will send the cities up in flames; millions will die from poisoned water; we will be stacked shoulder to shoulder in a country of a billion people; we will be overwhelmed by the revolutionary rage of the Third World; and so forth. If-you-don't doomsaying has its uses, although frequently weakened by overuse.

Then there is a purely descriptive school of doomsaying. Here are the people who have come to the cool and dismal conclusion that it is all over with America. When it is honest, it is a conclusion reluctantly reached. It can be based on innumerable evidences—political, economic, cultural, military. One of the strongest evidences is the loss of nerve reflected in and intensified also by the reluctant doomsayers. And of course these people may be right. That is part of being an experiment, being vulnerable to history.

The most problematic form of doomsaying, however, might be termed preventive purgation. During the Vietnam war American aggressive bombing strikes into the North were called anticipatory retaliation. In a similar way, many current assaults upon the American experience are rationalized not on the basis of present reality but on the basis of what may happen. In Luke 16 Jesus tells the marvelous story of the unjust steward. The fellow had been doing very well by himself through various kinds of cheating, but now his master has found him out and he is about to lose his job. Being a clever man, he calls in his master's debtors one by one and proceeds to juggle the accounts in their favor, thus setting up for himself some IOUs which he will be able to call in when he is unemployed. "The sons of this world," we are told, "are wiser in their own generation than the sons of light. I tell you, make friends for yourselves by means of unrighteous mammon, so that when it fails they may receive you into the eternal habitations."

The doomsayers who believe America is terminally ill and seem so eager to hasten the end may indeed be anti-American or even self-hating Americans, as is frequently charged.[7] But it is more complex than that. Like the unjust steward in Jesus' parable, they may have made a calculation about the future and are taking steps to secure for themselves a place in whatever new order will succeed the American imperium. There is solid Christian precedent in support of the wisdom of this intuition. Again in Luke 16, we have the story of the rich man and miserable Lazarus who begged at the rich man's gate. The Requiem Mass of the Western church includes this final blessing of the faithful departed: "Into Paradise may the angels lead you: at your coming may the martyrs receive you and bring you to the holy city Jerusalem. May a choir of angels receive you, and with Lazarus, poor no more, may you find eternal rest."

Between the rich man and Lazarus the tables are now turned. It is with the Lazaruses of history that we will spend eternity. If we have not been on good terms with Lazarus here on earth, it is likely to be an awkward meeting in heaven. Contrary to vulgar legend, it is not St. Peter but Lazarus who guards the celestial gates. If, as many believe, the United States is today in the place of the rich man and America's victims at home and abroad are Lazarus, it is not pathological self-hatred but cool common sense to strike a deal with the victims. Psychological identification with the oppressed against the alleged oppressor is like taking out an insurance policy. When the day of wrath arrives and the American Babylon falls, those who have been prescient enough to take out such insurance will be able to say, "There's nobody here but us anti-Americans."

It must be quickly added that of course few of the doomsayers under discussion consciously operate with the biblical metaphors suggested here. But the dynamics are nonetheless strikingly similar. There is among the materially privileged—which is to say most Americans and almost all American intellectuals—a widespread feeling of guilt. We are fearful of the envy of those not so privileged. The litany of America's sins, of our disproportionate use of the world's resources, and so forth, has become a veritable rite of confession encountered in any issue of any opinion journal even slightly to the left of center. Such ritual confession can be seen in terms of what Helmut Schoeck calls the "appeasement of envy."[8] We are tainted by our privilege, the poor are justly envious, we must be made clean. Purgation will come hard if it is forced upon us. Perhaps the pains of purgation can be prevented or at least ameliorated if we anticipate the turning of the tables. Thus the doomsaying of preventive purgation.

The dynamics in all this are excruciatingly complex. I do not mean to caricature this style of doomsaying. There is indeed intolerable injustice in the present distribution of wealth. We are all, to the extent that we possess power and privilege, in part responsible for that injustice. The Judeo-Christian tradition does indeed affirm that the poor shall inherit the earth. Having said all this, however, it does not lead logically to the doomsaying of preventive purgation. First, it is not clear that now or in the near future is the time in which the rule of justice is to be definitively established. To assume the contrary is an instance of historical pride. We should not confuse our nervous tremors with the final apocalypse. Then too, it is an instance of intellectual pride to be certain that the collapse of America is either imminent or is necessary to the advancement of justice. It may be that the American imperium is only in its beginning phases. We shall return to that possibility in a later chapter. It may also be, as we have noted earlier, that America may yet be more instrument than hindrance toward the establishment of justice. Although the prevailing images of America coming out of the Vietnam years make it seem implausible, America may yet prove to be, as the founders hoped, a blessing and not a curse to the nations of the earth. These are possibilities to be entertained. They can only be excluded by ideological dogmas about the inevitable decline of capitalism or by organic models of the rise and decline of empires.

A further problem with the doomsaying of preventive purgation is that it smacks of false consciousness, to borrow a Marxist term. Real identification with the poor may mean, as Jesus suggested from time to time, selling all one has and giving it to the poor. It may mean engaging in the life-and-death risks of revolutionary warfare against the oppressor. But it is bad faith, as Sartre might say, to assure the poor that their perceived enemy is also your enemy, while you continue to enjoy the privileges of being the enemy, that is, of being American. The credibility of one's identification with the victim is, I should think, best measured by the victim.

In black Brooklyn, Africa and Latin America I have inquired of those who perceive themselves to be oppressed by American power. They view much of what passes for North American radicalism as being self-indulgent, hypocritical and finally pitiable. The doomsayers of preventive purgation are, unlike the unjust steward, making few friends among the rulers of the new order, if new order there is to be. Talk about the end of the American era makes sense to people who see a signal of the apocalypse in a gasoline shortage that makes them think twice about rousing three hundred horsepower to go five blocks for a pack of cigarettes. But when American power is viewed from the bottom up, from the perspective of the victim, it appears to be an unchallengeable colossus, firmly controlling the world in its own interests.

It is small comfort to the victim to have American intellectuals tell him they sympathize with his complaint and he should take heart because the colossus is fast crumbling. Having a higher estimate of the durability of American power, he needs friends who will take responsibility for changing the uses to which that power is put. He does not need American friends who psychologically (but seldom economically) take out citizenship papers as members of the Third World. He needs friends who are, on his behalf, as emphatically American as he is Guatemalan, Nigerian or Brooklyn black.

These are but some of the ways in which we neutralize the power of the future to bring us to judgment. It is possible that the American experience has already been judged and found wanting. It is conceivable that there is no American future. But to wish this to be the case is, I believe, sickly and cowardly. Those who wish such an end are neither believable nor helpful to those who see themselves as the victims of American power. It is a cowardly wish because it is a refusal to accept responsibility for one's placement in history, it is an attempt to evade the judgment that will, sooner or later, surely come. The risk of courage is to identify with the promises of justice and freedom that are deeply and religiously rooted in what America has believed about itself. Only in this way do we lay ourselves open in vulnerability to the judgment of the future.

6

The Embarrassing
Burden of Empire

To say that we are all socially and historically conditioned is a generalization of less than stunning novelty. Yet we often resist when this unexceptionable insight is applied to particular historical and social conditionings. For example, most thoughtful people are at best ambivalent about their being identified as Americans. A person may say that her being an American is just not, in the hierarchy of all the things to be said about her, a very important thing to be said about her. I am a resident of San Francisco, a mother, an executive, middle-aged, Jewish, politically liberal, a movie lover and appreciator of good food, and, yes, somewhere down on the list I'm also an American. For many of us, being an American is not a very important component in our "identity kits." As we have seen, there are myriad ways in which we can try to eliminate it altogether from our consciousness of ourselves.

To be sure, there are many who uncritically celebrate their American identity, confident that America is the biggest and the best and that therefore they, as Americans, are superior beings. But I assume that people who are not troubled by ambiguities of being American will not be reading this book. Indeed an uncomplicated view of being American requires that one avoid much reading or thinking at all. If one does think about it, being an American is inescapably complex. The American identity is filled with such extravagant, and often contradictory, claims. If America had not claimed so much for itself it would be easier to be an American. It is tempting to relieve the tension by forgetting the claims, but then we would no longer be talking about America. Or at least we would no longer be wrestling with that historically conditioned definition of America that gives us so much trouble.

It might be possible, however, to forget the claims. Many have suggested that we do just that. Perhaps the 1970s mark the period of America's coming of age, setting aside the illusions of singularity which marked our idealistic adolescence. Yet, even were we able to do this, it is doubtful that being an American would be less troubling and ambiguous. To be part of an imperial power must always be troubling for the thoughtful person. America *is* an imperial power. A citizen of Denmark need not be troubled by the questions that trouble us. He probably has no illusions that Denmark is in the vanguard of history, and, if he does, they are harmless illusions that do not impinge upon the rest of the world. He does not have to fret about the ways in which Danish military, political, economic and cultural influences change the lives of others, for better or for worse. For Americans it is more difficult.

Suppose we could drop from our history all our self-images, ideals, notions of destiny and everything else that makes up what we have called America's public piety. America would still be an imperial power. In any conceivable scenario short of nuclear annihilation, the United States will for the foreseeable future be among the strongest, maybe *the* strongest, power on earth. The ways in which American influences are, for better and for worse, inextricably intertwined with the policies, aspirations and fears of other peoples defy enumeration. America may not be as omnipotent as many Americans and some others thought it was in the first twenty years after World War II. But neither is it the pitiful, helpless giant that Richard Nixon said it would become if it were defeated in Vietnam (as indeed it has been defeated in Vietnam).

The American empire is as morally ambiguous as is power itself. Only those who feel the pain of that ambiguity know what it is to crave for the innocence of the powerless. We have discussed some of the evidences of that craving in contemporary American thought, the ways in which we would dissociate ourselves from our identity as Americans. But Americans we are, like it or not, and in some small way responsible for empire. How American power is used depends in part upon how the American experience is defined. We may, by saying we are not really part of America, decline to take responsibility for that definition. But this is clearly an instance of false consciousness. The most poignant example of its failure is when black Americans identify themselves as Africans and go to Africa only to find that Africans insistently define them as Americans. We have already discussed the more ludicrous examples of upper-middle-class white Americans who identify themselves, at least in their own minds, as citizens of the allegedly revolutionary Third World. Another alternative to the ambiguity of being American is just not to think about it. But that is merely to say that there is always the alternative of not being politically conscious, which, perhaps unfortunately, is not an option for many people.

In the time of their empire Romans expended enormous energy on the question of what it meant to be a Roman. Only in recent history have the English been relieved of empire and thus also of the need to be always asserting the meaning of England. Power is not self-legitimating. Those who have power have a need to believe in the legitimacy of their having power. They must have some *right* to it. The problem of legitimation is more complicated than it has sometimes been in the past. Other empires could, for example, appeal to the notion of racial superiority. But such an appeal is passé, both because, after the Third Reich, it is in terribly bad taste and also because, in view of America's genetic stew, it is thoroughly implausible. Others could appeal to oracles, or to the will of the gods implicit in the possession of power itself. Frances Fitzgerald has brilliantly analyzed this legitimation as it relates to the "Mandate of Heaven" in Asian thought.[1] Such a notion of divine mandate, while present in some of the more simplistic versions of America's "manifest destiny," today seems absurd or, to the religiously literate American, even blasphemous.

It is America's misfortune to have assumed (some would say "seized") the mantle of empire at a time when thoughtful people are, to a perhaps unprecedented degree, suspicious of power. The possession of power can only be legitimated by the way in which that power is exercised. The public piety or belief system of America suggests the moral criteria by which the American experience, including the American exercise of world power, can be evaluated. Our problem is that too many of the most morally sensitive American thinkers have neglected, or given up on, the task of defining America.

We are at present in the unhappy situation of having largely abandoned the perverse idealism of the cold war only to replace it with a realpolitik based upon a narrow, nineteenth-century, European definition of national interest. The former was a distortion, the latter is a repudiation, of America's historically constructed understanding of itself and of its place in the world. The Kissinger version of realpolitik, with its casual indifference to the majority of the world that is poor, violates fundamental tenets of the American public piety. While Kissinger finds it "lamentable" that so much of the world lives in misery and hunger, he wants it clearly understood that the big boys cannot let sentimentality about the plight of their lessers distract them from the proper business of power politics.[2]

Any definition of "national interest" that is historically identifiable as American must take into account the interests of the rest of the world, especially of the world's poor and oppressed.

> Give me your tired, your poor,
> Your huddled masses yearning to
>   breathe free,
> The wretched refuse of your teeming
>   shore,
> Send these, the homeless, tempest-tossed, to me:
> I lift my lamp beside the golden door.

Today we are ambivalent at best about Emma Lazarus' grand sentiment inscribed at the base of the Statue of Liberty. In his 1968 campaign,
Eugene McCarthy suggested the statue and its invitation should be turned
around, since thousands of young men opposed to the Vietnam war could
find freedom only by leaving America. Quite apart from whatever merit
his suggestion may have had, Americans today find it difficult to believe
that for millions of people Emma Lazarus' poem described nothing more
than the obvious truth. Mass immigration from the Old World was a
powerful transfusion into the bloodstream of American public piety. The
plausibility of the "idea" of America was sustained and rejuvenated by
successive waves of immigrants who discovered, or thought they discovered, its truth confirmed in new freedom, prosperity and opportunity. To
this day the rituals of patriotism are celebrated in communities with living
memories of the great immigrations with less embarrassment than among
those who take "being American" for granted.

It should not be hard to understand why the people of Hamtramck,
Michigan, or the Greenpoint section of Brooklyn, many of whom have
close relatives in Poland or Sicily, find it easier to affirm the American
experience. It is not, as some would have it, because they are anti-
intellectual, or authoritarian personalities or latent fascists. The reason
for their patriotism is embarrassingly simple. They or their parents before
them knew what it was like to live somewhere else and find living in
America much to be preferred. They may not like being called "wretched
refuse," but the humiliation is more than made up for by pride in being
American. Activists who in the sixties forced a choice between being
American and being on the side of peace and justice were unconscionably
(although in some cases unconsciously) cruel, to say nothing of being
strategically inept. Compelled to choose between any cause and their
identity as American patriots, millions will not hesitate in choosing to be
American patriots. Insofar as the cause is just and humane, the patriotism
that is separated from it will be forced to the side of injustice and
callousness.

People whose basic metaphors for understanding America are derived
from the immigrant experience are not "naturally" less humane or less
concerned for justice, nor are they a peripheral minority in America. In
the notoriously liberal Northeast first-and second-generation immigrants
make up 48.6 percent of the population of New York City and 45.5
percent of Boston, for example. Such strongholds of political conservatism as Dallas and Houston have 6.9 percent and 9.7 percent respec-
tively.[3]

Obviously, patriotic passions have many sources. Some of the uglier
forms of patriotic chauvinism have been emphatically nativist, aimed at
maintaining a supposed racial purity by keeping out the foreigners. The

anti-Catholic, anti-Semitic and anti-outsider-in-general nativist movements of the nineteenth century were of this sort. Some of this may still be found among America's purest WASPs, the Southern whites for whom, for example, the U.S. military is still a noble vocation, as witness their disproportionate representation in the officer corps. At the lowest points in Richard Nixon's political fortunes they also supplied almost the only audiences in which it was safe for him to declaim on the greatness of America. The irony, however, is that the very foreigners whom the nativists would have excluded have become the nativists' partners in the championing of American patriotism. The triumph is that ethnics have, for the most part, resisted the forced and false bifurcation of patriotism from the quest for justice.

The triumph, I hasten to add, is not yet firmly secured. The uncertainty is dramatically illustrated in the curious affinity that blue-collar immigrant communities expressed for both George Wallace and Robert Kennedy. The political positions of the two men could hardly have been more different. They both, however, played on the themes of patriotic sentiment. The nativist Wallace, now accepting the ethnic worker as a "true American," called for a repudiation of the un-American hippies, draft-card burners and welfare cheaters and for a defense of "our" rights against the doubtfully American blacks. Kennedy, affirming the American experience, called for an expansion of its benefits and deplored the war and racial injustice which, he said, were unworthy of America. To the extent that liberals and radicals persist in the error of dissociating social progress from patriotic sentiment, the immigrant American will feel forced to the side of the George Wallaces.

The legitimacy of the idea of America is hinged upon its promised benefits to all of humankind, especially to the poor and the oppressed. This legitimacy was powerfully reinforced during the last half of the nineteenth century and into this century by the great immigrations. It may be that the believability of American patriotism began to decline with the end of mass immigration in the 1920s.[4] Perhaps taken-for-granted Americanism needs to be regularly refreshed by the Americanism of those who discover America all over again. The renewal of mass immigration seems very unlikely, although there are no doubt millions in Latin America and elsewhere who would eagerly respond to the opportunities given Europeans a century ago to become U.S. citizens.

The pervasiveness and plausibility of the metaphors of rapid growth and upward mobility made it possible for a previous generation of Americans to welcome, or at least tolerate, massive immigration. Both metaphors are in serious trouble now. It might be argued that Americans could still accept a large number of outsiders who would presumably come in at a much lower level and would therefore be safely behind those already here. It might even make the present bottom 20 percent feel better to have someone else under them. But this possibility is being foreclosed as the nation moves toward establishing some kind of income floor or guaranteed minimum for all its people. Such a step is just and long overdue, but one consequence of it is to make further mass immigration highly unlikely. An income floor automatically places the outsider beside rather than behind millions of Americans and thus creates a fear of competition that is politically potent enough to forestall any wider opening of Emma Lazarus' "golden door."

These, then, are some of the reasons why the American idea will not likely be revitalized again by immigrant discovery of the American promise. Another less reputable reason is the continued, maybe increased, vitality of very old-fashioned and very ugly nativism. We may profess concern for the poor countries and say the poor should stay there to help develop those countries, despite the fact we do not consult the poor on the matter, and despite the fact that many countries could well be shed of several million people. People of conservationist bent complain that America is already overpopulated and afflicted by myriad problems resulting from crowding, despite the fact that, compared with some of the more prosperous and liveable countries of the world, the United States is sparsely populated indeed, and despite the fact there is little evidence to support a causal connection between crowding and social ills.[5]

The distateful truth is that most Americans would be appalled by the prospect of ten or forty million Mexicans, Nigerians or Malaysians coming through the "golden door." Economics aside, they are so *very* foreign. They are not more of *our* people coming from *our* old countries. They are so decidedly *them*. They are as frighteningly foreign to us as were the huddled Irish, Jewish and Italian masses frighteningly foreign to the scions of the country's founders a hundred years ago. But today, unlike a hundred years ago, America has neither the necessity nor the will to take the risk of welcoming the stranger.

Then too, also unlike a hundred years ago, America is now and beyond doubt an empire. The legitimation of the American idea, also in its imperial phase, is hinged upon America's relation to the poor and oppressed. "An extensive empire," wrote Gibbon in *The Decline and Fall*, "must be supported by a refined system of policy and oppression; in the centre, an absolute power, prompt in action, and rich in resources; a swift and easy communication with the extreme parts; fortifications to check the first effort of rebellion; a regular administration to protect and punish; and a well-disciplined army to inspire fear, without provoking discontent and despair."[6] There are of course big differences between the empire of Charlemagne which Gibbon was describing and the American empire. Global communications, multinational corporations and nuclear weaponry are among the changes that have reshaped the face, if not the substance, of empire. Pertinent to our discussion here, one thing would seem to remain constant; the home base of empire—whether Rome, or England, or Russia or America—finds some evidence of its own legitimacy in the very exercise of imperial power.

At the same time that America was being re-legitimated by the immigrant experience it was asserting its legitimacy in imperial expansion. Among the more vulgar exponents of this logic was Theodore Roosevelt. In a September, 1899, speech in Akron, Ohio, he lauded the expansionist efforts of all the nations of Western Europe. "In every instance the expansion has taken place because the race was a great race. It was a sign and proof of greatness in the expanding nation, and moreover bear in mind that in each instance it was of incalculable benefit to mankind . . . . When great nations fear to expand, shrink from expansion, it is because their greatness is coming to an end. Are we still in the prime of our lusty youth, still at the beginning of our glorious manhood, to sit down among the outworn people, to take our place with the weak and craven? A thousand times no!"[7]

What appears to be a less self-serving and more benign version of the same logic is revealed in President McKinley's description of how he sought God's guidance in deciding whether the United States should take over the Philippines:

I don't know how it was, but it came; 1) that we could not give them back to Spain—that would be cowardly and dishonorable; 2) that we could not turn them over to France or Germany—our commercial rivals in the Orient—that would be bad business and discreditable; 3) that we could not leave to themselves—they were unfit for self-government and would soon have anarchy and misrule over there worse than Spain's was; and 4) that there was nothing left for us to do but to take them all, and to educate the Filipinos, and uplift and civilize and Christianize them, and by God's grace do the very best we could by them, as our fellowmen for whom Christ also died. And then I went to bed, and went to sleep and slept soundly[8]

That America is an empire is, as I have indicated earlier, a fact to be accepted. One need not approve of it and might wish it were otherwise. I accept it as I accept the fact that Saudi Arabia has more oil than Japan. It is a factor to be taken into account. Without agreeing completely with those who argue that power seeks a vacuum and therefore we should rush to fill every vacuum with our power rather than "theirs," I do not deny that American imperium is probably, by and large, preferable to the two alternative imperial powers, that of the Soviet Union and, sometime in the future, of China. But one must be much more hesitant in supposing there is a destiny that mandates America's imperial expansion.

McKinley, Roosevelt and others notwithstanding, much of America's public piety is not comfortable with imperial power. That stream of public piety is better represented in the words of John Quincy Adams: "Wherever the standard of freedom and independence has been or shall be unfurled, there will be America's heart, her benedictions, and her prayers. But she goes not abroad in search of monsters to destroy. She is the well-wisher to the freedom and independence of all. She is the champion and vindicator only of her own."[9] America's contribution was to inspire the world by fulfilling her own promise to her own people, not by imposing her rule on others.

But Adams' counsel can no longer be followed, at least not literally, for America has become an empire. Not just Americans, but all thoughtful people must be uneasy about the possession of imperial power. Writing during World War I, George Unwin said of the English: "Empire is congenial enough to the Englishman's temperament, but it is repugnant to his political conscience. In order that he may be reconciled to it, it must seem to be imposed upon him by necessity, as a duty. Fate and metaphysical aid must seem to have crowned him."[10] So today it is reasoned by the national security managers and foreign policy experts in Washington, in the universities and in the Council on Foreign Relations. Following World War II America had no responsible choice but to accept the mantle of world hegemony bestowed by a shattered Europe. In recent years "revisionist" historians have sharply challenged this orthodoxy. They accent deliberate calculation rather than destiny, economic greed rather than morality and seizure rather than acceptance as the modes by which the United States elevated itself to empire.

On whatever side, or in whatever mixture of sides, the truth may be, for most of us empire is, if not repugnant, at least troubling to our political conscience. Yet we must attend to the imperial realities lest America's global influence be left to those who suffer few qualms of conscience in the exercise of imperial power. In international affairs, as in its domestic behavior, America must be judged in terms of accountability to the poor. This can only happen, and even then very imperfectly, if there is a strong domestic constitutency exerting political pressure with regard to U.S. policies abroad. At present, after Vietnam, there is no such constituency. The building of such a constituency should have a major claim on the energies of the churches, synagogues and other voluntary associations in the country.

As important as it is to hold to account America's world influence, that is not finally where the American promise will be vindicated or repudiated. Neither the good America may be able to do in the world nor the good it offered the immigrant masses can vindicate the American experiment. As was once so eloquently stated at Gettysburg, the experiment is to test whether a nation conceived and dedicated as this one is can both endure and signal a new birth of freedom for mankind. Although both immigration and expansion are inseparable from what the American experience has been, they cannot legitimate that experience. Both immigration and expansion are dependent upon power, the power to attract people with material benefits, the power to impose one's will upon others. But, as we have noted, power is not self-legitimating, it requires a moral rationale.

Americans, as visiting observers have noted from the beginning, are incorrigibly moralistic. Not in the sense of being upright in behavior, but in the sense of being perpetually exercised about the rights and wrongs of things. During the great immigrations, the attractions of America's material benefits were reinforced by, legitimated by, what appeared to be America's moral stature in the world as examplar of liberty and concern for the world's little people. Until the Vietnam war, America's new imperial power appeared to be legitimated by her global defense of freedom. That banner of legitimation is badly tattered, perhaps beyond repair. Some new legitimation must be found, if indeed there is legitimacy to American power. It might be found in part through a changed role for American power in the world, especially in the Third World. But I suspect it will not be found abroad unless it is first, or perhaps simultaneously, found in the American character and in the quality of our own society.

The question with which the experiment began was succinctly put by the Frenchman, J. Hector St. John de Crèvecoeur, who settled in western New York and in 1782 issued his famous *Letters from an American Farmer:* "What then is the American, this new man?" He answered, "He is either an European or the descendant of an European . . . who leaving behind him all his ancient prejudices and manners, receives new ones from the new mode of life he has embraced, the new government he obeys, and the new rank he holds."[1] Almost two hundred years later much more must be appended to Crèvecoeur's description, but his question is what the continuing experiment is all about, "What then is the American, this new man?" Our uneasiness may be with the assumption behind the question, that there is something all that new about the American. Maybe we are right to be uneasy. America is, after all, an old nation as nations go. Maybe the sense of newness made sense in a time when the frontier was hardly imagined, not to mention closed. Maybe it was futile to think the newness could be sustained through the transformations of two centuries. Or, just maybe, we are reluctant to assume responsibility for our part in the continuing experiment.

7

The Covenant
and the Salvation
for Which We Hope

A covenant is a very troublesome thing. It consists in promise making and promise keeping and, things being as they are, promise breaking. It is relentlessly historical, and therefore vulnerable to the unexpected. Contract theories of social order, from John Locke to John Rawls, are ever so much more pleasant to contemplate. They are presumably constructed upon constants in the human condition; constants rationally ordered and secured by law and habit. Social contracts appeal to the romantic as well as to the business and technological mind. The answer to social ills lies in striking more rational deals according to the logic of enlightened self-interest, or, for the engineers among us, in fixing up the machinery of social interaction. Covenant, on the other hand, invokes the metaphors of adventure, pilgrimage and vulnerability to the unknown.

To be sure, much of the thinking that has been formative of American polity and policy has been of the social-contract variety. This is especially true of the eighteenth-century Enlightenment thinking that went into shaping such foundational scriptures as the Constitution. To expunge the influence of John Locke from American history would be as absurd as is the more common effort to expunge the influence of the Puritans. In either case one is left with a notion of America that has little to do with the America that has been and, *mutatis mutandis,* will be. Public philosophy in America is, at its best, a lively dialectic between contract and covenant. There are several reasons why I believe the present need is for an emphasis on covenant.

First, the emphasis on covenant is a necessary corrective to the more secularly respectable contract thought that dominates the discussion of such things today. Second, given the admitted crisis in American identity, some of the liveliest metaphors and conceptual resources for change are inseparably tied to the imagery of covenant. Experiment, judgment, forgiveness and renewal are all emphatically historical categories. They assume a transcendent point of reference to which we are corporately accountable, and they assume *times* in which judgment is rendered, forgiveness bestowed, renewal begun and the experiment either vindicated or repudiated. Then too, the alternatives to covenant imagery manifest an inherent addiction to the present or, more frequently, an addiction to seeking foundation in some past time. Contract theory, for example, often implies that human nature is now discoverable. Once we have discerned and catalogued its interests, conflicts and commonalities, we can with a degree of mathematical precision order its corporate existence, which we call society. An alternative approach in contract thinking acknowledged that man as he is is sadly distorted by perverse (irrational) social systems. One must revert to some idealized or hypothetical past to discover man as he *really* is. In political thought this conceptual regression can, as we have seen, assume both radical and conservative forms. In whatever form, I believe it is delusory and destructive of creative social change.

The truer vision, and the vision upon which covenant thought is hinged, is that man and his society are indeed profoundly distorted. The perspective from which one makes this judgment, however, is not from some rationally idealized past or present but from a hoped-for future. Man is man becoming. In the continuing debate over abortion, the fetus is often referred to as only a potential human being. The point here is that we are all only potential human beings. God, who is the power of the future, has made a covenant with his creation that he will bring to completion that which he has started. Whatever might be said about the American covenant must always be understood in the context of this larger covenant. The covenant relevant to America is but a specific instance of that covenant with the creation—just as whatever sense of covenantal accountability each of us may have about his or her own life is worked out, with greater or lesser awareness, within the social reality that is America.

In the last few sentences I have, of course, touched on one reason why covenant thought has been so neglected and the dialectic between covenant and contract so enervated. Covenant thought in America has historically involved talk about God. Such incisive critics as Daniel Bell can also call for a "transcendent ethic," a point of reference which might again offer a meeting point for our fast diverging cultural images, on the one hand, and social systems on the other. "The lack of a rooted moral belief system is the cultural contradiction of the society, the deepest challenge to its survival."[1] And yet, for him, the dilemma seems insoluble, given radical cultural pluralism and a regnant science that is incapable of dealing with values, a science that is, by its own ethos, committed to deal only with "facts."

Theoretically at least, there are several ways out of this dilemma. One is to seek secularized conceptual substitutes for the embarrassingly religious notions that have shaped covenant thought. This kind of conceptual sanitization or laundering has preoccupied much of what is called Christian apologetics. Another way out, taking a cue from Pascal, is to urge a kind of covenant gamble. We can act *as though* there is a covenantal purpose in our common life, grateful if the assumption turns out to be true but knowing we have not lost much if it turns out to be false. In either case we have had the renewing benefit of the lively symbols of the covenant.

Yet more cynical is the option for the scientific and political elite to invoke the covenant in all its religious tonalities, knowing that the great majority of Americans, being much less secularized than the elite presumably is, will thereby be guided, inspired and perhaps controlled. The leaders of ancient Greece and Rome and men such as Thomas Jefferson and Benjamin Franklin in our own history were uninhibited in appealing to God or the gods, acknowledging the public usefulness of beliefs they did not share. It is perhaps not unkind to suggest that much of prayer-breakfast and political oratory today falls into this category. It is just that it does not seem to work so well today. The public perceives such invocations of the sacred as implausible or (much worse in a culture addicted to subjectivity) as insincere.

Then too, the churches today, unlike the guardians of the temple mysteries in the past, are much more readily provoked by the suspicion that religion is being used to legitimate public policies in which they have no genuine religious interest. A good example of this was the inability, by and large, of political leadership to use the symbols of "Christian America" in selling the Vietnam war to the American people.[2] This was in stark contrast to the use of civil religion in past wars. One has no reason to believe that the theological integrity of the churches is that much stronger today. At another time and for another cause they may be as eager as ever to sacralize public policy, no matter how dubious. But right now church leadership is as unlikely to bless the American experience as is *The New York Review of Books* to come out for the gun lobby.

There is, of course, a large cluster of evangelical or fundamentalist churches for which this generalization does not hold true. Although large in numbers, their political potency is limited by their affirmation of an America that is alien to the mainstream of the nation's public piety, by their concentration on privatized morality, and by the fact that they are, with thinly veiled disdain, viewed as marginal by the politically potent mass media. They provide no foundation for a transcendent ethic or rooted moral belief system for the larger culture. Nor, I quickly add, would they want to serve as such a foundation. The business of the church, they insist, is not to meddle in the affairs of the world, unless it involves such clear "moral issues" as pornography and the licensing of liquor outlets.

We might note in passing that one of the ominous transitions in American public piety occurred when Christian revivalism lost its concern for shaping the culture. From the seventeenth through most of the nineteenth centuries, the great religious revivals engaged the most creative minds in the tasks of culture formation. Today we must live with the legacy of Billy Sunday and others, perpetuated by Billy Graham, in which revivalism is virulently anti-intellectual and anticultural. This has in turn led to the unhappy dilemma in which religious vitality is bifurcated from social concern, the dilemma analyzed by Dean Kelley and discussed in an earlier chapter.

Covenant thought, then requires a transcendent point of reference. But it is precisely such a point of reference that seems to be so irretrievably lost to culture-forming thought in our day. I have mentioned several theoretically possible ways out of this dilemma. None of them offers an answer to Bell's question about a transcendent ethic, the lack of which is "the deepest challenge to [our society's] survival." The more promising course is to challenge the prevailing notions of "science" and of "secularity." One hopes that books such as Andrew Greeley's recent *Unsecular Man* will encourage others to join in challenging the allegedly inexorable force of secularization. In *A Rumor of Angels*, Peter Berger threw down a gauntlet that has still to be picked up. He analyzed the constrictive, arbitrary and finally unscientific character of what today passes for secular scientific rationality. Most ambitiously, the theologian Wolfhart Pannenberg is engaged in an architectonic enterprise of reconstructing theology as a scientific discipline based upon public evidence and fully comprehending the insights of post-Enlightenment man.[3]

Such a recovery of nerve and such a reconstruction are essential if the church is to play a part in the renewal of public piety through the discovery, or rediscovery, of a transcendent ethic. Without the church's help such a transcendent ethic might be discovered nonetheless. But we ought not be looking for just *any* ethic that will provide a sense of communal cohesiveness and supply a point of reference for judgment. National socialism with its myths of blood and soil, and Soviet Russia with its myths of historical inevitability are both instances of transcendent ethics that, from a purely pragmatic viewpoint, supplied cultural legitimations for social systems. They are not happy precedents. In the absence of the Absolute point of reference that we speak of as God, some lesser and finally dehumanizing mythology will be enlisted to serve the needs of communal identity and cohesiveness which will not go unserved for very long.

We have touched upon some of the ways in which the religious vision of the covenant might be related to the hunger of the "cultured despisers of religion." Perhaps the single most important change required for the revival of covenant thought in our general culture is to overcome the secular prejudice against Judeo-Christian truth claims because they are thought to be nonrational or even irrational. We cannot be content to let these claims be consigned to the realms of subjective faith, poetry and religious feeling. We must liberate the Christian claims from their religious ghettoes so that they can enter into the world of universal reason and make their impact upon our public understanding of history's purpose, including, among other events, the American experience.

The symbol of covenant, like any symbol, must have some correspondence to reality in order to be effective. For an idea to have a sustained enlivening effect, it is not enough for the idea to be lively. (One may find being the richest man in the world a lively idea, but one doesn't need to wait for the monthly bills to realize its lack of correspondence with reality.) That America is to be conceived in terms of covenant assumes realities such as the purposefulness of history and the transcendent point of reference who is the Lord of history. Making the argument for the plausibility of those realities is not the immediate task of this book.

The more modest task at hand is to persuade people who subscribe to the Christian truth claims that these claims contain the resources by which the American experience can be creatively redefined. It is a more modest task than that of persuading nonbelievers of the truth of the claims, but it is in some ways as difficult. Among those who accept the claims there are conflicting ideas about how they are to be related to the American experience, if they are to be related at all.

There is a radical, often apocalyptic, school that sees America as Babylon already judged and found wanting. Thus lawyer and lay theologian William Stringfellow: "America is a fallen nation . . . America is a demonic principality, or conglomeration of principalities and powers in which death furnishes the meaning, in which death is the reigning idol. Enshrined in multifarious forms and guises, it enslaves human beings, exacts human sacrifices, captures and captivates Presidents as well as intimidating and dehumanizing ordinary citizens."[4] The writings of Jacques Ellul, another lawyer and lay theologian, go even further in repudiating not just the American but all social and political structures as idolatrous illusions. While the Stringfellows picture themselves in a prophetic tradition, calling down judgment that should issue in repentance and reform, Ellul condemns reform itself as a demonic delusion designed to blunt the sharp edge of the radical finality of divine judgment: "Judgment has been rendered once and for all: 'The Light came into the world, and the world did not receive it.' There is no use trying again. And if you see the powers of the world so well disposed, when you see the state, money, cities accepting your word, it is because your word, whether you are only a man of good will or an evangelist, has become false. For it is only to the extent that you are a traitor that the world can put up with you."[5]

Although Ellul's argument insistently, almost fundamentalistically, appeals to the Bible, it is not dissimilar in tone and import to some of the "secular" radicalisms of recent years. "In the dialectical view," Norman O. Brown writes, "demystification becomes the discovery of a new mystery. The next generation needs to be told that the real fight is not the political fight, but to put an end to politics. From politics to poetry. . . . Poetry, art, imagination, the creator spirit is life itself; the real revolutionary power to change the world."[6]

Less respectable, and not usually labeled as politically radical, are other apocalyptic schools such as the Jehovah's Witnesses. Here too it becomes impossible, indeed an act of blasphemy, to relate the Christian truth claims in a way that can shape the cultural metaphors of the American experience. Judgment has already been rendered upon the American and upon all principalities and powers. The imperative is not to reform or to reshape but to come out and be separate, to gather together the remnant to be saved in the awful Day of the Lord.

Closely related to this view, although usually less apocalyptic and less strident, is a privatized understanding of the Christian gospel that does not so much condemn existing economic and social orders as it bifurcates these orders from the realm within which the Christian truth claims hold sway. Christian existence is centered in the very personal world of subjective experience and its public expression is limited to acts thought to be specifically religious. In its more refined theological versions, this approach espouses some notion of two kingdoms. There is the kingdom of grace and the kingdom of power. Again and again, this approach has degenerated into suggesting that there is the kingdom of Christ, on the one hand, and the kingdom of the world on the other. Which finally comes out in its more vulgar form: religion and politics don't mix.

Such an approach makes it difficult, if not impossible, for Christianity to play its culture-forming role. The dynamics of grace and redemption are removed from the mundane stuff of everyday history and reserved to the distinct realms of the sacred. I hasten to add that the doctrine of the two kingdoms, which has been particularly prominent in Lutheran theology, does not necessarily intend these consequences. But it is historical fact that the distinction of realms has invited the bifurcation of realms, the church's failure in Nazi Germany being but the most horrendous example.[7] These may not be necessary consequences of the two-kingdom doctrine, just as revivalism need not reduce Christianity to privatized experientialism. The point here is simply to illustrate that, among those who accept the Christian truth claims, there is no necessary agreement on the culture-forming impact of those claims. Still today the most useful analysis and summary of these diverse viewpoints within the Christian tradition is H. Richard Niebuhr's *Christ and Culture.*, to which we will have occasion to return.

Covenant imagery, as we have seen, assumes a transcendent point of reference. Contract imagery has us making promises to one another, which is, of course, an essential part of any social order.The covenant has us, together, making promises to Another. He is, as the German Roman Catholic theologian Karl Rahner has taught us to call him, the Absolute Future. Our promises are in reponse to his prior promise, that he will bring to completion that which he has started. What he has started is, quite simply, history. Here the term *history* means the totality of all that has been, all that is and all that will be. History is synonymous with the whole of reality. All that has been and all that is is *realized* in what will be. That is, history is realized in the Absolute Future. Thus, in the Christian view, the plan of salvation is nothing less than the fulfillment of history. "And when all things shall be subdued unto him, then shall the Son also himself be subject unto him that put all things under him, that God may be all in all" (1 Cor. 15). The center of the biblical message and of the ministry of Jesus is the insistence that the Kingdom of God is at hand.

The American experience is an important part of the history whose fulfillment is promised. It is obviously important to us because we *are* part of the American experience. In a larger sense it is important because America is such a large part of this historical epoch. If the fulfillment of history bypasses the hundreds of millions of people whose lives have, in one way or another, been shaped by the American experience, it is not a very interesting fulfillment. The Kingdom which Jesus described is one in which every sparrow that has fallen and every hair that has gone down the washbasin is given its due. He knew nothing about a spiritualized Kingdom that drew back from the itching, sweating particularities of historical existence. Paraphrasing Jesus, we might ask, Are not the countless lives, dreams, hopes and tears that comprise the American experience worth infinitely more than sparrows and lost hairs?

But now we must back up a moment. Surely some distinctions are in order when we speak of the American experience. It is one thing to speak of all the people, all the human stuff, that has gone into making the phenomenon we call America. It is something else to speak of the political, ideological and social orders and powers that distinguish the *American* experience from other collective experiences. If, when we speak of the fulfillment of the American experience, we are referring only to God's redemptive love for individual persons called Americans, what we say would be equally applicable to Englishmen, South Africans and Chinese. It may be that people are "saved" *despite* the social and political orders that comprise the distinctively American experience. In the past, collectivities such as Babylon and Assyria came under divine judgment. They were, according to biblical witness, repudiated by God. Yet God's love for his individual children, including his Babylonian and Assyrian children, remains certain.

It is far from certain that God has made a covenant with the American experience as such. Babylon, Nineveh, Assyria and the Third Reich all fell under the divine wrath. The American empire may be today's Babylon. Only the future will reveal whether or not this is the case. The business of Christians is to try to anticipate and act upon the divine judgment. If we believe America to be Babylon, then we must act upon the warning of the book of Revelation and come out from her that we not partake in her sins. Such a decision is radical. One must then be anti-American for the sake of the Kingdom.

In a variant of this view, one must be anti-American not because of anything unique to America but simply because, at this moment in history, America represents power, and salvation is to be discovered in repudiating "the principalities and powers of the present age." This conviction is given eloquent expression by the pacificst R. V. Sampson:

To admit no violence whatever as legitimate is to repudiate all politics, all power, and thus expose to the light of day the unwanted truth that the responsibility for ending the evils in the body politic rests inescapably on each one of us, who can only contribute to moral progress by mending his own life. Those who make this truth clear are apt to experience difficulty in getting their voices heard anywhere. . . . We cannot all be born Thoreaus or Blakes, but their values are not esoteric ones. In so far as they lead to life—and to a life bearing within it the joy of endless renewal without robbing anyone else of a like joy—they are values which are desirable for their own sake and attainable by all alike.[8]

Such a posture over against the political order regularly reappears in Western Christian history and has indeed enriched our common experience. We have seen how in the case of William Stringfellow, for example, such a posture is bent to essentially reformist purposes. Ellul, Sampson and (with confusing twists and turns) Daniel Berrigan carry their equation of power and Babylon further, opposing the reforms that can only make the essential evil of power appear more seductively attractive. But in arguing for the American covenant, these are not the people against whom we must primarily contend. They have chosen a radically different option, and only the future will reveal if they are right. In affirming the covenantal character of American experience, one takes a deliberate risk, knowing full well the vulnerability to the future's judgment.

God has made a general covenant with his creation and a specific covenant with Israel and his church, the Body of Christ. It is not revealed that God has entered into the American covenant. Without the participation of the other party, of God, the covenant is only illusion. To believe in the American covenant is either an act of supreme arrogance or of supreme trust. My trust in the fulfillment of the creation and in the community of the church are also vulnerable to repudiation by the future. But at least with regard to the creation and to the Christian community we have an explicit word we consider revelatory, and upon that word we take our risks. We have no such explicit word with regard to the American experience. The American covenant is therefore derivative, to be accepted insofar as it conforms to the "revealed" intentions of God in history. The American covenant is therefore more tenuous, more contingent, more radically experimental. But such risk should not scare off people who are prepared to bet their lives upon the unlikely proposition that an itinerant rabbi who was executed in the boondocks of history almost two thousand years ago will be revealed as Lord of the universe.

The argument, then, is not primarily against the Elluls and others who have a radically different understanding of how God works in history. Their witness poses the question of whether God necessarily works through power, and systems and laws, and even through tragedy and violence to achieve his redemptive purposes. At a deeper level it is a question of whether the promised redemption is through history, apart from history or even against history. In Christ, we can act in the courage of our uncertainties. All bets are made in the name of him whose power of forgiveness is greater than our errors. One is a pacifist; the other reluctantly takes up arms in service to the neighbor. One remains untainted by the inevitable falsities of power politics; the other engages in contesting for the right, or at least for the lesser evil. One condemns the American Dream because it is a false hope for people called to seek the Kingdom; the other embraces the dream because there is within it the foretaste of the promised fulfillment. Each decides in the courage of uncertainty, in the gift of faith. As to who is right, "Let no man judge before the time" (1 Cor. 4).

The burden of the argument is not against those who try, as best they can, to come out from among the condemned of the American Babylon. The argument is rather with those who partake fully in the glories or abominations, as the case may be, of the American experience yet accept no religious responsibility for that experience. The lives of the vast majority of Christians in the United States are inseparable from the

American experience. Our language, our values, our career patterns, our attitudes toward personal worth, our manner of social interaction—all bear the unmistakable trademark of America. It is our placement in time and history.

Of infinite possible times and spaces, America is the time and space in which we are what we are. We as individuals are not abstracted souls but socially constructed persons. There is no self to be saved other than the self of historically conditioned time and space. Aside from being obscenely egocentric, it is an impossible abstraction to envision my individual salvation while all that made me *me* is either damned or viewed with indifference. Such an attitude is one of disdain toward the mystery of the incarnation in which God most dramatically and irretrievably made his very Being contingent upon the creation's fulfillment. In yearning for the creation's fulfillment (Rom. 8), we are but joining God in his suffering.

The American experience is an inescapable factor in our moment of history's yearning. There is cause for scandal in the suggestion that America may be a sacred instrument of divine purpose. It is but a small part of the scandal of God's becoming man. It is not to be compared with the scandal of God's throwing his very existence into doubt until his existence is demonstrated in his rule in the Kingdom of God, in the creation finally fulfilled.

We must be careful in speaking about the connection between individual and social salvation. I do not mean to suggest there is no personal salvation apart from the salvation of the society of which one is part. As a social system, as a way of ordering human behavior and aspirations, America might finally be condemned. That does not mean all Americans would be condemned, just as not all Germans of the period were condemned by virtue of the condemnation of the Third Reich. Those German Christians who gave themselves to what was evil in the Third Reich might to that extent expect to have their lives repudiated. That which participated in the evil also falls under judgment. To the extent that we ally ourselves with evil, we may be forgiven but not vindicated. We all hope for the vindication received by the servant in Jesus' parable to whom the master says, "Well done, thou good and faithful servant." But we must all finally rely upon the mercy shown the penitent thief on the cross. If that reliance, however, relieves the sense of urgency about being faithful here and now, we have fallen into the trap of what Dietrich Bonhoeffer called "cheap grace." We have then become historically irresponsible, indifferent to the history of which our lives are part. Being historically irresponsible may seem like a minor fault, until we consider that it is precisely to history, also to *our* history, that God has committed his all and invites us to commit our all.

Those who believe, and act upon the belief, that America is Babylon are being historically responsible. They may be wrong, I think they are wrong, but they are taking history seriously. The alternative is not to think that America represents God's design for the ages or is the unique agent of his purposes. We have no revelation to that effect and we do have a great deal of unhappy evidence to the contrary. The alternative is to sense a promise and hope within the American experience that are deserving of our devotion. The alternative is to meet the judgment of the future in the full particularity of our historical identity. To meet God, if you will, as Americans. To be sure, we meet him first of all as people redeemed by his saving love in Jesus Christ. Without that, there is no meeting that can be welcomed. We are not redeemed as platonic souls, however, but as historical persons who lived out the only history that is ours within the context of the American experience. We are inextricably part of that experience.

We might argue that, if we are redeemed, then part of the American experience is being redeemed. Since presumably there are many of us, a large part of the American experience is being redeemed. But that argument soon starts turning in circles. We could as well say that, since many Germans who lived during the period are redeemed, the Third Reich is in large part redeemed. We could also say in that case that the redemption of those Americans who lived out their discipleship in opposition to the American experience contributes to the vindication of the American experience. The tautology soon becomes evident. There is, by that logic, no way America can lose. As we have seen, covenant implies contingency, the possibility of losing.

No, when I speak of standing before God as an American, I mean standing before God as one who identifies with the American social experiment and accepts a measure of responsibility for America's influence in the world. If it turns out that America is indeed more Babylon than New Jerusalem, I will have made a very serious error indeed. But not, I hope, a fatal error. "American" is not the only nor the chief component in my identity. I would assert that I am human being and Christian before I am American, although I am not quite sure what the assertion means since I am inescapably an American human being and an American Christian. I just know it is a necessary assertion, not least because Christianity affirms a redeemed and redemptive community that knows no barriers of race, language, nation or culture. It is also a liberating assertion. Not because it liberates me from religious responsibility for the particularities of my placement as an American, but because it gives me an identity, a psychic "place to stand," from which I can deliberately *choose* to be an American.

Although, unlike the immigrants of yesterday and today, most of us had little to do with our being Americans, being American is not simply a matter of historical fatedness. To put it another way, fate is affirmed by decision, and is therefore not *mere* fate. If one is American by both circumstance and will, the salvation for which he hopes incorporates the communal experiment he has embraced. The ultimate hope for the Kingdom of God must be in some sort of continuity with what one has loved and celebrated in this our provisional moment in history. This is not to deny the freedom of God or that there are glories beyond the imagination yet to be revealed. But God has, in freedom, bound himself to history's yearning. His revelation of his purposes may be surprising, but he is not capricious. His aim is not to keep us guessing about what he is up to. He rather calls us to live lives of radical faithfulness to the signs he has given, preeminently in Jesus the Christ, and he, on his part, pledges faithfulness to his promises.

It is worth dwelling for a moment on this question of continuity and capriciousness. Christians have always been somewhat ambivalent about the use of analogies in trying to picture the Kingdom Come. We reject what is called an Islamic paradise (but is really a caricature of Muslim piety) which is depicted as a hedonistic heaven of endless revelry and debauchery, the best things of this life squared. Yet, if we are truly to hope for the Kingdom, it must be in some kind of continuity with what we partially experience and celebrate now—justice, love, truth, joy. We see through a glass darkly and know only in part, but we do see and we do know. We may be many millennia from the Kingdom's final realization, but we are part of the history that is in process of realization. There is no smooth, uninterrupted, upward and onward progression toward the Kingdom. Because of the sin that is radical to the human condition, there is tragedy and reversal and the experience of despair. But we are on the way. The children of Israel did not take the shortest route from Egypt to Canaan.

It is cognitively necessary to think of the Kingdom in terms of our present experience. We have no concepts that are not derived from what we have known. More to the point, God's promise invites us to analogize from our experience. His very revelation of himself and his final will has been within our collective experience, that is, within history. "And the Word became flesh and dwelt among us, full of grace and truth; we have beheld his glory, glory as of the only Son from the Father" (John 1). As the late Rabbi Abraham Heschel was fond of saying (admittedly, without the Christological reference), "When we think of God in terms of our experience we are not anthropomorphizing God; he has theomorphized our experience." That is, the believer does not make God over into his image but rather sees himself and the world in the image of God.

Some biblical scholars emphasize the discontinuities in eschatological

images of the End Time.[9] There is an abundance of imagery in the Bible
to support this emphasis: the day of wrath, mourning, and judgment, stars
falling, thrones tumbling, and pyrotechnics enough to make the most
dreadful nuclear holocaust seem like a Roman candle that fizzled. Some
of this more grotesque imagery reflects a strain of religious piety that is,
well, grotesque. It is the stuff of fire and brimstone preaching and of a
brand of orthodoxy that makes God's glory dependent upon the eternal
damnation of sinners.

Preferable is the school that seeks a Kingdom in which the sparrows
find their place and all get their lost hairs back. It is not simply that such a
Kingdom is more attractive. It is because that is the Kingdom God has
promised. To be sure, there are radical discontinuities. The Kingdom
Come will no doubt be radically different from anything we can know or
imagine in our very provisional moment of history. Different from, but
not in contradiction to, the love and truth and beauty which God has
revealed and in which our hope has taken form. God is no doubt surprising, but he is not capricious. He is not wanton or erratically self-indulgent, entertaining himself by playing tricks on those he calls to obedience.
Although we in our ignorance may at times think him capricious, the most
elementary statement of biblical monotheism is that God is a faithful God.
In view of the incarnation, he has made himself, so to speak, accountable
to history, and it is only on that premise that he calls us to join him in
a like accountability. Thus it is that God has something at stake in the
American experience. If this were not the case, if it were a matter of
indifference to him, then we who seek our life's purpose in doing his will
have no stake in the American experience.

Christians must learn from our elder brothers in living Judaism to again
argue with God. It is a necessary part of taking him and his promises
seriously. The nineteenth-century Hasidic rebbe of Kotzk cried:[10]

> Master of the Universe, send us our Messiah,
>   for we have no more strength to suffer.
> Show me a sign, O God. Otherwise . . .
>   . . . otherwise . . . I rebel against Thee.
> If Thou dost not keep Thy Covenant,
>   then neither will I keep that Promise,
>   and it is all over, we are through being
> Thy chosen people, Thy peculiar treasure.

To be sure, Christians believe that Jesus of Nazareth is the promised
messiah. In an anticipatory, proleptic way we already celebrate the End
Time, the Kingdom, in his abiding presence among us. But the promise
has not yet been fully realized. A mere look within ourselves or at the
world around us is evidence enough that history has not achieved its

promised fulfillment. Therefore the whole of the Christian life is a life of hope. "Now hope that is seen is not hope. For who hopes for what he sees? But if we hope for what we do not see, we wait for it with patience" (Rom. 8). Two thousand years after Paul—after countless wars, famines, failed revolutions and death camps—we should not maybe be so patient. They also wait who wait in protest and frustration, crying out of the darkness, "How long, O Lord? How long?"

When the early Christian community discovered that God was not keeping to the eschatological schedule they had set, his tardiness became something of an embarrassment. *Realized eschatology* is a relatively recent term in Christian theology, but the ploy has in one sense or another been a staple response to the Kingdom's delay. Whether in the systematic theologian's more sophisticated version or in the revival preacher's more vulgar version, realized eschatology comes down to saying that the Kingdom has come if you only believe it has come. There is erudite talk about a *Heilsgeschichte* ("salvation history") in which God has kept all his promises and the plan of salvation is neatly wrapped up. We are instructed not to be confused by the evidence of ordinary, secular history. But we all live in that ordinary, secular history where prisoners cry in the night, the unborn are killed for convenience, the useless aged are put out of their misery and ten thousand people die from hunger each day.

Rejecting the palliative of diverse realized eschatologies, there is the stubborn, persistent question, "How long, O Lord? How long?" We sing the Virgin's song, but we sing it as a song of hope, knowing that it describes not what is but what is to be. The proud have *not* been scattered in the imagination of their hearts, nor have the mighty been put down from their thrones, nor have those of low degree been exalted, nor have the hungry been filled with good things, nor have the rich been sent empty away. Not yet. Mary's hope and ours has not yet been vindicated, not fully, not the way he promised.

"If Thou dost not keep Thy Covenant . . ." Our collective situation is the situation of Job of old. Those who would relieve the tension between the Now and the Not Yet are the Eliphazes and Bildads and Zophars of our day. There is no relief short of the Kingdom Come. Every synthesis by which the world would be made acceptable as it is is a premature synthesis and the essence of idolatry. Every synthesis that is proffered—whether it be religious, philosophical, psychological or political—is a cheap substitute for that promised Kingdom, the search for which is the meaning of Christian existence. God neither needs nor wants our excuses for the trouble he is having in keeping his promise. He wants us to hold him to his word. Job asks Zophar, "Will you plead God's defense with prevarication, his case in terms that ring false? Will you be partial in his favor, and act as his lawyers? . . . Can he be duped as men are duped? Harsh rebuke you would receive from him for your covert partiality" (Job 13).

Job does God the honor of taking him at his word. "But my words are intended for the Lord; I mean to take up my argument with God." Then it all comes pouring out, a torrent of complaint, words tumbling over one another, laments elbowing their way to the front to gain the Lord's attention. But behind the words is Job's unbreakable confidence. Even though he goes down to Sheol in shame and misery, yet there will be another time. "Then you would call, and I should answer, you would want to see the work of your hands once more" (Job 14). "You would want to see the work of your hands once more"—God has a stake in Job's vindication. He cannot deny Job without at the same time denying part of himself, for Job is the work of his hands.

Commentators have noted that the question posed by the book of Job is not whether God's ways can be justified to man but whether man can love God purely. The opening chapter's dialogue has God asking Satan, "Whence have you come?" Satan answered the Lord, "From going to and fro on the earth, and from walking up and down on it." And the Lord said to Satan, "Have you considered my servant Job, that there is none like him on the earth, a blameless and upright man, who fears God and turns away from evil?" Then Satan answered the Lord, "Does Job fear God for nought? Hast thou not put a hedge about him and his house and all that he has, on every side? Thou hast blessed the work of his hands, and his possessions have increased in the land. But put forth thy hand now, and touch all that he has, and he will curse thee to thy face." Around this question turns the wager which is the drama of the book of Job: "Does Job fear God for nought?" Toward the end of the story, after Job has laid out his case before the Lord, the Lord "speaks out of the whirlwind" and takes a couple of chapters to put Job into his place, beginning with, "Shall a faultfinder contend with the Almighty? He who argues with God, let him answer it." The author has the Lord run through the differences between the Almighty and mere mortal man, rehearsing especially all God's great acts of creation, including the Behemoth and Leviathan and his control over the hoary deeps. At the end of this rehearsal, Job is properly intimidated: "I know that you are all-powerful, that what you conceive you can perform . . . I have been holding forth on matters I cannot understand, marvels beyond me and my knowledge . . . I take back what I have said, and I repent in dust and ashes."

At this point many commentators would bring the story to a close. Job's final submission is the answer to Satan's question, "Does Job fear God for nought?" The answer is yes, and this submission of utter self-abandonment is the measure of true religion. In *Purity of Heart,* Kierkegaard takes up the same theme in connection with Abraham's readiness to sacrifice his son Isaac. Abraham's obedience, says Kierkegaard, is pure because it is against his moral sensibilities and even against his understanding of God's promise, for God had promised that through Isaac Abraham would become the father of many nations. Thus Abraham and Job are pointed to as examples of existentialist heroism, surrendering all in a radical leap of faith. But to stop these stories at the point where Kierkegaard would stop them is like ending the narrative of the Christ event with Jesus' last words on the cross, "Father, into thy hands I commend my spirit." In wondrous fact the narrative ends (and begins) with the Father's vindication of Jesus by raising him from the dead. So also with Abraham, God intervenes before Isaac is killed and does indeed keep his promise to Abraham to make him the father of nations. And so it is with Job.

In the last part of the book of Job, the Lord restores all his fortunes several times over. "And after this Job lived a hundred and forty years, and saw his sons, and his sons' sons, four generations. And Job died, an old man, and full of days." This vindication of Job's faithfulness is frequently dismissed as a later appendage, a banal ending that spoils the profundity of the tale. Whether or not Job 42: 7–17 is an addendum, whoever wrote it may have been a better theologian than he was a dramatist. The heart of biblical religion has less to do with the existentialist heroics of self-abandonment than with the relentless quest for history's vindication, for the Kingdom of God. God cannot be finally glorified while his promises are so clearly unfulfilled. It is not a choice between being theocentric or being anthropocentric, between a religion centered upon God or a religion centered upon man. The central mystery of the Christian faith is that God has thrown in his lot with the human struggle. He seeks no glory apart from the completion of the work he has begun. "Then you would call, and I should answer, you would want to see the work of your hands once more."

At the risk of being misunderstood, we can say that the whole of the biblical message is premised upon sanctified self-interest. That is, it is sometimes necessary, through the mysterious and circuitous ways of history, that we abandon ourselves—our common sense, our moral sensibilities, our apparent self-interest—in order to submit to the will of God. But that submission is always premised upon the promise that God's will is to vindicate the human struggle of which we are part. *For the Lord's sake* we must seek our own vindication. This is the logic in the psalmists' incessant plea that the Lord would grant peace, prosperity and victory to the children of Israel. For if the children of Israel became "a byword and laughingstock among the nations," the God of Israel would be brought into disrepute. In our age, sated by psychological skepticism, we may wonder whether the children of Israel were really concerned about the

glory of the Lord or about their own advantage. The distinction would
have made little sense to them. God had inextricably tied his glory to their
vindication. The prophets warned that Israel would be tested and tempered by adversity, would be humiliated into repentance, but the promise
was not to be thrown into question. To throw that into question would
be to blaspheme against the Lord.

> For a brief moment I forsook you, says the Lord,
>   But with great compassion I will gather you.
> In overflowing wrath for a moment
>   I hid my face from you,
> but with everlasting Love I will have
>   compassion on you,
> says the Lord, your Redeemer (Isa. 54).
>   . . . Arise, shine; for your light
>   has come,
> and the glory of the Lord has risen upon you.
> For behold, darkness shall cover the earth,
>   and thick darkness the peoples;
> but the Lord will arise upon you,
>   and his glory will be seen upon you.
> And nations shall come to your light,
>   and kings to the brightness of your rising (Isa. 60).

Neither did Jesus call for *ultimate* self-abandonment. We do not need
to, indeed we should not, search what Yeats called "the rag and bone
shop of the heart" to see whether our devotion is utterly selfless. As
though anticipating the interminable anxieties of existentialism and psy-
chologism, the writer of 1 John says, "By this we shall know that we are
of the truth, and reassure our hearts before him whenever our hearts
condemn us; for God is greater than our hearts, and he knows everything." And what is the evidence that overcomes the condemnation of
our own hearts? "By this we may be sure that we are in him: he who says
he abides in him ought to walk in the same way in which he [Christ]
walked (1 John 3 and 1)." The way in which Christ walked was the way
of a covenant contingent upon a promise and its fulfillment. If his
abandonment on the cross had been ultimate, if it had been the last word,
then the covenant would have been broken, his trust fatally misplaced,
and we would have no reason to celebrate him as Lord. Christ's search
and the Christian's search is not for the act of pure self-abandonment, of
pure selflessness, but for vindication, for the Kingdom of God.

Of course Jesus called people to lose their lives in obedience to the
Father. But they were to lose their lives *in order to find their lives.*
"Blessed are the poor in spirit, *for theirs is the kingdom of heaven.*
Blessed are those who mourn, *for they shall be comforted.* Blessed are

the meek, *for they shall inherit the earth.*. Blessed are the merciful, *for they shall obtain mercy*" (Matt. 6). And so it goes throughout Jesus' teaching. "And every one who has left houses or brothers or sisters or father or mother or children or lands, for my name's sake, will receive a hundredfold, and inherit eternal life" (Matt. 19). Similarly Paul: "I consider that the sufferings of this present time are not worth comparing with the glory that is to be revealed to us" (Rom. 8).

The glory has not yet been revealed, except in a promissory way in Jesus the Christ. The poor are still poor, those who mourn still mourn, and the meek have not inherited the earth. We do not glorify God by "spiritualizing" his promises, nor by believing that they have been fulfilled when they have not been fulfilled. We honor God by taking him at his word. Our personal and collective covenant with the Lord is still contingent upon the future.

To illustrate the point: imagine a friend who promises most solemnly to do some great thing. He believes his very being, his sense of worth and self respect, depend upon his achieving this great thing. But you think he cannot or will not do it. In any case, you tell him it is not necessary for him to do it, since you love him as he is. But he is stubbornly set upon his goal. Having failed to dissuade him directly, you take another tack, assuring him, with expressions of great joy and congratulation, that he has indeed already achieved his goal. You share with all his friends your theory about "realized goal-achievement." But he is not fooled, nor are many of his friends. Far from honoring him, you have demeaned and patronized him with your patent lack of trust in his purpose. Thus we patronize God when we do not take with ultimate seriousness the covenant that is contingent upon the coming of his promised Kingdom.

Let us add another element to the illustration. Suppose your friend's goal is to be achieved through some great change in you. Its achievement requires some great sacrifice on your part, perhaps even your death. "If you join me in this endeavor," says your friend, "even though you lose your life, you shall in its success find a more abundant life." In this case, your attempts to dissuade him from his goal or to persuade him it is already achieved are clearly much more selfish and born from a manifest lack of faith in his promise. Thus it is when we refuse to join the divine pathos, when we prematurely relieve the tension between the Now and the Not Yet, when we decline to share in the way of the cross toward history's fulfillment. The irony is that what now appears to be in our self-interest leads to a dead end, leads to our missing out on the only hope for our lives. If Jesus is right, our real self-interest lies in abandoning everything and following him toward what is to be. *If* Jesus is right. That is yet to be seen. The Christian is one who gambles all on what is yet to be seen.

When I meet God, then, I expect to meet him as an American. The statement is not as impertinent as it may at first seem. It is simply to say that I look for the vindication of myself in my historical particularity, and of the American experience of which I am part. It is simply to say that the divine promise is attached to all of history, of which the American experience is a large part, or at least it is a large part of our limited moment in history. All of history is *Heilsgeschichte,* salvation history. All history is the history of redemption. There is not a sacred history and then a secular history. There is one, universal history to which God has irrevocably committed himself.[11]

"Then one of the elders addressed me, saying, 'Who are these, clothed in white robes, and whence have they come?' I said to him, 'Sir, you know.' And he said to me, 'These are they who have come out of the great tribulation; they have washed their robes and made them white in the blood of the Lamb. Therefore are they before the throne of God, and serve him day and night. . . . They shall hunger no more, neither thirst any more; the sun shall not strike them, nor any scorching heat. For the Lamb in the midst of the throne will be their shepherd, and he will guide them to springs of living water; and God will wipe away any tear from their eyes'" (Rev. 7).

History is the great tribulation. Its shape is cruciform and its signal of hope is the resurrection of Christ. We are now passing through the great tribulation. But we are not passing through history in general, we are passing through that slice of history which is twentieth-century America. I trust there is room in the vision of St. John the Divine for the emergence of a distinctly American division from the great tribulation. In my childish way, I imagine a highly differentiated state of affairs around the throne in the Kingdom. I find it hard to hope for a kingdom in which all differences would be submerged. C. S. Lewis once described such an undifferentiated heaven as a "tapioca pudding of Divine Being." No, I trust the Italians will be emphatically Italian, the Germans German and the Chinese Chinese. Men will be men, women women, and Plato will be unmistakably Platonic. Maybe there will even be time and change (I find it impossible to imagine their absence). The difference will be that differences will enrich rather than separate; the cacophany of envy and distrust will be transformed into a chorus of everlasting praise for him who finally brought history to its fulfillment in reverent respect for all its particularities. In any case, I'm going to the feast as an American.

There is admittedly something whimsical about all this. Yet whimsy and humor and play all have their place as resources in helping us envision, in small part, that for which we hope. Jesus also was chronologically far removed from history's completion (about two thousand years farther removed than we are) and often disappointed those who wanted a plain and lucid description of how things were to be, resorting instead to "parables and dark sayings." Although through a glass darkly, we see; although in part, we know. Martin Luther described the Kingdom to his four-year-old son Hans as "a lovely garden where many children in golden frocks gather rosy apples under the trees. . . . They sing, skip, and are gay. And they have fine ponies with golden bridles and silver saddles." At another point he assured his son that his lately departed puppy would certainly be in heaven, no doubt with a golden tail quite perfectly curled.[12]

It is more than whimsy; it is sound theology. As we grow older we are removed from the children only by degree, and golden tails are replaced by perhaps more pretentious hopes surrounding the ideas, projects and achievements to which we are attached. When Karl Barth suggested that in the Kingdom the angels will play Bach around the throne of God but will play Mozart when they get together by themselves just for fun, he was not taking time off from being a serious theologian. The best we have known here is a foretaste of what is to be. And not only the best, but also the trivial and routine. If we removed the quotidian from history, there would be very little history left to redeem.

The ordinary and frequently noxious stuff of history, then, is what God is ultimately serious about. As Jesus said, there will be some surprises in the end. The chaff will be separated from the wheat; in another metaphor, the weeds will be pulled out from among the good plantings; or, in yet another, the edible fish will be separated from the junk drawn in by history's net. But the whole point of Jesus' work with the disciples was to minimize the surprises, to alert them as much as possible to what history is really all about, as distinct from what their age (and ours) thought history was about. Even with such a teacher, they did not anticipate (as he perhaps did not anticipate) the cross and resurrection, which remains the central surprise in the dialectic of history's unfolding. We, like they, must in radical faith trust that God is faithful and not capricious. This is the faith that gives us courage to act in convenantal uncertainty.

Yet for many Christians the delay of the Second Coming for two thousand years since Jesus and for however many years more is an inexplicable phenomenon to be accepted "by faith." In any case, it is said, the fulfillment of history has nothing to do with our personal salvation. As Christians we allegedly live within the sacred circle, the sphere of the guaranteed, the realm of the "already realized." They pray the early church's "Maranatha!" not with a yearning for history's promised fulfillment but with the hope that God would quickly terminate the embarrassing persistence of a history that has no necessary place in the plan of salvation. After all, everything necessary has already been realized. They do not consider that, were history to be terminated now, with the world in the shape it is, God's promise would be proven false. Through such thinking, the church that ought to be putting the world on alert with a heightened sense of historical urgency has instead contributed to the enervation of a sense of human responsibility in partnership with God's work in history. When Marxists say religion is the opiate of the masses, this is the kind of religion they have in mind, and, in sorry truth, they haven't said the half of it.

I am well aware that much of what has been said about the connection between salvation and history will seem alien to the piety that dominates church life in America, and to the piety that has prevailed throughout a large part of Christian history. One has only to read the prayers, hymns and liturgies of the Western church to recognize the extent to which eschatological urgency has been gutted by dehistoricized notions of redemption. Nonetheless, while an emphatically historical understanding of the Kingdom is revolutionary in its implications, it is not in rebellion against the catholic tradition. It is not offered as a novelty to titillate the fashion-addicted world of American religious thought. It is proposed as a sorely neglected part of the biblical tradition that is rich in resources for renewing our religious understanding of the American experience.

I should at least mention another possible misunderstanding of what has been said in this chapter. If indeed the promise of salvation is contingent upon history's fulfillment, and if Christians are as far from the Kingdom as is the rest of the world, what then is the point of being a Christian? Part of the answer has already been given: Christians are those who have been alerted in advance to the meaning of universal history, and their mission is to alert the world to its destiny. There is also a sense in which Christians *now* participate in what is to be. This is the element of truth in the talk about "realized eschatology" that has, in one form or another, so enervated our sense of historical urgency. Because the End Time has already occurred in Jesus the Christ, those who live in obedient communion with him *now* know and celebrate the oncoming Kingdom.[13] But this knowledge and celebration is a *foretaste* and in no way a substitute for the establishment of the Kingdom.

Jesus said, "Behold, the Kingdom of God is in the midst of you" (Luke 17). He is telling them that *he* is in their midst, the one in whom the End Time is occurring, as evidenced by his resurrection from the dead. He is, to use again Wolfhart Pannenberg's favored term, the *prolepsis* of the Absolute Future. Jesus' ministry is proleptic signal and power, sustaining us on our pilgrim way toward the Kingdom to which he points. If in Christian piety Jesus becomes a substitute for history's realization, then the whole purpose and thrust of his ministry is aborted. It is clear from a reading of the gospels that Jesus consistently referred to the Kingdom as "coming," being "at hand," "near at hand" and so forth. The Kingdom is always future, yet the Absolute Future, God, is always breaking into the present. This dialectical dynamic runs throughout the biblical understanding of history. To be sure, there are different accents and even, as some scholars insist, different theologies within both Old and New Testaments. The New Testament clearly reflects the early church's confused wrestling with what seemed to many the inexplicable delay in Jesus' return in glory.

We, like people of other times, are frightened by historical contingency. A radically experimental view of our existence means the experiment may turn out badly. Above all, we would not choose to be vulnerable to a promise and a judgment that is not within our control. We all, at least at times and with a part of our heart, prefer a secure present to an uncertain future, even if that future be the Kingdom of God. In the next chapter we will examine some of the ways in which we exercise that preference.

8

Liberating the Future from the Past

The troubling thing about the future is that it is largely unknown. We are all engaged in time. Whether we see that engagement as a trap or as a road of pilgrimage depends upon our response to the future we confront. The most intense human emotions all relate to the future. Fear and hope, dread and anticipation, confidence and anxiety—all are responses to a real or imagined future. Every analysis of the present is a contingent analysis. We say this is the way we think things are, but it may "turn out" to be quite different. This is as true of our loves and careers as it is of our ideas and beliefs. Only at the end of an historical era do we know what the era is about; only then can we give it a name. Thus it is with the whole of our experience. Yet even when we say a period, or an epoch or an era has come to an end and we then give it a name, that too is contingent; it is vulnerable to yet another future which may radically revise the meaning of what we thought we understood. There are finally no endings before the End, there are simply points of reference, some more useful than others.

In speaking of time we touch upon a great mystery. St. Augustine wrote, "What, then, is time? If nobody asks me, I know . . . but if I try to explain it to one who asks me, I do not know."[1] Alfred North Whitehead found it "impossible to meditate on time and the creative passage of nature without an overwhelming emotion at the limitations of human intelligence."[2] The modern mind feels beset by uncertainty. Heisenberg's uncertainty principle and Einstein's theory of relativity, although perhaps seldom understood, have had an immeasurable impact upon our consciousness. Freud's equally potent relativization of human will and motivation is but another assault upon our desire for certitude. Little wonder that many resort to religion as the last refuge from uncertainty. "We preach a changeless Christ for a changing world," proclaims one Christian publishing house. Or in the words of a still-favorite nineteenth-century hymn:

> Change and decay in all around I see.
> O Thou, who changest not, abide with me!

Little wonder that we try to draw a sharp line between time and eternity, with our religious confidence securely ensconsed in the latter. We are outraged by the assertion that "the very essence of God implies time."[3] Classical theology has spoken about the immutability of God; popular piety has transformed it into the immobility of God. Such a God dwells secure in a timeless eternity, aloof from the terrors of history. Such a God would never find himself nailed to a cross, or driven into the gas ovens of Dachau. There is a species of piety that says we should not drag the majesty of God down into the itchy, smelly particularities of every day history. Indeed, we should not and we cannot. He has already made that decision by entering into covenant with his creation, most dramatically by his incarnation in Jesus the Christ. He seeks neither majesty nor glory apart from the healing and fulfillment of his wounded world.

We are outraged by the notion of a "timed" God, unless we truly seek first the Kingdom of God, that his will be done on earth as in heaven. Clearly his will is not now being done; time is our only hope. That is, the future, the Absolute Future, is our only hope. The promise is that time is on our side. To speak of the future is, then, to speak of the *mysterium tremendum et fascinans,* the mystery that inspires awe, terror and irresistible fascination. To speak of the future is to speak of God. When before the burning bush Moses asked who he should say had sent him to lead the children of Israel from slavery, God answered, "Say I AM WHO I AM has sent me to you" (Exod. 3). The Israelite name for God, YHWH, may, according to some scholars, be better translated "I will be what I will be," or "I am the one who brings all things to be." All names for God are by definition inadequate, but the "Absolute Future" is a fair rendering of God's answer to Moses and his answer to our own anxieties about what is to be.

The confrontation with the future, as we have said, arouses the most intense of human emotions. According to the biblical witness, hope triumphs over fear, anticipation over dread and confidence over anxiety, because the future can, ultimately, be trusted. Jesus named the power of the future he proclaimed. He called the power of the future "Father." In a time of less rigidly patriarchal structures, we may discover other names that communicate in our time what the word *Father* communicated in his—the person of utter authority, strength and trustworthiness. But we will no doubt also continue to address the Power of the Future as "Father," because of the centrality to our faith of what he has done in the man Jesus, who called him, and teaches us to call him, "Father."[4]

Until fairly recent times, observers almost universally remarked the hopeful sense of the future they discovered among Americans. Obviously, this sense had, in most of its manifestations, little to do (at least consciously) with the theological propositions sketched above. The American sense of the future has often been merely a naive optimism of the

"Smile, God Loves You" variety. America's hopeful sense of the future has sometimes been premised upon notions of racial or cultural superiority, vulgar material success or the pride of empire. The primary purpose here is not to analyze the ingredients and motivations that have gone into making—again, until recently—American culture a hopeful culture. The purpose rather is to affirm such hopefulness as a fundamentally correct intuition, although for perhaps quite different reasons than it has been affirmed in the past.

T. S. Eliot was only partly right in declaring it the greater treason to do the right thing for the wrong reason. While the wrong reason, consciously held, can corrupt the doing of the right thing, one may do the right thing for reasons that are better than one knows. The goal is not to search the "rag and bone shop" of the American heart to discover the motivations for American hopefulness. Rags and bones are as nothing compared with the vileness to be discovered and that many delight in exposing in order to discredit the American experiment. Yet there is also a reason for hope perhaps quite different from the reasons that now seem increasingly implausible and even morally objectionable. The intuition, if not the form, of the American hope may prove more sound than we suspect.

We must resist the temptation to exaggerate the uniqueness of the American experience, as distinct from other national experiences. All superlatives in this connection warrant our skepticism, whether they be negative or positive. "America is the most violent nation in the world, or the most materialistic, or the most hypocritical," or the most of whatever other sin the writer may be bemoaning at the moment. On the other hand, we hear that "America is the most generous nation in the world, or the most democratic, or the most compassionate." Such hyperbole can hardly sustain careful scrutiny and usually has slight support in empirical evidence. It is equally misleading, however, to suggest there is nothing distinctive about the American experience, that America is like all other nations on earth. While there are no doubt certain commonalities in what we call, for lack of a better term, the human condition, the communal manifestations of that condition are marvelously variegated. As elusive as satisfying definitions may be, there is an inevitability in our search for the American character, the American mind, indeed for America itself. It may be that, as Daniel Berrigan has suggested in the title of one of his poems, "America is Hard to Find," but the problems only intensify the pace of the search.

Something may well be characteristic of America without being unique to America. When we speak of America, we need not always be looking over our shoulder at other cultures, checking to see whether America has a copyright on her every characteristic. Every viable community is, as

Emile Durkheim suggests, in some sense a moral community. Ortega y Gasset asserts that in every nation there are beliefs; not so much the beliefs which we hold, but the beliefs which we *are*. From Benjamin Franklin to Sidney Mead, it has been said that America has given birth to a "Religion of the Republic," and in recent years Robert Bellah has given new currency to the idea of an American "civil religion."

All these discussions must be kept in mind when we speak about the idea of the future in American life. What is distinctively American, it may be assumed, is not one characteristic or another in isolation, but the distinctive clustering of characteristics that prompts us to say that something is American, rather than French, or Russian or Malaysian. Even if a particular attitude or pattern of behavior may be discovered in some other national experience, it does not prevent us from calling it American, nor is there any need to add in each instance that it is *also* American. After all, it is about the American experience we are writing. The biographer of Martin Luther does not play down the importance of constipation in his life and thought merely because the affliction was not uniquely his.

As we have noted, almost without exception, observers of the American scene have remarked the American sense of hopefulness about the future. Key concepts such as enterprise, opportunity, reward and experiment are all tied to the intuition of an open future. The very idea of newness—so omnipresent in the way Americans have been viewed and have viewed themselves—assumes the future is not captive to the past. From this assumption emerges the possibility of freedom. In moments of weariness we may agree with the Preacher of Ecclesiastes, "What has been is what will be, and what has been done is what will be done; and there is nothing new under the sun" (Eccles. 1). But, after a good night's sleep, we have set aside such subversive thoughts and affirmed again, "Remember not the former things, nor consider the things of old. Behold, I am doing a new thing; now it springs forth, do you not perceive it?" (Isa. 43)

So pervasive has been the sense of newness in American life that it has, from time to time, been thought the mark of sophistication to underscore the ways in which America is just like other nations. Harry S. Truman, wanting to present himself as something of a thinking man rather than merely the man on the street writ large, insisted to his biographers that he had all along believed that "the only thing that is new is the history you have yet to read." On a perhaps more serious level, pundits such as Walter Lippmann and Max Lerner regularly decried the American innocence implicit in the idea of newness, and delighted in emphasizing historical evidences to counter the presumptions of American novelty. Reinhold Niebuhr devoted a career to checking the moralistic propensities provoked by thinking of America as something so very special. And, at least for a time, under Nixon-Kissinger, Americans deemed it a sign of progress that we were able to exercise our national and international power according to categories of thought belonging to the European eighteenth and nineteenth centuries.

Historical modesty derives not from the fact that we are locked into the established patterns of "The nature and destiny of man," to cite the title of Reinhold Niebuhr's important work. Modesty derives from knowing that we can give only an interim report on the nature and destiny of man. The painter Van Gogh is said to have remarked that God ought not be blamed for history, "It is simply a sketch of his that turned out badly." We choose to believe that history's presently confused state is a work still in progress, perhaps hardly begun.

We are indeed deeply indebted to the work of Reinhold Niebuhr and others for tempering some of the more dangerous propensities associated with America's sense of singularity and innocence. The idea that America was a chosen people that could do no wrong was indeed a peril to ourselves and others. It would be easy to suggest that we are dealing merely with another instance of the well-known swinging pendulum. That is, we could say that today very few people, at least very few intellectuals, have any such illusions about America's virginity and therefore the accent now must be placed on what is upbeat and distinctive about America. But the swinging pendulum is usually a metaphorical device for lazy minds. I believe it is not a matter of degree or of shifting accents, but of a dramatically different understanding of the sources of historical modesty. One source of modesty is similarity with the past, the other is contingency upon the future. *Our hubris is checked not by the denial of newness but by the prospect of judgment.* "Every one to whom much is given, of him will much be required" (Luke 12). To assert that America has been given less than it has been given is not modesty but self-deceit. It is yet another instance of the desire to escape from judgment.

As in the past, foreign observers are often most reliable on this subject. Despite the success with which we have exported the slogans of anti-Americanism to the world, foreigners continue to encounter us with their belief that the United States is the laboratory of the future. The cultural, economic and political influence of America is almost all-pervasive. Intellectuals in other countries feel they have a ringside seat and watch avidly, not simply because America is such a fascinating show but because they see in what we are doing a preview of their own futures, for better or for worse. Following the Bolshevik Revolution, a number of Western intellectuals returned from Russia proclaiming, "We have seen the future, and it works." So people returning from the United States today say they have seen the future, and if it does not work, it at least has some interesting possibilities.[5]

It is not easy, in our current cultural climate, to gain a hearing for this viewpoint. The fashion now is self-denigration, the celebration of despair, the indulgence of the sense of ending. We would not know today how to respond to a Mark Twain or a Walt Whitman or a Carl Sandburg. Celebrants of the American present are, of course, always welcome at the Chamber of Commerce, but these great ones were celebrants of an American promise, as well as of an American present, and were uncompromisingly harsh about all the ways in which America was thwarting and defiling that promise. "The United States themselves are essentially the greatest poem," wrote Walt Whitman, and the writer must be "commensurate with the people." That a writer should today be commensurate with the American people would be considered another way of saying that he was mediocre, corrupted and unworthy of serious attention. Nathan Scott strives heroically to make the argument that Norman Mailer is "our Whitman." If so, our plight is more desperate than is commonly assumed. Mailer says he would discover the true America through exploring "the mysteries of murder, suicide, incest, orgy, orgasm and Time."

It is not that Mailer is unconcerned about America's healing. It is simply that, in his soteriology, things must become much worse before they can become better. "When the body is sick . . . a war goes on in the body, an inflammatory sickness, a fever, a crisis. The war decided, the organ subsides, different in size, stronger or weaker, it returns to its part of the body's function. *Acute disease is cure"* [emphasis added][6]. All organic models of society are suspect, but here we have an analysis even more seriously flawed. On the one hand, such an analysis of restoration through death suggests a christological imagery of cross and resurrection, and it is an exercise of monumental historical hubris to think that our moment—presumably because it is *our* moment—should be understood, in some singular way, in terms of the saving Christ figure. On the other hand, such analysis is the essence of decadence: the passion to shatter all differentiations between good and evil, baseness and nobility, disease and health. In either case, such an analysis must resist any suggestion of vitality, promise and hope in the American experience.

The roots of this resistance to positing hope for America are extremely complex. It is not adequate simply to dismiss it as anti-Americanism, as do the neoconservative writers who congregate around such journals as *Commentary* or *The Public Interest.* In some cases, as witness Mailer above, the denigration of America is tied to an almost mystical sense that the evil must be confronted, even heightened, before the first ray of redemption is permitted to appear. In a frightfully convoluted way that some might dress up as "paradox," such an approach is an equation of despair and hope. At a simpler level, there are those who feel that even the slightest acknowledgment of American merit might somehow compromise the radicality of their critique of America, or give aid and comfort to the reactionary enemy. At a more fatuous level, there are those who truly think that blasting the American experience is indeed, as the book blurbs say, "daring" and "courageous," when, in fact, within the circles of debunking authors the daring and courageous thing would be to underscore elements of value within the American experience.

The arrogance, innocence and assumptions of superiority that once accompanied and undergirded America's hopeful sense of the future are no longer dominant traits of our culture, or at least not of our high culture. To play upon Eliot's phrase, the assault upon "the wrong reason" (arrogance) has almost done in "the right thing" (an adventuresome trustfulness toward the future). The task now, to which the Christian gospel can make a crucial contribution, is to rediscover the hopeful sense of the American future upon quite different bases. It may at first be a hope only for those who share the biblical understanding of convenantal trust and accountability. Given the serendipitous ways of history, however, we should not underestimate the possible impact of such a hope upon the wider culture. If, as I think likely, the overarching "meaning systems" that have competed with the biblical world view—Enlightenment liberalism, positivist scientism and various Marxisms—continue to lose their hold, the possibility of that wider impact is greatly increased. Even if this speculation is proved wrong, however, and the biblically based view of the American promise is espoused only by a small minority, it is still worth pursuing. Indeed it is unavoidable for those of us who recognize no alternative to being both Christians and Americans and wish to be religiously serious about both vocations.

The sound American intuition, then, is that we have a future in our future. As Christians we anticipate that future not in a supernatural eternity above us but in time ahead of us. We know that some of the circumstances that used to sustain that hopeful sense of the future have dramatically changed. The great English political theorist A. D. Lindsay wrote of "all the immigrants of various nationalities who poured into the United States all last century and were united by their hopes for the future —their taking part in the great American experiment." We have already discussed why the sustaining power of mass immigration is not likely to be revived. Lindsay goes on to say that, in a variety of ways, "the United States has been made one nation by thoughts of its 'manifest destiny', but that look into the future was conditioned by the common inheritance of the original colonies. There has to be enough solidarity with the past— of tradition, of language, of ways of behaving—to make a framework for the hopes of the future."[7] Obviously, that framework cannot today be easily taken for granted. Yet, for all the disparateness that has been celebrated since the demolishing of the "myth of the melting pot" almost two decades ago, I suspect there is today more convergence of fundamental belief about the American experience than is usually recognized.

"Your taste is judicious," John Adams once taunted Thomas Jefferson, "in liking better the dreams of the future than the history of the past."[8] I note with hope that same judicious taste among the blacks, Puerto Ricans, Dominicans and elderly Jews of the Williamsburg section of Brooklyn, and among the old white stock of Cisco, Texas.

"Every one to whom much is given, of him will much be required." When, in a hungry world, one has a great deal, it is prudent to plead poverty. Thus also would we escape the threat of justice and of judgment. An America in which the hopeful sense of the future is revived will be an America that is hopeful about the good it might do, with its very real wealth and power, in a world that is terrorized by hunger and injustice.

We can state in brief summary form, then, the variety of ways in which people try to evade the judgment to come. Each is a ploy in defying or thwarting the future.[9] First is the belief that the goal of the future, the Kingdom of God, has already come if you believe it has come. Second is to substitute the securities and pleasures of the present for the hoped-for Kingdom. Third is to deny that there is anything really new, to deny that there is in fact a future. The fourth and more apocalyptic defiance of the future is to proclaim that the end is, for all practical purposes, upon us. The fifth defiance is to assert that the promise of the future is simply not very promising.

In these interrelated and frequently overlapping ways we would thwart the future. With the decline of America's hopeful sense of the future, it is not surprising that visions of change gravitate toward some idealized past. The effort to discover or reestablish a certain past is at the heart of many current social visions.

That the present is unacceptable is the starting point of all who seek change. There is wisdom in the observation that whatever is is false. The homeless mind and homeless heart cry out for a reality in which what we sense to be true will not be contradicted on every hand by experience. One way to say it is that we are alienated; or, in biblical language, we are pilgrims and sojourners on earth.

In times of uncertainty we look to the past. The past is what we can be sure about. We may think we understand the present, but the present becomes past as rapidly as it enters our consciousness. Thus the past, especially the near past, seems more certain. It is the foundation from which we can project alternative futures. Yet all futures remain speculative and all talk about the future seems to be in the realm of subjectivity. About the past, however, we think we can be objective. After all, we have reports, data and the evidence of experience to give us a grip on past reality. The future seems to consist of wishes, desires, dreams, fears and other gossamer stuff hardly fit for a firm foundation.

There is a bias toward the past built into our modern notion of objectivity. The bias is rooted in what we call the scientific method itself. In that method's approach to reality there is a determined resistance to entering into questions of ultimate or even penultimate meaning. The language of pure objectivity, of value-free or value-neutral science, is for good reason suspect today. The alternative, however, is not to revert to cognitive authoritarianisms of the past, nor to join in the antimodernity cults that have grown up around assorted pseudo-Orientalisms or around names such as R. D. Laing and Norman O. Brown. If there is to be a new form of confidence in the future, we must indeed be critical of the "objectivism" and "scientism" that have stultified our thought in the past, but we must be critical in a way that will preserve the benefits of the Enlightenment. That means we must see seventeenth-century Puritanism with its intimations of destiny and covenant as complementary to, rather than exclusive of, the eighteenth-century Enlightenment vision of rational order and contract. If the contractual is to be renewed by the covenantal, we have to rehabilitate, for use in public discourse, a covenantal sense of time and future.

A major problem with the scientific method as it is commonly defined is that it absolutizes relativity, thus excluding statements of ultimate meaning. If we are to entertain a more expansive understanding of reality, it is imperative that we "relativize the relativizers." The scientific method should not be permitted to cramp unduly our communal dreams. We dare not exclude "the rumor of angels."[10] Of course the angels of private or communal vision must be tested as to whether they are good or evil angels. One sure test is to ask whether such rumors of angels, if acted upon, would preserve the space liberated by the Enlightenment in which all rumors are subject to challenge.

Social man cannot live by contract alone. He needs covenant. But if the covenant is not to restore old oppressions or create new ones, it must be checked and undergirded by contract. One clause in the contract is that all covenants are open to communal deliberation and decision. A further clause is that the community can never agree to any covenant that would foreclose challenge by even the most marginal member of the community. Within these provisions we can entertain rumors of a promising and judging future calling us to covenant.

Classical liberal theory from John Stuart Mill through John Dewey and on to Bertrand Russell insists that we can only agree on what we can know. Since "knowing" is dependent upon a scientific method that is, in turn, dependent upon evidence of the past, we can posit no larger historical "meaning." In that case, every covenantal statement of meaning is finally arbitrary, relative and subjective. Such statements must be consigned, along with religious faith, to the realm of the infinitely moot. A hopeful sense of the future is then merely a matter of optimism, a question of private disposition, not a public proposition.

Our ideas of what is scientific and rational are today undergoing major change. We look for a way in which reason can overcome the dichotomy between fact and meaning, for we must speak rationally of both. If rational knowledge cannot deal with the meaning of history then it must, perforce, leave out the questions that matter most to us. The issues of value and meaning with which theology deals can no longer be relegated to some anteroom outside the arena where rational people debate the nature of reality and what should be done about it. The redefinition of rationality and of the "knowledge" that is appropriate to public discourse is perhaps the hardest and most urgent task facing contemporary theology.

To understand the nature of the problem it is necessary to understand something of its history. At one time the theologians dominated the play in what might be called the arena of the real world. They were the acknowledged experts in the acknowledged "queen of sciences." Everybody was to defer to those who had the best line to revelation, which was the authority by which truth and falsehood were measured. The Enlightenment changed all that, enthroning reason as the new authority. To be more precise, revelation was not dethroned, although some French zealots tried that for a time, but was rather picked up, throne and all, and moved to the sidelines. A strong fence was erected around revelation's assigned area to stop balls from flying on to the main field where they might interrupt, or even confuse, the game. Revelation's area was called religion and the main field was called the real world. The name of the game on the field was called reason, the name of the game in the other area was called faith.

To put it bluntly, religion's area was viewed as a kind of sandbox. It was assigned most of the big "meaning questions" that were not thought necessary for playing on the main field, but it was understood that none of religion's answers, if it had any, were allowed to impinge upon the game in the real world. Such questions and answers were in the realm of the private, the subjective, in short, in the realm of faith.

It would happen from time to time that players, even star players, on the main field would find the urge irresistible and wander over to religion's sandbox to indulge it. Much like an otherwise happily married man visiting a brothel on occasion, except in this case most everybody had nothing but nice things to say about what went on behind the fence—even if they didn't go in for that sort of thing themselves. When star players, such as world-renowned physicists and biochemists, would visit religion's compound during their off hours, they were much celebrated by the people who lived there all the time. They would accommodate the regulars by allowing as how reason didn't have all the answers and as how it was impossible to live fully without the occasional injection of faith.

Some said they needed the injection regularly, and that made the people in the compound feel very good indeed.

Life in the compound, it should be said, was anything but dull. Pondering the imponderable was both solemn business and marvelous fun. After a while it became so engrossing that the people there no longer resented having been shoved off the playing field. Some became convinced that they had the better part of the game and began to reinforce the fences. This time the purpose was not to keep revelation's balls from confusing reason's game, but the other way around. Thus what was designed as a sandbox to keep religion's children happy became, for those who had grown up in the sandbox, the main arena. And so it happened that theology made a comeback of sorts by making virtue of necessity. Its removal was not only not resented, it is celebrated. The dubious achievement of much modern theology—ranging in great variety from Barth to Bultmann—has been to legitimate the sandbox of subjectivity. Such theology cannot be interfered with by reason's game, nor need it contribute to it.

The fence must now be torn down. The biblical claims of a promising and judging future must be engaged in rational discourse about the business of the *polis.* Reason and faith, fact and meaning, contract and covenant are all essential to a more whole view of society—although each, to be sure, reflects the limitations of our placement in a universe that is not yet whole. This desired interaction requires the exposure of the inadequacies of a scientific method that would limit our reality to the cramped and fetid space of a secularized world. More positively, it requires asserting claims implicit in the gospel of the Kingdom, such as Pannenberg's concepts of "the ontological priority of the future." Above all, it means liberating ourselves and others from the mutual deprivation that is perpetuated by the fence between reason and revelation.

However it may be stated, Christianity inescapably posits the reality of the future. Otherwise, key Christian claims, such as a final judgment, make little sense. Judgment is not a matter of the past muddling through the present toward some time when everything goes out with a whimper or a bang or an alleluia. Judgment assumes a reality calling to judgment and exercising judgment. This understanding of the future opposes every effort to locate the future in the past.

The word *utopia,* as is frequently remarked, has a dual meaning. It means an ideal place, but from the Greek *ou* + *topos* it literally means "no place." It is clear to everyone thinking or writing about utopia that they are not describing an existing reality. The dreamer might say it is a place in his mind. But that is not very promising, not least because the dreamer's mind is mortal. Furthermore, we all have things in our minds that have no relation to what we call reality. Since utopia is clearly not in the present, utopia must, if there is no such reality as the future, be located in the past. Thus it is that visions of social change—whether ameliorist or revolutionary, religious or secular—so often seek the future in the past.

In the book *Conundrum,* James Morris describes the process, including genital surgery, by which he became Jan Morris. "I became the woman I always was," says James/Jan Morris. Our loss of the sense of a promising future has been replaced in large part by what might be called the conundrum syndrome. It is the notion of an idealized reality which has been distorted by the facts of history, but to which we can presumably return by rational engineering of our historical circumstances. The idealized reality may be called the State of Nature, true humanity, or the new man in the new society. Upon closer scrutiny, they all suggest not the fulfillment of history but the negation of history. When pressed, most utopian metaphors emit the distinct odor of nostalgia for Eden.

When biblical claims about the future are again permitted to engage public vision there may emerge a sense of covenant, of living by hope for the genuinely new. Such a sense of the future does not seek to restore, rehabilitate, revive or rediscover anything that is or ever has been. It is premised upon the confidence that history is not a mistake to be corrected or denied but the struggle of a future yet to be vindicated. "Behold, I am doing a new thing, says the Lord, do you not perceive it?" (Isa. 43.)

9

Detour to Apocalyptic Rock in the Cave of Despair

Erosion of confidence in the future is reflected in a variety of "defiances" which we have discussed. As we have seen, some postures of bold defiance are simply the facade for an evasion of responsibility for our moment in time, an effort to escape from judgment. It is obvious by now that evasion is not always a consciously chosen strategem. That is, some evasions are deeply rooted in habits of thought which are more or less taken for granted, such as the causal connection between past, present and future. What we have received as secularized and "scientific" ways of constructing reality militate against the covenantal consciousness that has been so formative for the American experiment.

Now we must turn to yet another, and an excruciatingly seductive, evasion of the future. We will call it decadence. Others may view it as liberation or as humanization—and for perfectly understandable reasons. The seductive character of decadence is precisely that it seems to represent a breaking of bonds, a rebellion against the limits placed upon reality. Most engaging is decadence's eager embrace of what is new. In the case of decadence, however, what appears to be a liberating openness to the future is frequently premised upon a species of nihilism. Yet it is not a true nihilism (if there is such a thing) since beneath it one frequently discovers another form of the conundrum syndrome. In other words, decadence too, for all its iconoclasm, assumes there is a base reality awaiting liberation from history's distorting overlays. That is the phenomenon we want to examine more closely in this chapter.

The language of covenant accents words such as *pilgrimage, contingency* and *adventure.* They are exciting words, but also frightening. Most of us discover we have a rather limited appetite for excitement and adventure. They relieve the monotony and deliver delightful surprises to the taste buds, but we would not want them as a steady diet. Excitement and adventure are welcomed as long as there is a "real world" to which we can return at will. Adventure, change, newness, surprise—in the music of life they are the counterpoint to regularity and predictability.

80

Unrelieved adventure leads to the edge of the abyss where we peer into the void of nothingness, it leads to the experience of terror.

A mother comforts her child who had a nightmare and awoke screaming in the dark. She assures the child that in the real world there is no bad man chasing her. The mother is warding off the terror. Supreme Court justices fret about drawing the line between individual liberty and society's legitimate interests. They too, in trying to order reality within concepts such as "rights," "obligations" and "laws" are warding off the terror. In much of our culture today, the tasks of ordering reality are denigrated as reactionary, or repressive. At least on the surface level, spontaneity is valued above discipline, confrontation above conversation, and there is little interest in anything that cannot be proclaimed as "New!!!" We are, as Christopher Booker argued in his book of the same title more than ten years ago, *The Neophiliacs.* Such an apparently adventuresome atmosphere would seem to be a good time for calling people to the high adventure of covenantal thinking. It is not necessarily so.

Decadence can be described in various ways. At the most obvious level, it simply means that a phenomenon is marked by signs of decay and seems directed toward death. From another angle, decadence is the hollowing out of symbols, conventions and values. Kierkegaard spoke about the revolutionary rage that violently overthrows society's institutions and values. He spoke also of a different kind of revolutionary who, in a mixture of boredom and resentment, quietly empties everything of meaning. The symbols of law, order, civility, honor and merit are emptied, left exposed as hollow shells of pretense and inauthenticity. It is, I believe, the essence of decadence not simply to empty symbols of their meaning but to celebrate their emptiness. Decadence is the celebration of absurdity.

Now I think it true that the only people who can celebrate absurdity are those who have not experienced the terror of absurdity. A kind of ultimate frivolity about life may be the product of an ultimate despair about there being any meaning to life. Laughter and mockery seem the only alternatives to crying and perhaps slitting one's wrists. A recent art show in Venice included the exhibit of an American artist, lying naked in a bathtub to which were attached two dozen or more plastic phalluses. Another exhibit was of a large canvas smeared, admittedly indiscriminately, with the artist's feces. Theater of the absurd and literature of the absurd regularly appear in times that are called decadent. Scholars who write on the origins of authoritarianism have frequently noted the role of decadence in revealing the fear to which authoritarianism is one answer—thus D'Annunzio in helping Mussolini to power and Otto Gross and his Munich circle as prelude to Hitler.[1]

Yet our own American situation differs in several respects from what happened in Europe a half-century or more ago. For one thing, the celebration of absurdity, the defiance of convention, has become to a large extent a pop culture. It is not limited to the relatively small group of the jaded, world-weary sophisticates who comprised the Bohemias of other times. Michael Harrington makes the point in describing, with loving remembrance, the Bohemia of New York's Greenwich Village in the 1950s. "Free love and all-night drinking and art for art's sake were consequences of a single stern morality: Thou shalt not be bourgeois. But once the bourgeoisie itself became decadent—once businessmen started hanging nonobjective art in the boardroom Bohemia was deprived of the stifling atmosphere without which it could not breathe." He disagrees with those who saw the counterculture of the sixties as a force extending Greenwich Village across the country: "That is to miss one of the most crucial and Hegelian truths about contemporary culture: that increases in quantity eventually mean a change in quality, that a Bohemia that enrolls a good portion of a generation is no longer a Bohemia."[2]

While the popularization of decadence may not have created a national Bohemia, neither did it leave the larger society unaffected. It might be argued, as Herbert Marcuse and others do, that the widespread acceptance of decadence, with its defiance of social patterns and authorities, is simply an instance of "desublimation," our society's way of taking the sting out of the radical critique of society. When the picture of the would-be revolutionary appears on the cover of *Time* magazine ("the most revered stained glass window in what used to be Christendom," according to Malcolm Muggeridge) it is an instance of what used to be called co-optation. And yet, no matter how cleverly the society may think it is stage-managing decadence's exposure and celebration of the society's absurdities, the society does not come away from this encounter untouched. In subtle ways we are changed even by what we think of as entertainment. The nuanced ways in which life imitates art is a subject of almost infinite fascination. It is not the decadence of Europe fifty years ago. Nor is it the Bohemia Harrington recalls. Nor is it, in this respect, truly a counter-culture or, as Lionel Trilling calls it, an adversary culture, since those adversaries who have not been converted are effectively isolated as being "out of it."

To be sure, the popular culture we have been discussing is not nearly so popular as its celebrants suppose. Those who are dismissed as being out of it no doubt constitute a majority of the population. They draw from other cultural wells, whether it be country music or the traditions of urban ethnicity. These sources may be generally affirmative of their social circumstance and outlook. The opposite of decadence, they are "solidly American." But this "middle American" majority is also affected by what they consciously reject. The pop Bohemia, which is so often indistinguishable from what is called the high culture, has its inevitable impact. When values that seemed absolute are seen to be challenged or parodied, the process of relativization has gotten a foothold. When, in response to the challenge, one determines to affirm such values, the process of relativization has made a significant advance. One's decision to affirm the values in question distinguishes one from those who repudiate them. Such values (behavior, habits, institutions) are no longer self-evident. They no longer make up a taken-for-granted everyday world. Now he must construct, make up, that world by decision. This erosion of taken-for-granted values is, for all the possibilities it may open up, a form of decay.

Obviously, such an opening up of possibilities does have many positive aspects; one might almost say liberating aspects. It may be viewed as an invitation to reorder social facts and meanings in a more humane and just manner. The serious question of decadence arises, however, when the protest is against the process of ordering itself. This is sometimes viewed as the line between the reformist and the radical or revolutionary approaches to change. In that vague realm we call culture, in the realm where values are born and die, the radical approach is marked by a strong strain of nihilism, by a delight in defiance, by a fascination with the apparently infinite freedom of an absurd world.

In the neophiliac's world the new is equated with the progressive. There is little or no discrimination to be exercised. The neophiliac's world is ruled by what might be called the determinism of time sequence. That is, in thinking about the future, we do not choose among options, but surrender ourselves with abandon to that which seems least precedented. Promise and hope are tied to the appearance of originality. Guided by no higher value than newness, this course inevitably invites the decadence in which we strive to outdo one another in doing or speaking or proposing the unprecedented. After a time comes the pessimistic wisdom of the Preacher of Ecclesiastes that "there is nothing new under the sun." To whatever might be proposed, the answer is, "It has already been done."

Because there are memory gaps between different periods of decadence, revivals of decadence are possible. New people do the same things again in the illusion they are breaking new ground. When they are made aware of their counterparts in other times and places, and thus of their unoriginality, or when they exhaust their imaginations and can think of no new thing to do, such people face a dilemma. If newness is life, a world without newness is intolerable. The logical consequence of decadence gone sour is suicide. Or else one may be driven to an even more feverish decadence, having discovered that not only are society and self absurd but that decadence itself, the celebration of absurdity, is absurd.

Decadence, absurdity and death are closely related. Even the break
with the logic of decadence may end up serving the purposes of decadence. That is, one may break with decadence by accepting any system,
any way of ordering reality, that will impose some meaning upon an
absurd world. The latter way of breaking with decadence has been chosen
in the past by societies in crisis. It is an invitation to, indeed a hunger
for, authoritarianism. And in its repressive coming, authoritarianism
serves the purposes of the decadence it was designed to counter, for it
too leads to death.

To speak of the connection between decadence and death may seem
excessively solemn when related to what is happening in American
culture. Perhaps so. There is certainly a difference between what might
be called earnest decadence, the orgiastic celebration of absurdity, and
playful decadence, the occasional enjoyment of defying the conventions
by which we live. Topless waitresses may be an instance of playful
decadence. One topless bar in the Midwest advertises itself as "wickedly
decadent." It is an invitation to be titillated, to toy with possibilities
usually excluded from one's everyday world. Limits are carefully built
into such an exercise in playful decadence and, most important, it is
assumed there is an everyday world to which one can and will return.
Earnest decadence is the naked artist in his phallus-studded bathtub, the
sadomasochism of an Andy Warhol porno flick, the Götterdämmerung in
which political radicals, yearning to put an end to politics, invoke the
forces of death. The line between earnest and playful decadence may
seem clear enough. While different in intention, however, they may have
similar consequences.

Both playful and earnest decadence focus heavily upon sexuality.
Today's "sexual revolution" would hardly seem to be a form of decadence at all. It purports to be a positive, life-affirming movement of
liberation. It is not necessary to make a defense of rigid sexual codes,
however, to recognize that sexuality is the latest sphere conquered by the
school of positive thinking associated, admittedly in other connections,
with the name of Norman Vincent Peale. Sex is good, wholesome,
beautiful; to do what you really want is to be what you really are. What
is denied is that sex is also filled with the mystery of interpersonal dreams
and nightmares, a thicket of egoism, a weapon with which to hurt and be
hurt.

Societies carefully circumscribe the space permitted to explicit sex. It
is the oldest theater of the absurd in which people do, think and say mad
things they would hardly admit to outside the prescribed space. Many see
the breaking down of the prescriptions as an expansion of liberated space.
Others view it as the destruction of the fences that made a liberated space
possible. Defenders of social mores generally deplore the sexual revolu-

tion as a sign of decadence. The revolution's proponents admit it may be decadent, but, if so, it is a playful decadence aimed only at enhancing joy and exposing the pretences of an uptight society. For all their priggish ineptitude, the defenders of morality may be less guilty of trivializing sexuality and more perceptive of the complex dynamics that sex engages. In other words, they may be more aware of the seriousness, even the political significance, of "play." Ironically, the defenders of the fences agree with the more politicized activists of the sexual revolution who see in the destruction of sexual roles and restrictions a major, even revolutionary, force for social change.

Oswald Spengler, in his analysis of the decline of the West, was much preoccupied with public symbols of decadence. We will be in very serious trouble if and when Spengler's gloomy and sweeping prognostications return to vogue. Yet elements of Spengler appear troublingly pertinent to some current cultural developments. At a point in the decline of civilizations, Spengler said, the *Seelentum* or spirit of the age reflected a sense of "encavement."[3] Because the future seemed unpromising, even threatening, people erected a barrier against it. This was, according to Spengler, architecturally symbolized by, for example, the domes over the Christian basilica, the Muslim mosque and the Mazdaic fire temple. Whatever these architectural forms may or may not have symbolized, the metaphor of encavement, of psychic entrance into a cave as security against the future, is provocative. It has its parallels in the assumptions that underpin and pervade much "no-growth" thinking in our day. It is closely related to the sense of endings that we noted at the opening of this essay, to the feeling that we live in a time that is post-everything.

On the face of it, there would seem to be major contradictions between the manifestations of decadence we have noted. For example, the sexual revolution and other movements that march under the banner of liberation seem to suggest a wide open and inviting future. It is, after all, the age of Aquarius. The encavement of the no-growth mentality, on the other hand, seems profoundly pessimistic, suggesting our dreams must be limited to the hope for survival, at best. The cultural liberationists strike up the tunes of youthful exuberance, the doomsday prophets seem to reflect the disillusionment of old age. Yet there is a nexus between the two cultural strains. Both are premised upon the belief that our history has been a grievous mistake, that our orderings of reality are at heart absurd.

The one perceives the ecological, moral and political absurdity of capitalism's committment to unlimited growth. The economist Robert Heilbroner has given currency to the notion that humankind faces the choice between global ecotastrophe or an authoritarian control of resources that may be able to ward off the end.[4] In such arguments (and

Heilbroner is by no means alone in holding this view), one detects striking similarities to many books written forty or fifty years ago in this country and in Europe. The crisis of democracy and the superiority of authoritarian government was a common theme, beguiling many readers into welcoming the alternatives offered by Stalinism and Hitlerism.

The youthful liberationists offer a much more undifferentiated protest against all the allegedly repressive pretenses of "civilization." Those who do not want to take the youthful cultural revolution seriously frequently observe that rebellion is endemic to youth and nothing to get excited about. They may be right in part, but that does not explain why, at particular moments in history, youthful rebelliousness is granted the degree of cultural dominance we have witnessed in recent years. Both disillusionment and high-spirited rebellion are, in our case, evidences of decadence and are symbiotically related. In both, the symbols of order and social meaning are hollowed out, emptied, cast aside as useless or even dangerous. Neither can envision a promising future in continuity with our past and present construction of reality. The disillusioned invite us to join them in the cave where the young people will provide the entertainment. *Carpe diem;* there is no tomorrow, or at least no tomorrow we are in a hurry to get to.

The picture of an encaved culture, hunkering down and seeking distraction in the rock tunes of the apocalypse may, again, seem excessive. Perhaps so. It is the picture that emerges if the logic of decadence is followed to its end. More often than not, its proponents do not intend that the logic should be taken all that seriously. (Indeed the cultural liberationists would protest that it is precisely that kind of uptight logical consistency they are repudiating. You haven't gotten into the swing of decadence, it might be said, if you take decadence all that seriously. One must be decadent about decadence.) The fact that they may not intend to be taken all that seriously, however, is not necessarily encouraging. Some may indeed be just playing around. Others, as we noted earlier, may see their extravagant statements in a strategic and reformist light: If we proclaim that it is all over and there is no hope, maybe it will shock people into doing something that will provide reason for hope. This approach is, I believe, a strategic error. For every person shocked into thought and action, there are more who accept the invitation to despair. And for every person who chooses either of these options, there are many more who dismiss the doomsayers as being slightly unbalanced, and thus also dismiss whatever real reasons for concern there may be.

Behind the celebration of decadence is the confidence that there is a base reality awaiting exposure.

In the late sixties one was often struck by the gap between the rhetoric and the expectations in certain styles of political radicalism. With high public passion and fearsome solemnity people called for the destruction of the society; a wasteland was the necessary prelude to the new society rising phoenixlike from the ashes. When pressed about the likely military and political consequences of a violent revolution launched by a small minority, such people would often admit that they depended upon the much-despised "liberal establishment" to protect their elementary liberties and amenities in the course of the revolutionary overthrow.[5] In their minds, the risk was not so risky as the rhetoric suggested. Similarly, it has often been noted that the most radical manifestations of the "youth movement" had its base in the most secure, middle- and upper-middle-class sectors of the society. This gave rise to pejorative remarks about "credit-card revolutionaries" and "spoiled children of the affluent society." While it is not an exhaustive explanation of the youth movement, the light-hearted and popular character of the movement cannot be explained with reference to the fact that, push come to shove, its participants had a relatively secure world to which they could return.

I have often noticed, although I cannot explain, that people seem to fall into two quite different personality structures with two quite different attitudes toward social structures and meanings. The first discovers himself in a world of order and feels repressed and limited by it. The second perceives a world of frightening disorder and earnestly seeks a way to make sense of things. For the first, liberation is liberation from order; for the second it is liberation in the discovery of order. My unscientific research on the subject suggests the difference cannot be explained by reference to childhood experience. People with the most wholesome and untroubled childhoods frequently fall into the second group, while some who emerged from snakepits of familial terror fall into the first.

People in the first group cannot understand what is meant by "the burden of freedom." They find it inconceivable that one might sympathize with the Grand Inquisitor in Dostoevksy's *Brothers Karamazov*. Freedom in the sense of contingency and adventure must always be asserted against what they take to be the dominant realities of order, rules and restrictions. They know nothing of the terror of freedom, they have not peered into the abyss of nothingness, they have not perceived the universe as a floating crap game. Their liberation movement is from the absolute to the relative, from the self-evidently true to the discovery of absurdity.

The people in the second group could never, from their earliest moments of conscious reflection upon the nature of the world, take the absolute for granted. They perceived in some early and formative way that society's orders and rules, rights and wrongs, truths and falsehoods were in no way self-evident but apparently determined in a fickle, arbitrary manner. They understood that things could be quite the opposite of what they are said to be. They were never fully persuaded by the adult world that the fantasy of fairy tales was necessarily less real than the "real world" from which the fairy tales were to provide relief.

As adults themselves, they are rather bored by the adults of the first group who chatter excitedly about their latest discovery that the emperor has no clothes. The people of the second group respond, "Of course, what did you expect? What do you suppose we might do about it?" In short, the people of the second group early discovered that the world really is absurd, or at least it appears to be. Because they have experienced the terror of absurdity, of absolute contingency and arbitrariness, they are not able to celebrate absurdity. They do not deny that there may be an order and meaning in the universe waiting to be discovered. Indeed they search for it, knowing it is always elusive and, when discovered, their hold on it is fragmentary and fragile. Pending its full revelation, the interesting thing to do, the great achievement, is to find some provisional rules by which the threat of absurdity may be held at bay.

In their understanding of society, the radicalism of the first group assumes that, at some primordial point of rootage, the givenness of society is safely secured. One can therefore afford to be reckless, extravagant and decadent about the social order. Indeed such indulgence of recklessness is the expression of freedom over against the given. The people of the second group see themselves as living in a reckless universe in which little is given and almost everything is up for grabs. For them, freedom is *from* absurdity, not freedom *in* absurdity. They have no confidence that there is at the base of things a true self or a true socieity that must be freed from the absurdities of civilization's repressive superstructure. Civilization is what makes freedom possible, protecting us from the tyranny of absurdity that is at the base. Their radicalism starts with the radical perception of absurdity and aims at more secure and more humane constructions of meaning.

The second group's search for security frequently leads to political conservatism. Those who have taken the full measure of the absurdity perceived, however, must be oriented toward constant, even radical, change. That is, they recognize that the terror of the base absurdity can only be countered by the development of social virtues such as compassion, justice and communal loyalty. Since these virtues are at best fragile and ambiguous in our present social order, major changes are required. Opposition to change is a shortsighted response to the perception of base absurdity. The indiscriminate celebration of change, on the other hand, reveals a disastrous failure to take seriously the absurdity that is the beginning assumption rather than the end conclusion of wisdom about society.

Those who begin from the assumption of absurdity are not eager to return to any "natural" state of the really real. On this score they agree with Thomas Hobbes' description of the state of nature: "No arts; no letters; no society; and which is worst of all, continual fear and danger of violent death; and the life of man, solitary, poor, nasty, brutish, and short." The people of the first group repudiate such a view as excessively pessimistic. If only history can be repealed, paradise may yet be regained. In the radical vision of this first group, civilization and all its works are not seen as protection against the terrors of the jungle. Civilization is rather the angel east of the garden, turning this way and that with flaming sword in hand, guarding the way to the tree of life, barring the return of Eden's exiled children. For them, radicalism means to overthrow the angel and at last return to our future in the past.

10

The Eden that Awaits Us

Birthdays and anniversaries—a nation's bicentennial, for example—are correctly viewed as occasions for reflection. Of course we give thanks for blessings, the most elementary of which is sheer survival, and try to reinforce the bonds of friendship that make life more than tolerable. But we also reflect. The most conventional and perhaps inescapable question posed for our reflection is, Who am I? or, Who are we? Since our identity is shaped by what has happened, by history, we quite naturally place our life into retrospective, trying to understand the events that have formed our present selves. The assumption is that truth is to be discovered in our origins. If we can somehow understand our origins, it is thought, we will then be able to bring present reality into line with the truth to be discovered there.

Among the most elementary beliefs promulgated by the Enlightenment, perhaps going as far back as the work of Francis Bacon, is the confidence that knowledge is power. Knowledge is the weapon with which the most recalcitrant realities can be changed or exposed as unreal. Usually the two meant the same thing: to expose as unreal was to change. Thus the confidence of many liberals still today that, if only education, knowledge's Mercury, could be more effectively spread around the world, then the plagues of war, nationalism, race prejudice and self-seeking could be expunged from human history. Admittedly and deservedly, that liberal confidence has been badly shaken in the last fifty years and is now widely viewed as naive. The shaking of the foundations has resulted primarily from the undeniable horrors perpetrated precisely by those people and nations most enamored by the gospel of progress, best endowed with the knowledge that was, like John the Baptist, to make straight the way of the utopia of the messianic age.

Bertrand Russell somewhere remarks that no one who did not grow up before 1914 can really know what happiness was. Of course he was speaking out of the experience of a very privileged part of the nineteenth-century British bourgeoisie, but his remark nonetheless has the ring of truth. It is too easy today to put down the supposed naiveté that permeated the American social gospel movement of sixty and more years ago. Yet it is impossible to read Walter Rauschenbusch, for example, without being struck by key assumptions which can only be described as extraordinarily naive. Contrary to accepted opinion, popularized by H. Richard and Reinhold Niebuhr, Rauschenbusch did have a place for original sin and was, in fact, strongly critical of the more fatuous notions of automatic progress. He wrote, for example, "None of us individually drifts into purity, justice, and unselfishness, as we all know. And humanity as a whole would likewise, if let alone, by no means roll into the millennium, but by a broad and easy track into a hell on earth, into rottenness, beastliness, and self-destruction "[1]

Nor did Rauschenbusch accept at face value the idea that education was the invariable servant of reform. As he wrote, "Even education does not lift man. It enhances his power either for good or evil. It refines his good or evil enjoyments. But it does not make him good. France is the living demonstration of that to our day. They dress better and converse better at Paris than the rest of us do; they write a more brilliant style, coin cleverer epigrams, and see plays more intelligently. But in spite of that, France supplies the world with lasciviousness and with virulent unbelief."[2]

Yet, for all that, Rauschenbusch and his colleagues shared the earlier world to which Bertrand Russell alludes, except, of course, theirs was a singularly American world. "There are only a few nations whose track through the last two thousand years seems headed toward the Kingdom of God. It is a wavering, lagging line, yet it goes forward. And they seem to have the faculty also of planting new and vigorous societies and of putting a thrill of life into the paralytic sister nations."[3]

Such a view of reality, Rauschenbusch admitted, was frequently not supported by empirical evidence. But he seems to suggest that there is something of a Pascalian wager in his assertions; that, even when the evidence is to the contrary, the belief is worth asserting. "To do the right against all considerations of utility is the categorical imperative of duty. To believe in the triumph of right against all appearances of defeat is the categorical imperative of faith. To deny the former is moral suicide. To surrender the latter is religious suicide."[4] There is more wisdom here than the proponents of the social gospel are generally given credit for. Unfortunately, despite the bold arguments of categorical imperatives to be maintained come what may, their engagement in history's tasks seemed to need the support of a certain reading of our modern age, a reading that today does not seem very plausible.

Rauschenbusch acknowledges that the New Testament holds out very modest hopes indeed for social reform. He explains this in the usual, and essentially correct, manner, underscoring the peculiar problems afflicting the early church and its expectation that the time before the final coming of the Lord is so brief as to make the work of social reform seem unnecessary, perhaps even a sign of unbelief in the impending Eschaton. It is in his statement of what has changed, however, that many of us find it difficult to accept the social gospel's confidence in the worthwhileness of social reform. "Affairs have changed [since the New Testament period]. Christian men are a power in the world."[5] At another point he explains the significance of this great change: "Despotisms are passing away. The greatness won by force is gaining less and less of admiration. The discernment of humanity is growing clearer. Men love heroism, self-sacrifice, love. Jesus has himself been the foremost force in bringing about this change, and in turn he reaps the reward of his work. The less men acknowledge the sovereignty of brute force and the more they yield their willing loyalty to the spiritual power of character, the more will Jesus become King of humanity."[6]

That all these are great goods much to be desired, there is no doubt, or at least most Christians would not doubt. That such developments actually mark the unfolding of our era seems doubtful in the extreme. True, there are intelligent people who today believe "the discernment of humanity is growing clearer." One thinks of the late U Thant, former secretary general of the United Nations, and Norman Cousins, editor of *Saturday Review/World,* and their campaign for "world citizenship." Or of the more facile appropriations of the thought of Teilhard de Chardin by those who see such things as the Nazi holocaust, Stalinist terrorism and massive famine as but ripples on the smooth sea we sail through humanization to the noosphere of our dreams.

As implausible as all this may seem, people of good will are generally tolerant of such "idealism" in a world that has run all too short of hopeful dreams. Such an optimistic reading of our times is, however, not only unwarranted; it is dangerous. It is an instance of the historical hubris we have discussed earlier. It invites us to construct our commitment to history upon the foundation of grand illusion. More important, it makes almost inevitable the bitter disillusionment which, in turn, invites the apocalypticism that would negate history.

It is not necessary here to recite the horrors that shattered the happiness of Lord Russell's world. The lessons to be drawn were spelled out in T. S. Eliot's "Wasteland" and in the "theological revolution" of which Karl Barth was the chief champion. I suspect those cultural historians are correct who see our time on a continuum of descent from 1914. World War II, the "crusade in Europe," as General Eisenhower called it, and its briefly buoyant aftermath (at least for Americans) was an exception, a momentary relief from the sense of the cave. Even that was marred by Hiroshima and the mushroom cloud that rose to hide the sky that had symbolized the expanse of human hope. By that shadow the dome of the cave was reinforced, and many felt compelled to confess the foolishness of their illusion that there could be even brief respite from the sense of ending. Assassinations, Vietnams, perduring racism and failed revolutions confirmed for many the ugly suspicion that there are no alternative routes to the path of descent on which history embarked by a tragic misstep one August day in 1914.

Some despair, others engage in what Martin Marty called "the search for a usable future." On birthdays and bicentennials it may happen that the search becomes more fervid. We who live in a Freudian (or, as some insist, a post-Freudian) time, assume the truth about the present is to be discovered in the past. Rummaging through the dark and murky sewage in which the present was germinated, we hope to find the knowledge that is the Excalibur by which we might vanquish the dark knights of the present. Too often we find only dark and murky sewage, and can envision no future other than its continued seepage into the void of that which is not yet. To push the metaphor a little, it is as though we were doomed to search, like the detective in Victor Hugo's *Les Misérables,* forever sloshing about in the labyrinthine passageways of the underworld of the past. Like Hugo, we may be in passionate search of justice and the secret of why it has been denied, but there seems to be no end to the ebb and flow of the excrement with which history honors hope. The cave takes many forms.

Pushing yet a little further, there may be some symbolic nuance in the place of tunnels and underground passages in the literature of romance and revolution. The charge that occasioned the 1971 trial of Philip Berrigan and others is that they were planning to blow up the underground passages beneath the Pentagon. Thus would we explode our way out of the cave into the future. I have not heard anyone remark on it, but in recent years New York City has stopped using manhole covers on many streets. Instead they just pave over the openings and jackhammer through to them when repairs are required. Could there be some sinister reason, something or someone they are trying to keep in, or, more likely, someone they want to keep out, someone who might descend into the bowels of our discontent and there plant a charge that might liberate us all? But now we have gone too far. Metaphors, especially confused metaphors, should be kept on a short leash.

Since we do not find in the past either blueprints or materials for the construction of utopia, we must go beyond the past. If the future has no reality, if the future is no place, we cannot place our utopian "no place" in the future. Since we cannot go beyond the past by going ahead of the past (or of the present which is, of course, fast becoming past), we go beyond the past by going behind the past. In searching for the future that is the "past" of our past, we challenge the angel who guards the way to the tree of life. This is the direction of defiance that has marked revolutionary movements, religious and secular, from antiquity up to the present.

It is the direction brilliantly described by Norman Cohn in his *The Pursuit of the Millennium.* In his chapter "The Egalitarian State of Nature," he discusses the ways in which the passion for equality is morally legitimated by appeal to the idea that egalitarianism is the true (that is, the original) condition of humanity. What he says about egalitarianism can, *mutatis mutandis,* be applied with equal merit to other ingredients that go into most utopian formulas.

The revolutionary eschatology of Europe, and consequently of America, can, Cohn writes, be traced back to the ancient world. "It was from the Greeks and Romans that medieval Europe inherited the notion of the 'State of Nature' as a state of affairs in which all men were equal in status and wealth and in which nobody was oppressed or exploited by anyone else; a state of affairs characterized by universal good faith and brotherly love and also, sometimes, by total community of property and even of spouses."[7]

In the "Reign of Saturn," a long lost Golden Age, Greek and Latin literature had a much happier state of affairs than we have known since. In his *Metamorphoses,* Ovid offers a description of that time which was later to be echoed during the Middle Ages. According to Ovid, in the time before Saturn had been deposed by Jupiter "men used to cultivate good faith and virtue spontaneously, without laws. Punishment and fear did not exist. . . . Earth herself, untroubled and untouched by the hoe, unwounded by any ploughshare, used to give all things of her own accord." Later, "shame and truth and good faith fled away; and in their place came deceit and guilt and plots and violence and the wicked lust for possession. . . . The wary surveyor marked out with long boundary-lines the earth which hitherto had been a common possession like the sunshine and the breezes. . . . Men lived by plunder . . ."

Ancient philosophy had an even greater influence than ancient literature in shaping the utopian thought of the Middle Ages. As early as the third century B.C., the beginnings of Stoic religion developed a notion of the sun god under whom the world was once ruled according to its true order. Such ideas entered Christian thought and were translated dozens of times during the Renaissance. It is a picture of unquestionable appeal:

[On the Isles of the Blessed] seven islands are dedicated to the sun and are inhabited by the Heliopolitans, or sun-men. Each day throughout the year the sun passes immediately over the islands, with the result that the days are always exactly as long as the nights, the climate is invariably perfect and the season invariably summer, abounding in fruit and flowers. The population of each island is divided into four tribes, each 400 strong. All citizens have the same perfectly healthy constitution and the same perfectly beautiful features. Each takes his turn to perform every necessary task as hunter or fisherman or in the service of the state. All land, livestock and tools are thus used in turn by every citizen and therefore belong to nobody in particular. Marriage is unknown and sexual promiscuity complete; the tribe is responsible for bringing up the children, and this is done in such a way that mothers cannot recognize their own. The consequent lack of heirs removes any cause for competition or rivalry; and the Law of Nature, operating in undistorted souls, produces amongst these people a complete and unfailing concord. And indeed in so equitable an order dissension is inconceivable. Even in their expectation of life the Heliopolitans are all equal, for all die voluntarily and peacefully while at the height of their powers, at the age of 150.[8]

The reader cannot help but note the parallels with many aspects of reform and revolution advocated today; from the more extravagant proposals for day-care centers, to the obliteration of sexual institutions (although not, apparently, of sex roles), to the movement for "death with dignity." The avant-garde is very old. The worthiest dreams may be, simply by virtue of being the worthiest, the most recurrent. The more significant point is that the dreams are premised upon the belief that the ideal is the really real, it is the natural way that history has distorted. This theme reverberates throughout contemporary cultural laments over what humankind has done in its exploitation of nature.

The church father, Clement of Alexandria, cites an early Greek document, *On Justice,* offering a picture of the Golden Age similar to the above. The conclusion is that "man-made laws have undermined the divine law and destroyed the communal order in which it was expressed. It was these human laws which created the distinction between Mine and Thine, so that things which by right belong to all can now no longer be enjoyed in common. And it was this violation of community and equality which gave rise to theft and to all crime." And so forth.

While Christian theologians operated more specifically from the Genesis account of the Fall, they expounded its meaning in a way that reveals their assimilation of the earlier myths. Slavery, for example, was legitimated in the present fallen order, in full knowledge that it was not part of God's original order. Thus St. Augustine: "This the order of nature has prescribed and thus God has created man. For he said: 'Let them have dominion over the fish of the seas, and over the fowl of the air, and over every creeping thing that creepeth upon the earth.' Having made man in his own image, a rational being, he meant him to be lord only over irrational beings; not man set over man, but man set over beasts. . . . The first cause of servitude is sin, by which man is subjected to man by the bonds of his condition. . . . But by that nature in which God formerly created man nobody is slave either to man or to sin."

The ideal of the "original condition" with its communal life, voluntary poverty and the such, found expression in medieval monasticism. But the church was "realistic" about the limitations imposed by a "fallen" creation. While monasticism was promoted as "the more perfect way," it was clearly understood that it was for an elite. Already in the Middle Ages, some millennialistic and revolutionary movements attempted to carry "the more perfect way" all the way, applying it to the reordering of the whole of society. The full social impact of the idea of reviving the Golden Age was to come centuries later. "It produced a doctrine," Cohn writes, "which became a revolutionary myth as soon as it was presented to the turbulent poor and fused with the phantasies of popular eschatology."

We began this chapter by looking at a species of optimism, associated with the "social gospel movement," that not only fails to grip us today but seems downright frivolous in its implausibility. Again, it is too easy to caricature people like Walter Rauschenbusch and Washington Gladden and this is frequently done by writers who evidence little of their concern for social justice or of their seriousness about the tasks of history. That concern and seriousness is desperately needed today, but it cannot be sustained by the delusion that, in a variety of forms, is evident at every point on the social and political spectrum, namely, the delusion that there once existed a true human nature and social order that can now be revived or liberated, whether by liberal education or by violent revolution.

The argument for a covenant contingent upon a real and promising future raises, I am well aware, many questions that cannot be adequately resolved within the scope of this book. The present chapter may have raised at least two questions and I should at least mention them before moving on. The first is: What if, in fact, civilization has been an horrendous mistake, quite apart from whether there was once something better that civilization "distorted"? The second, perhaps of greater concern to orthodox Christians: Do not the creation accounts in Genesis and their use throughout the Bible make mandatory some notion of paradisal bliss from which humanity has "fallen"?

The response to the first question can be brief; it is simply unanswerable. The question itself is part of "civilization," dependent as it is upon the infinite complexity of human language, humankind's most elementary social construction, and assuming as it does sophisticated judgments of value and fact. I am not simply influenced by civilization or part of civilization, I am inexplicable apart from civilization. If the promise of the coming Kingdom does not speak to the vindication of the enterprise we call civilization, then it is meaningless to all of us who are civilization. Obviously, this does not imply a carte-blanche endorsement of everything in any particular "civilization." The whole point of critical reflection is to be discriminate about what history is revealing about the possible and desirable—and about the impossible and undesirable. As indicated earlier, especially in the discussion of the book of Job, I am of the fallen-sparrows and lost-hairs school of Christian belief. If, as is of course possible, Jesus and others are quite wrong about the nature and destiny of history, then we are thrown into a very different and thoroughly pragmatic line of reasoning aimed at making the best of a very bad deal.

As to the question of the "fallenness" of the creation, I can here do little more than indicate a general disposition toward the question as it relates to the argument of this essay. I would in no way disagree with the intent of many who insist upon the historical reality of the Fall in order to underscore the radicality of evil and to exculpate God of responsibility for the sorry state of the world.

The Edenic myth as recorded in Genesis is part of a general religious phenomena, amply testified to in numerous religious traditions, albeit with significant modifications. Mircea Eliade speaks of the myth of the great return which is, he suggests, part of the very nature of religion itself.[9] The British sociologist of religion Bryan R. Wilson speaks of the "thaumaturgical persistence" of such a myth in contemporary native religions, from American Indians to the Zulus of South Africa.[10] Even the cargo cults, such as those that thrive in the South Pacific, expect a magical restoration of treasures that were somehow rightfully theirs in the beginning. Lest we think ourselves terribly superior to such primitivism, we should note the best-seller status of books such as *Chariots of the Gods?* which are but more technological versions of the cargo cult. No matter how bad things may seem, there is yet to be a happy ending when those who once had the world in happier order return to set things straight.

At the most profound level, the story of Eden must be seen as a serious response to the shape of history by those who take history seriously. It is simply intolerable that this world—a world in which the wicked prosper, the innocent are oppressed, suffering knows no limits, and death appears to be the last word—should be all there is. This cannot be the final statement on the nature of reality itself. A world that is more Auschwitz than Elysium is intolerable because it negates what man would say about God. The Edenic myth is at its heart a response to the problem of theodicy, the problem of justifying God to man. Without denying the support it gives in the human quest for meaning, the Edenic myth is more for the sake of God than for the sake of man. It is designed to exculpate an all-powerful and all-good God of any responsibility for what is called "original sin," the radical evil that pervades our historical existence.

We shall in another connection return briefly to the question of theodicy. Here it is enough to note that the idea of an historical Fall, while dominant in the Christian tradition, is not the only way Christian thinkers have tried to come to terms with the apparent contradiction between the shape of historical fact and what they say about the power and love of

God. I do not think the Edenic myth is a very happy way. There are the obvious problems posed by the endlessly discussed conflict between the sovereignty of God and human free will. For all the monumentally imaginative explanations offered through the centuries, the mystery of freedom versus determinism cannot be resolved by reference to the Edenic myth. Even more important, the idea of a Fall provides little meaning for subsequent history. If God is already sovereign, if his rule is independent of history, what is he waiting for? Surely the "Great acts of God" which theologians say make up "salvation history" (as though there were two histories, one for God's great acts and another for the rest of us) are all very nice. But as conventional Christian piety views them, all these great acts, from the Exodus through the Resurrection, are only minor repair jobs.

There was a deacon in my parish—we will call him James Johnson—a model of black nobility and Christian devotion. I held his hand as he died a painful death at age forty-three. Through the blood that bubbled from his hemorrhaged lungs he formed his last word, very quietly, not complaining but profoundly puzzled, he looked at me and said, "Why?" The reader may think I am being unfair, enlisting melodrama in support of an argument. No, this is precisely, this is inescapably, this is finally what it is all about. Every statement about meaning, about hope, about the purpose of history, must be tested against that "Why?" With him and with many, many others, I hope that what was said about the great acts of God changed the manner, the degree of confidence and perhaps peace, in which they died. But there was no great act of God there and then. They died. And that is intolerable.

If he is able, why does God not get on with the job of repairing this wretched creation? There are those who think such a question impious, despite its echoing through the prayers of psalmist and prophet. There are those who say such questions must be referred to the realm of unfathomable mystery. But we cannot stop thinking about them. As rational beings, we offer God no service by escaping into a "faith" that confuses mystery with obfuscation. But, it is said, we cannot understand what God may be doing, for we are mere mortals. True enough, if he is God, we cannot comprehend the fullness of his mind or his ways. But I dare say I do know some things God should do, if he is God, if he is able. The millions of victims of the Black Plague, of the Nazi Holocaust, of Stalinist terror, of Maoist rectification—they all saw more clearly than do the theologians who manage his public relations what God should be doing, if he is God, if he is able.

There are those who say that history is not to be taken all that seriously, that there are larger, spiritual, realms in which the truth is to be found. But, again, history is all we have. History is us. We do not honor God by despising his creation or by dissociating him from his project. The trouble his project is in should not be belittled. To relativize or to diminish the death of one innocent child—not to mention uncounted millions of men, women and children—is obscene. To put it quite bluntly, there is no possible good that God might be up to that can justify his not stopping, if he is able, the absolute evil to which history witnesses.

That may seem an extravagant statement, for how do we know what is the possible good? The answer is, We do not know, but neither is it a very useful question. All that we know we know from history. Facing certain evil, we know that a God who is all-powerful and all-loving would prevent its happening. If we do not know that, we do not know anything. If we do not know that, we do not know, for example, that there is a God worthy of our trust and love. If, on the other hand, we think we know that God is able to prevent such evil, but he does not prevent it, then he is to be feared but we can neither love nor trust him. The Edenic myth of a free and sovereign God who created a perfect world that then fell into sin cannot, I believe, provide an adequate response to James Johnson's question. The Edenic myth is a powerful and poignant, but finally unsuccessful, attempt to acquit God of the charges history brings against him.

But of course there is no adequate response to history's horrors. There are only less inadequate responses. A less inadequate response is the concept of the divine pathos, of history as the process of God's Self-realization. In connection with the present discussion, it is appropriate to ask what that implies for the Genesis accounts and for all the traditions of "paradise lost." The very pervasiveness of such traditions suggests that they are anthropologically rooted and must be taken seriously. In some very important respects they must be affirmed. They are necessary protests against things as they are. They correctly underscore the radicality of evil. They are desperately serious efforts to exculpate God from responsibility. In these ways, the Edenic myth must be affirmed, at least in its intention. But it need not and should not be understood as a description of what once was. It is rather a proleptic vision, a "future flash," of what is to be. The Genesis accounts should be viewed not as prehistory but as eschatology. To put it another way, the prehistory and the end of history are the same. The beginning and the end is the Word of God who both initiated and will fulfill the creation we call history. In this sense, Genesis is as much eschatological literature as is the book of Revelation. "Behold I am coming soon, bringing my recompense, to repay every one for what he has done. I am the Alpha and the Omega, the first and the last, the beginning and the end" (Rev. 22).

As the stories of a Golden Age must be viewed eschatologically, so must all the biblical statements about the freedom and sovereignty of God. When biblical writers spoke about God holding in derision the principalities and powers of the present time, or about God ruling the whole of creation in justice, they were speaking in hope. Clearly they were not describing the state of affairs existing then or now. When today worshipers, in song and liturgy, acclaim God as almighty and all-power-ful, they too have reference to hope. They sing the songs of Zion in a strange land which little resembles the world for which they yearn. If, as the believer trusts, things will one day be as the songs describe them to be, then God will be vindicated in the fulfillment of history. In that case, it will turn out that we were right all along to call him all-powerful and all-loving. Then too, the Edenic myth will, at least in its most profound intention, be vindicated. Then we will understand that the angel guarding the way to the tree of life was our own fear of the future, our fear of the Absolute Future who calls us to absolute trust in his victory and ours.

11

Choosing Between
the God of History and
the Engineer Emeritus

"When in the course of human events it becomes necessary for one people to dissolve the political bands which have connected them with another, and to assume among the powers of the earth, the separate and equal station to which the Laws of Nature and of Nature's God entitle them, a decent respect to the opinions of mankind requires that they should declare the causes which impel them to the separation. We hold these truths to be self-evident . . ."

Here we find the elements that glue together the contract, as distinct from covenant, approach to understanding society. It is assumed that there is at the base of all reality a "natural" way, a way approved by Nature and by Nature's God. If there be progress in history, it is through the historical task of discovering and unfolding what is natural. What before was hidden is revealed as "self-evident" because it is found to be rooted in nature.

Today we witness a revival of subservience to nature. It is widely believed, and not without reason, that the modern world with its technological exploitation of nature has run amuck. It must be checked by the truth of nature. There are enormous differences, however, between the eighteenth-century's view of nature and the view that is now current. The American founding fathers offered a highly political reading of Nature's Way. Today many of the acolytes of the natural would "put an end to politics." The founding fathers had an extremely optimistic view of nature; their themes were new beginnings and possibilities. Today's rediscovery of nature is dominated by pessimism; its themes are endings and limitations. In Enlightenment thinking, the human enterprise was befriended and liberated by nature. Today it is suggested that humankind and nature have become enemies and that both are, in all likelihood, doomed by that enmity. Although they draw dramatically different conclusions from the fact, the Declaration of Independence and *Wilderness* magazine agree that the truth is to be found in nature. Historically and psychologically this belief is tied to one version or another of the myth of Eden. And that, in turn, is related to the belief that the truth about the future is to be discovered in the past.

The discussion of the ecological crisis today frequently assumes that the concept of the mastery of nature must be replaced by that of the liberation of nature. We are offered the stereotype of man the ruthless and mindless exploiter of a nature he mistakenly assumes to be inexhaustible. As with most stereotypes, there is enough truth in it to keep it in circulation. In more extreme arguments we are offered the alternative of nature untainted by the human enterprise, of which the wilderness is the ideal type. There nature is liberated from human mastery. There the "domination of nature" mandated in the book of Genesis is replaced by service to nature, the best service being to let Nature have her way. In this now common view, it is forgotten that the biblical mandate called humankind not to unlimited domination but to accountability. Man was not so much the master as the steward and caretaker of the creation, answerable to creation's Lord. Nor could humankind be separated from nature. If we are faithful to the biblical insight, we will not become bogged down in conceptual conflicts between man and nature, or between history and nature. We are part of nature, and nature is part of the history which is the process of God's Self-realization in time.

Human beings are, however, a very special part of nature. We are so special a part of nature that we can sympathize with the slight hyperbole of the late Marxist philosopher, George Lukács, who called nature "a social category."[1] Obviously, we cannot make nature anything we want it to be. This is as true of human as of nonhuman nature. There are, so to speak, objective limits, although these limits are not so absolutely fixed as both premodern and postmodern people believed and believe. In our yearning for the fulfillment of nature, and of humankind within nature, we encounter limitations. These limitations are not inherent in nature, as though the creation were in *stasis.* Rather, if the gospel of the Kingdom turns out to be right, such limitations are to be explained in terms of our provisional moment in history. What we might call the true nature of nature is yet to be revealed. Human beings have, within nature, the singular task of interpreting the history of which nature is part. Indeed this process of interpretation is what is meant by history in a much narrower and admittedly more conventional sense than we are using the term here.

To say that nature is a social category is to say there is no nature apart from history. To put it another way, there is no fact or event apart from the interpretation of that fact or event. This means we do not come to nature as though it were a book to be read, as though it contained ideas and lessons which we human beings are to learn. We do not approach nature "objectively" or as pupils who come as blank slates on which Nature might inscribe her wisdom. Appeals to Nature and to Nature's God are in fact appeals to particular human ways of constructing reality. If we interpret such metaphors in a literal way (and this is frequently done), we deceive ourselves most dangerously.

Some claimed to discover in the "laws of nature" human equality or the self-evident right to life, liberty and the pursuit of happiness. Others have, with an equal sense of certitude, discovered in nature the iron laws of the survival of the fittest. The most antithetical of social and political theories appeal to the laws of nature. No proponent of any party likes to admit that his proposals are unnatural or contrary to nature. Yet, what the Christian gospel proposes would seem to be very close to that. In saying that the truth is to be discovered not in what is but in what is to be, we defy any reading of reality that would absolutize the lessons to be drawn from present or past, whether they be drawn from history (the human enterprise and its interpretation) or from nature (extrahuman nature).

In fact, the Christian proposition is not unnatural or contrary to nature; it simply asserts that the truth about nature has not yet been finally revealed. The truth of this assertion can be indicated or repudiated only by the future. For the present, we understand nature to be a social category which is, like all social categories, contingent upon the future fulfillment of promise. Without denying the extrahuman objective reality of what is called nature, the meaning of nature is a human construction. We discover in nature what we have imposed upon nature. We find the treasures that we first hid. Nature has limits but it has no lessons, unless the lesson be the limits which are common to all reality in this provisional moment of its unfolding. It is the singular task of humanity to defy such limits in our yearning for the new heaven and new earth of divine promise. That for which we hope is beyond the past and present of nature. Only when we have lost confidence in the Power of the Future do we ground our hopes in nature. Nature's God is not simply the religious term for what in secular language is called nature, although that may be what was intended by those who so smoothly linked the two. Nature's God and ours is nature's future and ours. He is the Power of the Future with whom we are called to struggle for the fulfillment of past and present. This is at the heart of covenantal existence.

Social-contract thinking has over the years taken many forms and appealed to many sources. There are those who have urged that a serviceable contract can be devised and sustained purely on pragmatic or utilitarian considerations. Others, such as John Rawls in our own day, have correctly seen that a strong social contract, strong enough to survive the vagaries of individualism and historical turmoil, must be grounded metaphysically (even if they are hesitant to use the term *metaphysical*). Those who seek such grounding almost inevitably turn to nature or to what is natural.

Our argument is for a primarily covenantal approach to society. It assumes there is no existing point of reference—neither a general will, nor common sense, nor utilitarian consensus, nor laws of nature—that can provide final rules for our present action or future hopes in society. History (which is to say, all of reality) is struggling toward a promised eschaton, a hoped-for fulfillment. Again, we do not repudiate all thought about a social contract. Indeed, the ambiguities of history make some contract necessary if life together is to remain human. But the terms of the contract are at best proximate and always provisional. All contracts are contingent upon the promised fulfillment and remain under judgment. The conditions of the contract are provisional rules for pilgrims along the way. The contract is for the sake of the Kingdom. We noted earlier, for example, the utterly crucial character of the contractual agreement that freedom of thought and opinion be encouraged. Our insistence upon this point is not grounded in laws of nature nor in any of the other sources to which social contract theory might appeal. Our insistence upon such liberty is for the sake of the Kingdom. Because ours is such a provisional and partial moment of history, because we see through a glass darkly, because the Spirit blows where he will, it is essential that we maintain maximal openness to diverse sightings of the Kingdom's coming. Thus, as people of the covenant, we concur in some of the affirmations of classical liberalism, but such concurrence is always provisional and is reached through a quite different line of reasoning.

For the Enlightenment thinkers Nature's God was, to use Peter Gay's term, the Engineer Emeritus. After the timepiece of creation had been made and wound, Nature's God could safely retire to his celestial pastimes. In covenant thinking, God is the Power of the Future and knows no sabbath rest until creation's project is realized in the Kingdom Come. In Enlightenment thought, Nature and Nature's God were, for all practical purposes, the same thing. To understand the way of Nature was to perceive the intention of Nature's God. Indeed even the mention of Nature's God was something of an appendage, tacked on as a gesture toward the religiously inclined. All the truth that matters was accessible in Nature alone. These assumptions still dominate what we call modern thought about nature, reason and truth. Biblical religion must regain its nerve to challenge them at their very foundations.

Today we have every reason to be skeptical of the assumption that the good, the true and the beautiful are to be located in the natural. This is still the assumption of modern science that sees itself "unfolding the secrets of nature." One need not agree with the antitechnology faddism of our time nor join up with the Luddites of ecologism to acknowledge that one of the hard lessons of recent history is that scientific progress is not necessarily human progress. What is called objective, value-free science is not enough as final guide. There is much that can be done scientifically that should not be done. The "secrets of nature" when revealed can invite cosmic destruction, as in the field of nuclear energy, or can be profoundly misleading, as in the case of social scientists who would understand society in the light of insights gained from studying the sexual or territorial habits of orangutans.

The truth by which science must be checked is not contained within nature nor within the scientific method itself, at least as presently understood. Neither is it enough to say, as is commonly said today, that science and its technology must be critically checked by the realm of values. If we simply leave it at that, the problem arises that people seek values and the principles of moral judgment in the "laws of nature." Thus the perilous narrowness of a scientific method that limits itself to the search for truth in nature's past and present is monitored by an ethic that is just as perilously narrow. The truth is in the future and is yet to be fully revealed. It can now be apprehended by reason, sustained by hope and acted upon in faith. The truth is hinged upon a promise and gives birth to a moral discourse by which a covenantal community must keep under judgment all that is called science.

Social-contract thinking that emerges from the "Nature and Nature's God" school assumes that the purposes of history are implicit in what already is. It requires only the application of reason to discover and elaborate what is already there. The Engineer Emeritus has done his work and now leaves it to us to draw the proper inferences. For this grievous distortion of Christian teaching the church itself is no doubt in part responsible. We have already discussed the facile Christianization of the myth of the "Golden Age" that did so much to erroneously locate in the past and in nature the "truth" about the human condition. It would seem also that orthodox Christianity has been guilty of overreacting to the heresy of Manichaeism. In rejecting the idea of a dualistic cosmos divided between Good and Evil, Light and Darkness, orthodox Christianity asserted the sovereignty of God in a way that often left little room for the "divine pathos" engaged in history's struggle for fulfillment. Whatever the route may have been, and whosoever the fault may have been, Western thought arrived at the point where the idea of the sovereignty of God was transmogrified into the notion of a creation in *stasis.*

It is but a short distance from that point to Pierre Simon De Laplace's famed response to Napoleon Bonaparte. "You have written this huge

book on the system of the world," said Napoleon, "without once mention-
ing the author of the universe." "Sire," Laplace answered, "I have no
need of that hypothesis." Thus does reference to Nature's God become
little more than a rhetorical flourish, an attempt at moral reinforcement,
in much social-contract thinking. Nature's God is finally superfluous.
When one has said "Nature," one has said everything, or at least
everything we need bother our heads about.

Throughout modern history there have been intellectual subcurrents
expressing profound suspicion of science, technology and modernity
itself. But this suspiciousness was usually viewed as marginal and even
kooky; it was submerged under the tide of confidence, based on osten-
sible improvement in the human condition, that inevitable progress at-
tended the reign of a science that was continuously unlocking nature's
beneficent secrets. Hiroshima symbolizes the point at which what had
been marginal misgivings about this optimistic world view began to carve
out a place in popular consciousness. The much-publicized soul-search-
ing of Robert Oppenheimer and others involved in nuclear development
infiltrated the public mind with the idea that there was no inherent logic
of science that could be trusted. Scientific progress could mean human
regress, or even annihilation. Today this viewpoint is no longer novel,
indeed it is the conventional wisdom among those deemed to be thoughtful persons. In recent years biological and medical sciences have come
under increasing scrutiny and, perhaps for the first time, the scientific
community is imposing self-limitations upon research in areas such as
genetic engineering and bacteriology.

What we have discovered is that, contrary to Francis Bacon and the
Englightenment, science and the nature it reveals are not innocent.
Nature is possessed neither of inherent logic, nor of inevitable progress,
nor of superior morality. The irony in current awareness of the limitations
and dangers of "scientism" is that, in seeking some point of reference by
which science might be checked, the appeal is commonly made to nature.
Thus we are brought full circle. Beginning with the idea that knowledge
of nature is power, we discovered the paradox that with increasing power
we not only became more powerless but threw into question our very
survival as a species. Now it is widely touted that knowledge of nature
is wisdom, that from nature we will gain the wisdom to check and control
our misbegotten pursuit of power. In coming full circle, we have only set
ourselves up for further disappointment. Nature has no more inherent
wisdom than it has inherent power. The putative secrets of wisdom that
are to be unlocked will turn out to be as disappointing as, and even more
dangerous than, the secrets of power that led to our present feeling of
powerlessness.

Nature is as locked in to this provisional and largely distorted moment of history as are we ourselves. Indeed we human beings are but the interpreting party within an incomplete nature within an incomplete history. The power and wisdom we seek is the Power and Wisdom of the Future whom believers call God. In seeking a transcendent referent by which to bring science under check and control, we delude ourselves if we look for it in any existing reality. It is not to be discovered by scientific rummaging through past and present but by the powers of imagination, reason and faith to reach toward a promised future. The scientific technocrat and the wilderness enthusiast are equally guilty of assuming that nature is in some sense innocent. That one would exploit nature and the other adore it makes little difference. Both trust nature as the goddess who holds the secret of human happiness and fulfillment. One would unlock the secret with scientific technology and the other would court the goddess into revealing it, but both assume she has the secret. Neither takes seriously what is intended by the ancient metaphors of original sin and the pervasive fallenness of the creation. Neither understands that our hope for the future lies not in the past, nor in extrahuman history, but our future, and the future of all that is, is ahead of us in time.

In an important book, *The Domination of Nature,* William Leiss describes the ploy by which Francis Bacon gained respectability for a kind of scientific curiosity that had previously been associated with alchemy and various "satanic arts." "Bacon perceived that behind the reluctance of society to encourage scientific innovation was the fear that man might incur God's wrath by interfering with the natural order of things. Thus he took great pains to stress the 'innocence' of the scientific endeavor." In trying, unsuccessfully, to persuade Queen Elizabeth to give royal support for scientific research, he argued that of all the exercises of the mind, "the most innocent and meriting conquest was the conquest of the works of nature." In an early essay, he wrote that discoveries in the arts and sciences (the two were not clearly distinguished then) were part of a game that man played with God, "as if the divine nature enjoyed the kindly innocence of such hide-and-seek, hiding only in order to be found, and with characteristic indulgence desired the human mind to join Him in this sport. And indeed it is this glory of discovery that is the true ornament of mankind, In contrast with civil business it never harmed any man, never burdened a conscience with remorse. Its blessing and reward is without ruin, wrong or wretchedness to any. For light is in itself pure and innocent; it may be wrongly used, but cannot in its nature be defiled."[2]

Such extraordinary naiveté about the consequences of scientific discovery may seem incredible to most people today. Yet many, with Bacon, would still offer the facile explanation that whatever horrors science has perpetrated are due to nature being "wrongly used." Man is guilty, nature is innocent, or, as some would prefer it, nature is neutral, equal in its potentiality for good or evil. The Christian insight is that extrahuman nature is as compromised and distorted by the incompleteness and unfaith called sin as is human nature itself. Nature is no zone of innocence unaffected by the sway of the principalities and powers of the present time. Our hope for the future stands over against nature as much as it stands over against our present human condition.

It is in our trust toward the Power of the Future, or, as Jesus puts it, in our seeking first the Kingdom of God, that we anticipate the new heavens and new earth of our nature's yearning. In this connection, a radically different way of thinking about our relation to extrahuman nature is suggested by early Christian tales of saints who tamed wild animals. The early Christian fathers took seriously the idea of Genesis that man was to share God's universal dominion over nature, including the animal kingdom. The fact that there were wild animals unresponsive to human bidding was but another indication that the consequences of the Fall had thrown into disorder the whole creation, not just the human condition. The saints, those who had entered into a more perfect union with God's will, are depicted as going into the wilderness where they encounter and tame wild lions and other beasts. This was perceived as an eschatological sign of that messianic age in which man would be fulfilled in perfect obedience to God and nature fulfilled in perfect obedience to man.[3] The conquest, it is important to note, is not, as with Bacon and the Enlightenment, through scientific knowledge but through personal holiness.

It is notoriously difficult today to speak of holiness. But whatever term we might use, it is that disposition of radical devotion toward what is to be, to the promised future that is, in biblical language, called the Kingdom of God. Devotion to God and devotion to the Rule of God are the same thing, for God's Being is inseparable from his Rule. It is only as we join God in history's struggle toward his Self-realization that we discover the transcendent referent by which science and the nature it serves are fulfilled in the new order for which they were made. Now that is, of course, always a partial fulfillment, but in the promised End Time it will be complete. The crucial point is that the alternative to present discontents and horrors is to be discovered not in "getting right with nature" but in—for all the unhappy associations the phrase may have—in getting right with God. (The unhappy associations are, of course, the revivalist's pitch that places God outside history, thus enervating the dialectic between present and future.)

There is a profoundly antipolitical bias in appeals to nature as the transcendent point of reference by which human affairs are to be ordered. This is as true of those who appeal to nature in the temple of technology as it is of those who offer their prayers in the temple of ecology. Of the revelations of nature, Bacon wrote "[they] never harmed any man, never burdened a conscience with remorse." It is significant that he says this is the case, *"in contrast with civil business."* In the realm of politics, we posit concepts such as justice, the public good and truth against the way things are. It is assumed that the right ordering of society and the world is singularly and emphatically the human task. In the temples of nature, however, it is thought that all such concepts, to the extent they have any merit, are inherent in the natural order. Thus in Bacon's utopian *New Atlantis,* the scientific research establishment is the repository of truth and exercises an element of independence from the rest of the society: "And this we do also: We have Consultations in which we decide which of the inventions and experiences we have discovered shall be Published, and which not. And we all take an oath of secrecy to conceal those which we think fit to keep secret; though some of these we do reveal to the State, and some not."[4]

The language has a strikingly modern ring. Indeed it is the ideal still espoused today by many social critics and reformers who, in the name of science and efficiency, tend to view politics as a necessary evil in order to gain the masses' assent for the exercise of power by those who, by virtue of scientific expertise, know best. Bacon's utopian vision is present in varying degrees in contemporary social prescriptions associated with names such as John Kenneth Galbraith, Daniel Bell and Clark Kerr. The idea of social management of technocrats, by a scientific establishment, by the products of the university's knowledge industry—all demonstrate the perduring power of Bacon's understanding of the connection between truth and nature. After the Vietnam war, which was preeminently the experts' war, and the exposure of the military-industrial-university complex, such social analyses have encountered severe challenge, but they can by no means be counted out.

William Leiss speaks of Bacon's concept as being one of "mastery over nature." It would be more precise, I believe, to speak of mastery over history through obedience to nature. The crucial point, however, is that the truth is located in nature and revealed through the science that explores nature's way. "So definite was [Bacon's] work," Leiss writes, "that the history of all subsequent stages in the career of this idea down to the present can be arranged as a set of variations on a Baconian theme."[5] The "naturism" that today protests the still regnant "scientism" of our time agrees with the first part of the Baconian theme, namely, that truth is located in nature. It differs only in its conclusion that science and technology distort rather than reveal nature's way.

The revitalization of covenantal politics requires a metaphysical reaffirmation of the centrality of the human enterprise as it encounters and shapes historical change. The idea of drawing lessons from nature is, for the most part, an exercise in false consciousness. The significant lessons are not inherent in nature, deposited there in order for us to play hide-and-seek with Nature's God. Rather they are human constructions. What we read in nature has been written by the hopes and dreams and fears and fantasies of humankind. Our hope for progress is in our own dreaming and daring in relation to a hoped-for future which, Christians believe, is also a promised future. Progress is not the inevitable unfolding of the Original Playwright's scenario but the vindication of a struggle in which we are called to play a part.

A covenant view of history assumes that human beings are uniquely possessed of that consciousness that reaches toward a future in opposition to an intolerable present. Except as we sentimentally anthropomorphize nature, trees and animals do not live in a sense of accountability to Another, nor do they protest the inevitability of death, nor do they dream of new heavens and new earth. To be sure, biblical language envisions the rivers clapping their hands and the mountains leaping for joy. Jesus even suggests that there is wisdom to be discovered in observing the ways of the flowers of the field and the birds of the air. But none of this suggests that nature is the repository of truth or that it is in creative dialectic with nature that humankind may find salvation. Rather such biblical language suggests that the whole of creation will share in that salvation which is uniquely perceived and celebrated in human faithfulness to a covenanted future. St. Francis of Assisi, who is frequently nominated as patron saint of nature's devotees, spoke of sun and moon and animals as brothers and sisters. To think of nature or any part of nature as mother and father, however, would be entirely alien to his world view. Francis may serve as a magnificent example of humanity as the cantor, caretaker and interpreter of the whole creation. His example underscores, and in no way denigrates, the centrality of the human role as the vanguard of the future for which the whole creation yearns.

Before leaving this topic, a word should be said about the place of contemporary Marxist thought on nature and history. There are so many versions of Marxism current today, and they are frequently so contradictory, that it is hard to find a common denominator beyond their self-designation as Marxism and the common appeal to the sacred writings of that tradition. We are all influenced to some degree by the thought of Karl Marx, just as we are all influenced by, for example, the insights of Sigmund Freud. My intention, however, is to rest the argument for covenantal existence on non-Marxist foundations. While practitioners of the theology of liberation such as the Latin American Gustavo Gutierrez speak eloquently of human freedom, it is not at all clear that, in order to affirm freedom, they have not simply jettisoned the notions of historical determinism that are such an important part of what might be termed more orthodox Marxism. While participants in the "Christian-Marxist dialogue" such as Roger Garaudy find functional equivalents for "God" that can sustain "Christian Marxism," it is far from clear that they have not done mortal violence to the atheism that the founding father viewed as essential to a correct analysis of historical reality. While democratic spirits such as Michael Harrington celebrate the virtues of individual liberty, it is only with great charity that one can accept his ingenious interpretation of the "dictatorship of the proletariat" as anything other than an intellectually desperate effort to be rid of a Marxist embarrassment.[6] But to enter into the mare's nest that is contemporary Marxism's world of Talmudic tedium in the service of infinite revisionisms is an invitation to be respectfully declined. To paraphrase Laplace, "I have no need of that hypothesis."

To summarize, then, the desired dialectic between contract and covenant thought is frequently hindered by efforts to secure the social contract in something other than the future to which the covenant points and with which the covenant is made. The contract is not the last word, it is not ordained by Nature and Nature's Engineer Emeritus. The contract, any social contract, is a provisional arrangement. At its best, it is pragmatically based upon experience and in service of the hope by which it might be transcended in covenantal fulfillment. In this and previous chapters we have explored briefly some of the ways in which the dialectic with the future is evaded, and sometimes aborted, by preoccupation with an ultimate truth to be discovered in the past or in nature. In such thinking, past and nature represent two essentially similar aspects of the Edenic myth.

Lest it seem we have been too harsh or sweeping in our critique of Enlightenment thought and its modern progeny, we now turn briefly to some of the ways in which pre-Enlightenment Christian thinking contributed to the future-evading and covenant-destroying preoccupation with the past. We will then note some of the parallels in contemporary instances of secular social thought, notably in John Rawls' immensely important *A Theory of Justice*. After that, we will be able to take up the ways Americans have thought about their social experiment and ask whether covenantal vitality can be restored in American public piety. That line of inquiry will lead to a careful look at the currently widespread discussion of American civil religion, asking whether it is disease or cure for a culture encaved in its sense of endings.

12

Vulnerability
Along the Way of Hope

In his parting address to the Pilgrim fathers, John Robinson declared his confidence "that God hath more truth yet to break out of his Holy Word." That address and others like it are frequently cited as reflections of the naive optimism or even arrogance that marked the start of the American experiment. Today it is hardly necessary to list all the ways in which notions of America's manifest destiny may have reinforced policies and attitudes that led to the oppression of others and the blighting of America's own promise. But those who declaim the dangers implicit in John Robinson's declaration have frequently misrepresented the basis upon which he and others viewed America as an experiment of revelatory significance. They have also failed to weigh the import of the antithesis to Robinson's confidence: God hath *no* more truth yet to break out of his Holy Word.

As we have emphasized above, the idea that God has a hand in the American experiment does not underscore the uniqueness of America. It does not suggest an American innocence that is somehow exempt from the ambiguities of history. True, the ideas of uniqueness and innocence were prominent in much religious interpretation of the American experiment. But they are not necessary to the affirmation that the American experiment is of revelatory significance. To the contrary, any statement about America is derived from a prior affirmation about the revelatory significance of history itself. Far from exempting America from the historical process, Robinson's statement can be understood as tying America into inextricable unity with the divine and human struggle for history's vindication. Only because the American experiment is such a large part of the historical moment for which we are accountable is it necessary to inquire into its revelatory significance.

British-American Protestant thought from the seventeenth through nineteenth centuries developed many lively metaphors for understanding America's role in history. Redeemer Nation, the American Adam, the New Israel—these metaphors and others are today almost universally lamented as signs of historical hubris or ridiculed as signs of historical naiveté. It is the conventional wisdom among commentators who make the smallest pretention to historical awareness to explain everything from Vietnam to welfare policies in terms of the hubris and/or innocence inherent in America's founding ideology. As with most clichés, there is enough truth in the stereotype to sustain its currency. As with all clichés, this one calls for critical reexamination.

The logic in the idea of America as a covenanted nation induces humility rather than arrogance. Covenant is a relationship of mutual accountability. A nation that is accountable is vulnerable to history, it is always under judgment, it is held to account by the Power of the Future. The idea of "a nation under God" can, of course, be vulgarized. It can be, and frequently has been, transmogrified into an equation of divine purpose with American policy. This transmogrification, however, is not a consequence but a direct contradiction of what is meant by "a nation *under* God." Among literate Americans today there seems to be little danger that American interests will be equated with divine purpose. Much more respectable is the suspicion that anything in America's national interest must of necessity be demonic.

The God-fearing people who reflected on the revelatory significance of the American experiment and who molded the controlling metaphors had a peculiar reading of their moment in history. That reading made it not only possible but necessary to link closely divine purpose and American interests. That linkage, in turn, made it not only possible but inevitable that less scrupulous men would assume they had God's blessing to do almost anything they wished in the name of America. As Ernest Lee Tuveson has most eloquently described it in *Redeemer Nation,* at the heart of the founders' peculiar reading of history was the idea of the millennium.[1] The absolute uniqueness, the millennial definitiveness, of our historical epoch is no longer manifest to most of us today. That America has no *manifest* destiny, however, does not mean that America has no destiny. If the American experiment has no destiny, it would seem to follow that history has no destiny. The destiny of history however, is precisely what the gospel of the coming Kingdom is all about.

Speaking at Yale in 1855, Henry Boynton Smith of Union Theological Seminary declared it "the unique privilege of the nineteenth century" to realize fully what Jonathan Edwards had seen a century earlier. Now we recognize that "the whole of human history, according to Edwards' unrivalled scheme, becomes one body of divinity, presenting to us an untroubled mirror of the wisdom of God, and the image of his goodness."[2] Living in the century of Auschwitz and the Gulag Archipelago, such a description of history must seem to us obscene. If this history is the mirror of God, it is the mirror of a monstrous God. That earlier

reading of history, with its specificity of millennial schedule, was profoundly mistaken. But the truth of the Kingdom's coming does not
depend on the schedules we contrive. The mistaken readings in the past
do not deny the prior insight that history is possessed of divine passion
and purpose leading to a fulfillment yet to be revealed. Indeed, sobered
as we are by the horrors of our time, we are thrown back in more radical
faith to that prior insight.

The same Henry Boynton Smith declared, "The most diligent investigation of Christian History is one of the best incentives to the wisest study
of Christian Theology. The plan of God is the substance of both; for all
historic time is but a divine theodicy; God's providence is its law, God's
glory its end."[3] It is an intriguing proposition. It is easy to dismiss it, but
more interesting to examine it.

Today we are not so confident that a diligent investigation of history
will lead to conclusions supporting theology's claim that all is conducted
according to the plan of God. It is not apparent to us that God's
providence is the law of history. Yet precisely because we may be more
aware of the ironic and even the demonic in history, we need more
urgently to declare the hope that is within us. Modifying Smith, we might
say, "All historic time is a divine theodicy; God's suffering is its form,
God's glory its end." If history is not theodicy, if the promise and the
hope are not to be vindicated, then history is absurd and Christians are
of all people "most to be pitied" (1 Cor. 15). We have, in short, every
reason to agree with John Robinson "that God hath more truth yet to
break out of his Holy Word."

Today we must dissent from the founding fathers' certitude about the
significance of the American experiment in the divine economy. Or at
least we cannot share the certainty in their reading of the particularities
of that significance. When we say that history seems to us more ambiguous than it apparently did to them, it does not mean we are necessarily
more intelligent or more sophisticated than they. We are simply more
confused. A tide of reversals that can be conveniently dated from a
certain day in August, 1914, has challenged, if not discredited, a world
view premised upon the notion of continuous, even automatic, progress.

Then too, for a host of reasons, we no longer find authoritative reinforcement for the view that our epoch is of definitive millennial significance. Whether we stopped reading the Bible in terms of historical
"dispensations" because such a reading was so monumentally contradicted by historical events or whether a nondispensational reading of the
Bible emerged from the logic of scriptural study and theological thought
is a moot question. It seems both likely and healthy that there is a
symbiotic relationship between our reading of world history and our
reading of the scriptures. In any case, the two readings today coincide

in a way that deprives us of the millennial confidence that permeated the thinking of earlier Americans, both those of the Puritan and of the Enlightenment worlds.[4]

The novelist Henry James is today frequently admired as the prescient exception to the vulgar optimism of nineteenth-century American thought. James made no secret of his elegant disdain for almost all things American. Dying as a British subject, his life's work was indeed the refined forerunner of the vulgar anti-Americanism celebrated today by American intellectuals who would be mortified to be thought insufficiently alienated from the American experiment. James' was not a more accurate or plausible reading of the nineteenth-century American moment. Of course there was the vulgarity, pollution and mindless belief in technology, all of which he lamented. But his refusal to enter into the promise that was also present in that American moment reflected not so much a reading of the external events of history as it did his personal propensity toward the aristocratic style that marked the older and, he thought, better world of Europe.

To set Henry James against the more sanguine interpreters of an earlier American moment is fundamentally unfair. His interpretation had less to do with evidence than with personal disposition. So do many of the doomsayers of our time manifest a disposition toward endings, they seem to want the American experiment to turn out badly, they would be embarrassed were it to turn out any other way. Obviously, the more euphoric spokesmen of those earlier times also had personal dispositions, but they tended to rest their interpretation upon the "objective correlates" in historical events external to themselves. Many things have happened in the twentieth century to refute their happy reading of their historical moment, especially the variations on the theme of inevitable progress. Reinhold Niebuhr once remarked that it was a great blessing that Walter Rauschenbusch died in 1918 before it became evident how completely his hopeful world had been shattered. Had he lived to see it, "It would have broken his heart."[5] Niebuhr made the remark in criticism of the social-gospel movement's view of the Kingdom of God.

The same observation might, however, be made to the credit of Rauschenbusch and others who shared a more optimistic reading of their historical moment. The possibility that historical events might have "broken his heart" reveals the degree to which his thought was indeed vulnerable to history. It is the sin of much contemporary thought, both religious and secular, that it has made itself impervious to historical event. I use "sin" advisedly, for it is the essence of sin to refuse to enter into the pathos of history, which is the pathos of God.

Moreover, earlier and more optimistic Americans were not ignorant of the presence of evil nor of life as struggle.[6] They were often mistaken about the particulars of the historical timetable. Our hope must be of a different quality. It must be sustained without their perception of almost uninterrupted progress, and without their confidence in millennialistic immediacy. Yet, although our particular reading of the historical moment may be dramatically different, our hope is at heart one with theirs. Again, it is, quite simply, the confidence "that God hath more truth yet to break out of his Holy Word." The opposite is to say that God hath no more truth yet to break out of his Holy Word. Which is to say that it has all been said and all been done. In which case history is robbed of any *ultimate* meaning, it cannot properly be taken with *religious* seriousness. In which case we are waiting for Godot after all—or, if we are believers, for a God who is criminally dilatory in letting his creation in on the benefits of a victory already achieved.

13

Resisting the Sirens
of History-less History

There is a proper sense in which the revelation of God in Christ is changeless. But this changelessness is to be understood not so much in terms of immutability as in terms of utter reliability. There is, we believe, an utter constancy and reliability in the promise of history's meaning, the promise signaled by the resurrection of Jesus of Nazareth. But promise is by definition a statement about the future, about what is not yet. The realization of the future requires change, the realization of the future proclaimed by Jesus requires radical change. Were God indeed changeless, in the usual sense of that term, he would be the chief obstacle to the fulfillment of his own promise. Unhappily, Christians have often spoken of the immutability of God in a way that is indistinguishable from the immobility of God.

St. Augustine derives God's immutability from his absolute plenitude of being: "Being is a name which connotes immutability. For all that changes ceases to be what it was and commences to be what it was not. True Being, Genuine Being is possessed only by Him who does not change."[1] It is not possible, nor is it necessary, to here enter into the complex discussion of the ways in which the Hebrew God of history became, in early Christian thought, the Eternal Being of Greek philosophy. For more than a hundred years now it has been a commonplace to deplore the Hellenization of biblical thought. The historical was transmuted into the eternal, the dynamic into the static, and the great acts of God were replaced with metaphysical speculation—or at least that is the way the indictment usually reads.

To suggest, as some do, that we jettison the fruits of Hellenization and return to Hebraic dynamism is to ignore our own historical placement and formation, to sacrifice many riches of postbiblical religious reflection, and, above all, to perpetuate the Myth of Return. The idea that we should try to wipe out centuries of Christian thought and piety in order to return to the more historically dynamic concepts of the Hebrew Bible is itself a violation of historical dynamism. Unless, of course, one is prepared to assert that sixteen or more centuries of Christian thought and devotion constitute a monstrous distortion of revealed truth. In that case, it is hard to see how or why one would continue to do theology in any distinctively Christian sense.

The Hellization of Christianity, if that is what it was, must be seen as the consequence of a necessary encounter in the testing of the universality of the Christian gospel. Since that gospel proclaims a universal promise, its truth is contingent upon its universality. It is true for all or it is not true at all. Therefore the history of Christianity must continue to be a history of encounters. We may anticipate the Hinduization and Islamization of Christianity, even as we have already begun to understand the secularization of Christianity. (I hasten to add that in recent years much that has been called "secular Christianity" forgot that in the encounter in which the gospel is tested the gospel also tests what it encounters. As a result, many statements on Christian secularization were little more than uncritical capitulations to the unreflective godlessness of much modern thought.)

There can be, then, no "return" to Hebraic dynamism, as though we could leapfrog the intervening history of Christian thought. Neither is it true, however, that there is an uninterrupted progress in Christian thought, as though the present point of development is superior to all that has preceded it. Even a mildly critical survey of the current theological scene makes one shudder at the thought. Rather, there is a cumulative tradition containing a growing variety of ways in which reality may be understood in light of the promise. Some of the ways are mutually contradictory, choices must be made, but all the ways are provisional, all point to a definition of reality yet to be revealed. Different and even contradictory traditions within the tradition must be kept in play, each checking, countering and correcting the other.

It is necessary even to keep alive the memory of antique "heresies," as each possesses a truth that in its mistatement enlivens the tenuous consensus we call orthodoxy. Arianism, Adoptianism, Donatism, Sabellianism, Monarchianism—they seem as irrelevant as the old chestnut about angels on pinheads, yet they are the necessary counterpoint to Christian thought. Certainly they are more intellectually interesting than some current theological options. In any case, as much as possible the totality of the tradition should be kept in play in a catholic and comprehensive manner. If we have not thought through the alternatives to what we call the truth, we have not thought through what we call the truth.

In sustaining the lively interaction between strands of the tradition, we inevitably make judgments of accent and substance as to what is needed for Christian witness in our day. My judgment is that the renewal of Christian social engagement requires a redefinition of convenantal exis-

tence, and that, in turn, requires the assertion of the emphatically historical character of revelation. Such an understanding does not mean that we
simply toss out what, for example, Augustine says about the True Being
of God. While one should not fear disagreeing with Augustine, it is both
more agreeable and more rewarding to reinterpret his thought in terms of
what we believe about revelation and history. Augustine's statement
about the True Being of God can be seen as an eschatological statement.
The True Being of God is not yet realized. Yet, as we discussed in an
earlier chapter, what is now said about God in the community that
believes the Kingdom promise is said in hope. There is an "as if" quality
to life in such a community; we speak and act "as if" God rules. It is
not a matter of delusion but of dialectic. That is, we are always aware
of the "as if" quality of our existence, painfully aware as we are that the
world is not now ruled by the God whom we worship. We live in the
confidence that our hope will be vindicated; it is a confidence that does
not evade hope's vulnerability to history's possible repudiation. All
historic time is indeed theodicy.

Paul wrote, "The last enemy to be destroyed is death" (1 Cor. 15).
Many Christians have believed that the last enemy to be destroyed is time.
In a sense, they are saying the same thing, for the message of time would
seem to be death. "Change and decay—*and death*—in all around I see."
Instead of living in the tension of time and hope, looking forward to the
destruction of death, they would eliminate time and thus make hope
superfluous. The abiding temptation of religious thought is the temptation
to timelessness. We may explore the far reaches of space and even think
we have conquered it, but as we have seen, time remains ever a threat.
It is the threat of the unknown.

Christians should make no apology for the "timed" character of our
hope. A hope that is not conditioned by time is no hope at all. This does
not mean there is nothing distinctive or rewarding about Christian existence *now*. To the contrary, the life that is entrusted to the future is a life
ahead of its time, a life of anticipatory experience of what is to be.
Heschel speaks of the believer's "sense of the ineffable" in present time
and mundane experience: "The ineffable inhabits the magnificent and the
common, the grandiose and the tiny facts of reality alike. Some people
sense this quality at distant intervals in extraordinary events; others sense
it in the ordinary events, in every fold, in every nook; day after day, hour
after hour. . . . Slight and simple as things may be—a piece of paper, a
morsel of bread, a word, a sigh—they hide and guard a never-ending
secret: A glimpse of God? Kinship with the spirit of being? An eternal
flash of will?"[2]

The question marks toward the end are deliberate. The believer answers each question with a yes, but only the future can remove the

question marks. The great temptation of all religion is to erase the question marks before the questions have been answered.

Christianity has been plagued by the notion that, as God is immutable, so must the truth about God be immutable. Thus even sophisticated notions of doctrinal development or, as some would have it, "progressive revelation" bog down in the insistence that nothing new can be added to the *depositum fidei,* to the truth once revealed. Here one must be very careful. On the one hand, if *God* was revealed in the Christ event, then it must have been a complete revelation. If it is not complete, it is not God who is revealed, since completion is essential to what we mean by "God." We can recognize the necessity (in terms of theological language) of making that statement, while, in the same breath, confessing that we are not very sure what it means. On the face of it, this may seem distressing, until we ponder the fact that, if we knew the full meaning of a revelation of the future, it would no longer be future. What is said now in theological necessity is said in hope of future revelation. The fact that we hope for further revelation does not mean that past revelation is incomplete, although we can readily see why it might be misunderstood in that way. Since revelation is always the Self-revelation of the *one* God who appeared in Jesus as the Power of the Future and is to us still the Power of the Future, there can be no question of his incompletion. Such at least is the assertion of Christian faith. When we speak of "further" revelation, therefore, we are speaking of historic time in which, we believe, that assertion will be proved true.

While it is theo-logically fitting to say that revelation is, in one sense, complete (since Jesus is God), there is neither need nor warrant for saying our perception of revelation is complete. Some theo-logical statements must be made "from above," as though we view reality through the eyes of God, so to speak. Obviously, that is extremely tentative speculation since the very minds with which we would view reality "from another perspective" are inescapably conditioned socially and historically. True, there are the mystics who ascend the mountain, and their reports (to the extent their perceptions can be reported) are to be received with utmost respect, indeed with reverence. Yet in the world of reasonable discourse our perceptions are "from below." Wolfhart Pannenberg writes: "No one now has an experience of Jesus as risen and exalted, at least not an experience that could be distinguished with certainty from illusion. . . . The *experience* of the presence of Christ is promised only for the end time. Therefore, also, whatever concerns the certainty of the present life of the exalted Lord is based entirely on what happened in the past."[3]

The full meaning of "what happened in the past" is yet to be revealed. It has not been fully perceived by anyone in the past, not by the biblical writers, nor by the church fathers, nor by councils. Orthodoxy, the full and correct understanding of God's Self-revelation, is reserved for the End Time. It is not a past treasure to be protected nor a present achievement to be vaunted, but a gift for which we hope. If we say that someone is an orthodox Christian, we are saying he is in the company and tradition of those who long for what is yet to be revealed. Orthodoxy is not so much a matter of possession as of identity, it signifies a placement within a believing community. Orthodoxy is not so much a matter of what we know as it is a matter of the tradition within which we ask our questions, entrusting ourselves to the Unknown who is both pursued and pursuer.

Unfortunately, the quest for certitude in timelessness has often won the day in Christian thought and devotion. Jaroslav Pelikan describes this phenomenon as it gained ascendancy in Eastern Christianity:

Underlying this definition of divine truth as changeless was a definition of the divine itself as changeless and absolute. Because God transcended change, the truth about him also had to do so. . . . The changeless truth of salvation was therefore not subject to negotiation. . . . Doctrinal controversy was a difference not over vocabulary but over the very substance of Christian faith. . . . Sometimes it was suggested that the two sides in the controversy over the wills of Christ differed "not at all except in mere formulas," but this suggestion was repudiated as a betrayal of the true faith. To those who were faithful, there could be no distinction within the tradition between those things that were primary and those that were secondary, ... for the doctrine had come from the fathers and was to be revered. This was the ancient and changeless faith of the church. Those who accepted it were "those who graze on the divine and pure pasture of the doctrine of the church." The church was "pure and undefiled, immaculate and unadulterated," and in its message there was nothing alien or confused. The truth of the gospel was present in the church as it had been in the beginning, was now, and ever would be, world without end.[4]

It comes as no surprise to note that religion is as subject to exploitation as any other dimension of human enterprise. Because, however, it deals with the ultimate meanings by which we try to order reality, the consequences of religion's distortion can be especially dangerous. In speaking of the dangerous distortions of religion, many people have in mind the dangers of religious fanaticism. There is no question that fanaticism is a very real danger, as many ugly historical instances amply testify. At the same time, much that status quo forces condemned as fanaticism turned out to be the agent and harbinger of needed change. No matter how obsequiously the church may at times bow the knee to things as they are, it can never shed itself of the embarrassment that the one it calls Lord was and is widely perceived as a fanatic.

The fanatic is one who closes himself off from evidence or reason outside his private and, he believes, inspired vision. That the vision may be reinforced by a community in no way detracts from its essentially private character. It is invulnerable to what we call objective reality, it is invulnerable to history. The word *fanatic* is related to the Latin *fanum,* meaning "temple." The fanatic's world is hermetically sealed, securely encaved, in the temple of subjective inspiration. Jesus was, in this sense, the very opposite of a fanatic. His gospel of the Kingdom called people to radical exposure to the contingencies of change. The cross is the ultimate sign of his vulnerability, the resurrection the ultimate sign of his vindication.

The Christian fanaticism most in need of challenge is not the fanaticism of those revolutionary zealots who would "take the Kingdom of heaven by force" (Matt. 11). The fanaticism most prevalent and in need of challenge is the fanaticism, the "sanctuary existence," of those who believe the Kingdom has already come and therefore seek it not at all. The zealot, fanatical though he may be, at least recognizes the evidence of the intolerable in the present order. In his windowless temple, the pietist permits no such evidence to disturb his devout tranquility. This is the more prevalent and more dangerous fanaticism that is peddled by religionists in the name of Jesus. It offers stability in a world of turmoil, certitude in a world of doubt, contentment in a world of pain. It calls people away from the tasks of history and offers a seductive alternative to joining God in his suffering. It erases the question marks before the questions have been answered, it calls off the pilgrimage before the promised land is reached, it relieves us of the burden of uncertainty and makes superfluous the search for the Kingdom. It is fraudulent. It is fanatical. It is the piety of countless millions.

"Because God transcended change, the truth about him also had to do so." Thus it is that Christian belief has tried to make itself impervious to history. In *The Historian and the Believer,* Van A. Harvey demonstrated how Christians have tried to exempt from historical criticism their beliefs about what happened in the past.[5] With some modification, his argument can illumine the ways in which Christian thought has attempted to make itself invulnerable to history itself, including the future.

After surveying the various models by which historiography operates, Harvey suggests that they have in common an insistence "that all responsible claims [about history] be candid and that reasons be given for them, reasons commensurate with the degree of assent they solicit from us. . . . We honor this principle in daily life, in law courts, politics, and newspapers, and we praise and blame men for their responsibility or irresponsibility in conforming to it. The same holds true of history, and it is just because this critical ideal has grasped the modern imagination that historical thinking is one of the most impressive triumphs of the human spirit."[6]

The liberation of Christian thought from the sandbox of subjectivity depends in large measure upon its willingness to celebrate this "triumph of the human spirit." In discussing earlier the "arena of reason" and the "sandbox of religious faith," we referred to the late Karl Barth in a manner that, in the way of parables, may have seemed simplistic or even flippant. Only gross ingratitude born of ignorance could fail to acknowledge the greatness of Karl Barth in helping to stiffen the backbone of Christian faith in the face of modern unbelief. And yet. And yet, he must be credited also with having offered among the most sophisticated of Christian evasions of the hazards of history. With architectonic scholarship he further sealed the walls of the *fanum* in which the true believer can dwell secure.

Barth made Christian truth claims about Jesus exempt from historical reason. He appeals to the New Testament resurrection stories, for example, to argue for the historical nature of these events. Yet at the same time he concedes that the stories cannot, from a historical viewpoint, stand up to critical scrutiny. Belief in a historical resurrection is presumably warranted by evidence that is historical in nature but which, when asked to submit to historical reason, begs off as being "imaginative-poetic." This procedure, says Harvey, "leaves the inquirer in the position of having to accept the claims of alleged eyewitnesses or risk the state of being a faithless man. Insofar as [the historian wants to be a believer] he has to surrender the autonomy of critical judgment. Barth, in effect, claims all the advantages of history but will assume none of its risks."[7]

Harvey, as we noted, is primarily concerned about the role of historical thinking in evaluating the claims made about Jesus. He is dealing with past events and the present significance of those events. He draws the conclusion that there are "two kinds of belief, and, accordingly, . . . two kinds of certitude." The first is the belief that the actual Jesus was as the church's image pictures him. That means things really did happen the way the catholic interpretation of the New Testament says they happened. The second belief is that the image we have of Jesus "does illumine our experience and our relationship to that upon which we are absolutely dependent." The first belief is "remote" from our own lives and the certitude we may have about it is dependent "on the data and warrants." The second kind of belief is "of a different order." It is not a belief *about* a past event but a belief "that an image cast up by a past event illumines some present experience. Consequently, this belief has to do with the present and can have an immediacy no remote event can acquire. . . . It is not a belief about one unique contingent event but has to do with the adequacy of an image for interpreting the structure and character of reality itself."[8]

Harvey's conclusion is an interesting example of what he himself calls the effort to "salvage" belief from the destruction wrought by historical reason.[9] We cannot here enter into a detailed critique of the suggestion

made by Harvey and many others regarding two kinds of belief, the one
dependent upon historical event and the other dependent upon its usefulness in illumining our experience. The problem is that such an approach
does not get us out of the sandbox of subjectivity. In its own way, it also
offers an invulnerability to historical contingency. That is, there is something pragmatic, arbitrary and finally subjective in deciding what does and
what does not illumine our own experience. There are innumerable
images, myths and constructions of reality cast up by the past. There
must be a reasonable connection between what can be said about the
historical event of Jesus and what we claim about the present significance
of Jesus. Otherwise, the image of Jesus becomes little more than my
choice of what "works for me." For someone else it may be the Buddha,
LSD, Mother Nature, the quest for power or Sly and the Family Stone.
This kind of pragmatic subjectivity is not enough to sustain the life and
mission of the Christian church. More to the point, I am persuaded it is
not the basis of Christian existence.

One frequently encounters in this connection a vulgarized version of
the Pascalian wager. That is, it is said that the Christian really cannot
lose. If the Christian faith turns out to be right, the reward for being a
Christian is eternal happiness; if wrong, there is still the reward of having
lived one's life enriched by the liveliest and most satisfying of myths. In
either case, what happens in history cannot finally touch me. The issue
is acute if one's primary concern is not muddling through this life in the
most satisfying way possible. If one's primary concern is seeking the
Kingdom of God, the meaning of life becomes utterly dependent upon the
Kingdom's coming. In other words, our concern must be for the truth and
not simply for the image or belief system that we find most "useful" to
our present existence. I might choose any mythopoetic bit of imagery and
entertain it as enriching whimsy, or even let it become a formative
fantasy, but I could not entrust my very existence to it, I could not *believe*
as Christians say they believe in Jesus. Not unless I am persuaded it is
true and prepared to risk my life on that persuasion.

But what, it might be asked, is really the risk? The answer is that to
have lived my life, and to have encouraged others to live their lives, by
a myth that I do not believe to be true is to have lived a lie. It is the
essence of inauthentic existence. No amount of temporary usefulness can
bridge the divide between truth and falsehood. It would be more authentic
and possibly more rewarding to abandon the myth of the Kingdom
altogether, to nakedly confront the apparent absurdity of existence and
to seek alternative ways to make the best of it without the dishonesty of
beautiful lies.

Christian faith is vulnerable, as Van Harvey so well describes, to historical thinking about past events. But Christian faith is most vulnerable to the history that is yet to be. That is, the very heart of Jesus' message and of Christian faith is that history is purposeful and will be vindicated in the Rule of God. Whether this turns out to be true is precisely that, namely a question of what turns out to be true. If death is the last word, if history is absurd, then, no matter how well intended we may have been, we have failed to see the truth and have lived a falsehood, albeit a falsehood not untouched by grandeur.

This is the courage of uncertainty that we are ever tempted to trade in for a fraudulent certitude. As with all science, historical science can demonstrate only a greater or lesser degree of probability. Honest science claims to "prove" nothing, everything is subject to further demonstration. Ironically, the church, whose extravagant claims are most in need of demonstration, often boasts of having an alternative way of knowing and knowing absolutely. Perhaps it is because the claims are so extravagant that Christians are not prepared to await God's demonstration of their truth. We do not wish to look foolish. We want some way, *here and now,* to prove the truth of our extraordinary assertions. Or at least we want to be able to claim that we have some such way, even if others and, most of the time, we ourselves do not find that way very plausible. Infallible Bible, infallible church, infallible religious experience, infallible faith—there is no end to the substitutes we have devised for the coming of the Kingdom.

In his *The Myth of Christian Beginnings,* Robert L. Wilken notes the frequent claim that Christianity, unlike other religions, is "a historical religion." The claim is made, he says, to distinguish the Judeo-Christian tradition from other religions, or to protest the transference of Hebraic thought into the categories of Greek philosophy, or to underscore a particular theology about how God acts in history. But, Wilken writes, "whatever the merits of calling Christianity a historical religion, I am convinced that few Christians are willing to take with complete seriousness the proposition that Christianity is indeed a historical phenomenon."[10] As the earlier quotation from Jaroslav Pelikan illustrates, when many Christians speak about history they are, in Wilken's phrase, speaking about "history without history." That is, they are speaking about history without change.

Wilken traces this propensity to the fourth-century Eusebius, the first church historian. In his *Ecclesiastical History* Eusebius set forth a defense of the Christian faith to its Roman despisers. Christian apologetics was, of course, nothing new. But in his *History* Eusebius took a different tack. Until that time, most apologists defended the faith by appealing to the reasoned arguments that had some leverage with their non-Christian readers. Eusebius, on the other hand, approached the apologetic task in what, at least on the face of it, seemed to be a more historical manner. He offered a systematic and continuous account of Christianity from its beginnings. The reason for this approach is not immediately obvious. As Wilken notes, "Three hundred years would hardly impress the Romans with the great antiquity of the Christians." But Eusebius is not talking just about three hundred years. He sets out to demonstrate that Christians "can trace their history back through the Jews to creation itself." "Even though the revelation in Christ took place relatively late in human history, Christ himself exists eternally, and the Christian religion is 'none other than the first, most ancient, and most original of all religions, discovered by Abraham and his followers, God's beloved.' The new name, the new way of life, and the new teaching are deceptive, for what Christians teach and the way they live are not recent 'inventions' but the 'natural concepts of those whom God loved in the distant past.'"[11]

If authenticity is guaranteed by antiquity and truth is certified by changelessness, it follows that the true faith cannot be new. We arrive once again at the dream of the Golden Age, we confront again the perduring power of the Edenic myth. This is the power that draws us back from entrusting ourselves to the struggle and promise of history, the power that so severely cripples the church's witness to the coming of the Kingdom. "Therefore, if any one is in Christ, he is a new creation, the old has passed away, behold, the new has come" (2 Cor. 5). Paul's apostolic daring was based upon the dawning of the new age he saw signaled in Jesus' victory over death.

If the church is less daring today, it is not simply because we lack the courage. It is also because in our very definition of Christian existence we have lost the sense of the pathos and promise of history. "Our hope for you is unshaken," Paul writes the Corinthians, "for we know that as you share in our sufferings, you will also share in our comfort" (2 Cor. 1). His sufferings are one with the sufferings of Christ. Paul wishes, he tells the Philippians, "that I may know him and the power of his resurrection, and may share his sufferings, becoming like him in his death, that if possible I may attain the resurrection from the dead" (Phil. 3). Not only Paul, and not only the Christians, but, again, in the majestic hymn of Romans 8, "The whole creation waits with eager longing for the revealing of the sons of God . . . because the creation itself will be set free from its bondage to decay and obtain the glorious liberty of the children of God."

This is the vision so fatally compromised by the constricting search for certitude. In whatever forms the Myth of Return or the idea of changelessness may appear, they are invitations to defy the call to entrust ourselves to the Power of the Future. Wilken suggests the better way:

The Christian realizes that his history goes back to the time of the apostles, but he also knows that the Christian hope did not come to fulfillment in the age of the apostles; nor did it reach perfection at the time of Constantine, nor in the Holy Roman Empire of the Middle Ages, nor in the sixteenth-century Reformation, nor in the social gospel of the late nineteenth century or the revivals of the American frontier, nor in the movements of renewal in our own day. The history of Christianity is the history of imperfection and fragmentation, but it is also a history of hoping and striving for an end men cannot see but that draws them on. The future constantly opens up new possibilities that make the past look pale by comparison.[12]

He cites a fourth-century theologian, Gregory of Nyssa, who compares God to a spring bubbling from the earth:

As you came near the spring you would marvel, seeing that the water was endless, as it constantly gushed up and poured forth. Yet you could never say that you had seen all the water. How could you see what was still hidden in the bosom of the earth? Hence no matter how long you might stay at the spring you would always be beginning to see the water. For the water never stops flowing, and it is always beginning to bubble up again. It is the same with one who fixes his gaze on the infinite beauty of God. It is constantly being discovered anew, and it is always seen as something new and strange in comparison with what the mind has already understood. And as God continues to reveal himself, man continues to wonder; and he never exhausts his desire to see more, since what he is waiting for is always more magnificent, more divine, than all that he has already seen.[13]

"As God continues to reveal himself." An immutable God is not playing hide-and-seek. A capricious God has not staged history as a striptease show in which he exposes his purposes bit by bit. No, a suffering God has engaged his creation in a labor of love and invites us to join him in bringing his project to completion. In the community of faith we speak and sing of him as omnipotent, omniscient, and maybe even immutable. That is because we are a community ahead of its time, a community of hope. We sing and speak and act "as if," sometimes with the accent on the "as," sometimes on the "if." We are utterly, unequivocally, desperately, daringly dependent on the Power of the Future, dependent on him.

14

Justice in a
Provisional World

The argument must of necessity keep returning to the tension between contract and covenant. How we think about America—past, present and future—depends, to a large extent, upon which of these metaphors is given priority. Covenant thinking envisions America as a lively experiment with promises to keep and a destiny to be realized within universal history. The contract metaphor, on the other hand, suggests a rational ordering of processes and goals, a bargain struck and adhered to for mutual advantage. The covenant appeals to the future for its ultimate legitimation. It can finally be "proved" correct only by the vindication of reasonable hope. Contract thinking, again, must seek its legitimating foundations in what already exists. In its search it turns toward a Golden Age to be reestablished or to some other version of what is "natural." Contract doctrine is closely linked in one way or another to the Edenic Myth.

In the dialectic between covenant and contract, priority must be given to the covenant. This is so not only because it is necessary to redress an imbalance in contemporary thinking about the American social experiment, but it is so absolutely. That is, the contract exists for the sake of the covenant; or, in theological language, the contract is for the sake of the Kingdom. This does not mean that there is nothing of absolute value in the contract. The contract's provisions for the protection of human rights and liberties, as well as its processes for the pursuit of justice, partake of the absolute. They are "intuitions of the ultimate," that is, of the future, in our past and present. They are, in short, of revelatory significance. The phrase "the American revelation" means simply that also in the American experiment there are these signals or intuitions of the ultimate. Some provisions and processes that have been codified, so to speak, in the social contract (notably in the Constitution and its laws) cannot be violated without in fact defying the future they signal.

It is sometimes said that covenant thinking marked the Puritan begin-

nings of the American experiment and was replaced later by the eighteenth-century social-contract thinking of the "founding fathers" who
were so very much under the influence of the Enlightenment's confidence
that it had attained the wisdom of Nature, and thus of Nature's God.
While the distinction between Puritan and Enlightenment thought is both
necessary and useful, it is by no means inflexible. The Puritan fathers,
largely out of their realistic assessment of human evil, knew the necessity
of compacts and contracts as provisional measures short of the Kingdom's final establishment. Similarly, the most religiously liberated of the
Enlightenment fathers nonetheless insisted upon their intuitions about
historical destiny and a future that would vindicate the social experiment
they were launching.[1] A covenant is premised upon a promise. Promises
are by definition contingent upon the future. Contract theory generally
appeals to an idealized past or to the eternally valid laws of nature. Thus
the structure of contract thinking does not require the future in the same
way, it has a self-contained integrity.

It may be that one reason we have such difficulties today with the
notion of an American destiny is that the reigning social theory does not
contain (and perhaps cannot accommodate) the idea of historical purposefulness. That is, contract theory has much to say about procedure but
little or nothing to say about ends or goals that are contingent upon the
future. Whatever ends or goals there may be are "values" mutually
agreed upon and already existing (or at least realizable through the
adoption of more "rational" procedures). Thus in much American social
thought the idea of historical purposefulness or destiny is quite apart from
the foundations of social theory which are located exclusively in past and
present. Thus the idea of destiny, with its vindicating future, is not
integrally related to the sources of social theory; it is unrooted and
therefore unchecked. As a consequence it was thought that the destiny
of infinite expansionism, economic and otherwise, was somehow automatic, that progress was inevitable. It is as though these "destinies" were
built into the very nature of things. What seemed to be the "natural"
unfolding of the processes agreed upon in the contract could not itself be
checked by reference to the contract, since the contract only has reference to what is "natural." As a result, it was impossible to bring the
experiment under judgment. An experiment that is not under judgment,
may become an empire in which notions of destiny that are not checked
by some idea of destiny *for what* have a way of running amok.

In arguing that all social contracts are to be viewed as provisional and
for the Kingdom's sake, I am well aware that I have made many assumptions that are not widely shared. First there are assumptions about the
meaning of biblical religion that certainly are not shared by all religiously
serious Christians and Jews. What would seem to be even more of a

problem, they are religiously particularistic assumptions that appear to have no place in the "secular" marketplace of ideas where the meaning of the American experiment must be formulated. These objections are not as conclusive, however, as they may seem at first.

Even if the argument offers nothing more than one way of viewing the American experiment from a specifically Christian perspective, it is worthwhile. Of course it would not be persuasive for the non-Christian or for the person who understands Christianity in quite different terms, but the worthwhileness of perspectives that illuminate our own experience are not subject to majority vote. In fact, however, this covenantal view of the American experiment is more than a privately helpful way of looking at things. It is, as we shall see, still very much part of what is now commonly described as America's civil religion or, as I prefer, America's public piety. In addition, to the extent covenantal thinking is revived in the church's theology and piety, it can have an important impact on the church's role in shaping the general consciousness and public piety of America.

The discussion of the dialectic between covenant and contract is neither theoretically esoteric nor so dated as to be antique. It deals both with the way we feel about America and with the way in which we approach public policy. The dialectic is powerfully, although often subliminally, present in Supreme Court decisions on everything from privacy, to abortion, to the rights implicit in equal opportunity. It affects most directly our thinking about the American future, both in terms of domestic problems such as the plight of the cities and in terms of the overriding question of the meaning of justice as it relates to the gap between poor nations and rich nations.

For the last few years and probably for some time to come, one of the thorniest issues of public policy in America is the meaning of equality. Inequalities have always raised difficult questions of legitimation. Why should some people have more than others? Whether the specific question is about money or about status or about power, the fact of inequality poses in most people's minds an elementary challenge to the notion of justice. Perhaps this has always been the case. There are specific reasons why the issue of equality looms so large today, however.

In a time in which our social structures have come under relentless scrutiny, it is inevitable that one of the most elementary facets of any society, namely, how it distributes its goods, would also be challenged. Is there any morally sound basis for the way in which wealth is distributed? Obviously, those on the bottom end of the distribution system have most reason to press the question. In fact, however, the issue is often pressed most urgently by intellectuals, academics, "populist" politicians and others who are distinctly not on the receiving end of the injustices they perceive. In some cases they press the issue out of feelings of guilt, or because it serves an ideological commitment to some form of socialist egalitarianism, or, as in the case of the politician, because there is a lode of popular discontent to be exploited. But it is a conservative cheapshot to explain away the egalitarian concern by reference to such motivations, although such motivations are undoubtedly present in some instances. Another and more heartening explanation of the rising concern about equality is that more and more people are morally offended by what they see as the injustice of the present system.

The new discussion of equality comes at a time when it may be increasingly pertinent to external developments quite apart from what is or is not in fashion among the mongers of ideas. Until the very recent past, the egalitarian impulse was subdued by the general feeling that the "system" was working more or less to the advantage of all concerned. Sometimes this was called the "trickle-down" effect. That is, it did not seem offensive that the rich got richer because the benefits would inevitably trickle down even to those on the bottom of the heap. Another version, although with reverse verticality of metaphor, was John F. Kennedy's favored axiom, "All boats rise with the rising tide." Perhaps the most common version, however, is that of the growing pie. As long as the economic pie kept getting bigger, even those with the smallest slice had an absolute stake in helping the system to go on working.

For some time there has been a popular awareness that these metaphors were not very helpful in understanding global justice. The gap between rich and poor nations grew wider, as did the gap between the many poor and the very few rich within the poor nations. More recently it has been widely proclaimed that there is little more equity within the United States itself. The maxim that the poor get poorer and the rich get . richer has the force of self-evident truth in many circles today. Until now it could be countered that, even if the *relative* share of the poor was getting smaller, the expanding pie meant their *absolute* share would increase. This was comfort enough to take the edge off moral anxiety about inequality and, not so incidentally, to defuse the political threat that might be posed by the resentment of the poor. Now, however, we are confronted by the twin prospects of no-growth ideology and economic depression.

In what ways no-growth consciousness and the moods of encavement may affect the presumably hard facts of the economy is a question best left to the metaphysicians of Wall Street. The myriad current and contradictory analyses offered by economists tend to confirm the suspicion that economics is, after all is said and done, a branch of rhetoric. On the other hand, the candor with which many economists now admit they have not the slightest idea of what is happening is a model of modesty that might

well be emulated by other professions. Be that as it may, if we are indeed
moving toward a no-growth economy, whether out of willfulness, ecological necessity, or both, we can be sure that the arguments over distributive
justice are just beginning to emerge.

Pundits and preachers proclaim that we have all been sated by consumerism and would all benefit from the leaner diet of a "new asceticism."
Unless there is a dramatic reordering of our social and economic system,
however, it is the poor who will pay the price for the new fashions of
austerity. More serious proponents of a no-growth world are aware of this
unhappy fact; thus the growing literature on distributive justice. In that
literature there are few books so deserving of attention as John Rawls'
A Theory of Justice.[2]

Published in 1971 and summarizing Professor Rawls' many contribu-
tions to date, A Theory of Justice has been hailed widely as one of the
most important books on social theory to have appeared in America in
recent years. I would not quarrel with that assessment. Its nobility of
purpose, grace of style and elegance of intellectual structure all commend
it to our attention. Most pertinent to the discussion at hand, is its
formidable restatement of contract theory as it relates to one of the most
pressing problems in American public policy, namely, the meaning of
justice in the distribution of society's goods. Among variegated egalitar-
ianisms now current, Rawls has become a standard point of reference.
Our purpose at the moment is not to treat the whole debate now raging
over "equality of opportunity" versus "equality of result," "meritocracy," "egalitarian leveling," and the such. Rather it is to focus only
on the most distinguished contribution to that debate to date, and that
only insofar as it illuminates the contrast between contractual and covenantal thinking about society.

Rawls argues that justice is, for all practical and theoretical purposes,
a question of fairness. The problem then is how to decide upon what is
fair. Since each person has a different historical and social placement and
has private interests to be served, it is obviously quite impossible for one
to be entirely objective or fair about who should get what at whose
expense. We must therefore imagine a situation in which people are
divested of all their social and historical particularities. This is called the
"original position." In this, he says, easily imagined position, people
must operate behind a "veil of ignorance." That is, they do not know
their level of advantage or disadvantage in the social order, they do not
even know their age or their place within the succession of generations.
In such an original position, behind the veil of ignorance, they are asked
to agree upon the principles for a just social order. Since no one knows
his placement in the society, and therefore which principles would likely
work to his self-interest, it is assumed that everyone will aim at a

maximum of fairness or justice. The principles agreed upon are then the foundational terms of the social contract and the measure of justice in the real world outside the original position.

Professor Rawls concludes that the exercise would indeed be successful and would arrive at contractually binding agreement. The General Conception that would be agreed upon is that "all social primary goods— liberty and opportunity, income and wealth, and the bases of self-respect —are to be distributed equally unless an unequal distribution of any or all of these goods is to the advantage of the least favored."[3] In line with this general conception, and indeed derived from it, are two main principles and several explanatory rules. "First Principle: Each person is to have an equal right to the most extensive total system of equal basic liberties compatible with a similar system of liberty for all. Second Principle: Social and economic inequalities are to be arranged so that they are both: (a) to the greatest benefit of the least advantaged, consistent with the just savings principle, and (b) attached to offices and positions open to all under conditions of fair equality of opportunity."[4]

Such a brief statement of Rawls' thesis can hardly do justice to the care with which he develops his argument. But the above description states the heart of the matter, and there is much in it that can be wholeheartedly affirmed. There is a commonsensical persuasiveness in the idea of justice as fairness. It removes the idea of justice from the ethereal world of conceptual specialists and asks that the issue be debated in an arena where it can be assumed that most people have some notion of what is fair. The approach has a democratic flavor that is fully compatible with the American democratic ethos.

Then too, Rawls assumes that justice has a kind of "reality" to it. Against the utilitarians (and the book throughout is an argument against utilitarianism), Rawls insists that "the priority of justice" is more than a "socially useful illusion."[5] He comes close to saying there is an ontological basis to the idea of justice as revealed in the original position. The ordering of society is not simply a floating crap game in which we ask only what is most "useful" in terms of the "values" now in play. Rawls is not so persuasive when he says his approach is superior to utilitarianism because it represents a "social choice" rather than the "principle of choice for one man."[6] In fact utilitarianism frequently contains a strong measure of social agreement and has produced its own versions of social contract. For our purposes, Rawls' dispute with utilitarianism is peripheral. Whether they pledge allegiance to Rousseau, to John Rawls or to Jeremy Bentham, our argument is with all who would finally establish the social order upon a contractual rather than a covenantal base.

Yet another attractive element in Rawls' main theses is the emphasis upon the "least favored." Justice must always be measured in terms of how it affects those at the bottom. This insistence is in line with the biblical emphasis upon the poor, the *anawim,* and their central role in the divine economy. It also accords with what we have said earlier about a society being measured according to its fault lines rather than by its successes.

The idea of justice as fairness has an agreeable democratic feel to it and reflects what I view as an admirable sensibility on the author's part. The idea of the reality of justice is, on the face of it, more comforting than the notion of justice as useful illusion. But, since he eschews the task of metaphysics, the reality of justice can finally be given no ontological status. It remains at the level of subjective intuition. The central role given the least favored seems equally to rest upon sentiment, although no doubt laudable sentiment. Unlike the biblical version of the role played by the *anawim,* Rawls acknowledges no "final good" that gives such priority standing to the poor. Rawls protests vigorously that he is not to be accused of sentimentality or intuitionism. He wants above all to rest his case upon hard reasoning and a moral logic that aims at the precision of mathematical theory. "We should strive for a kind of moral geometry with all the rigor which this name connotes."[7]

Rawls rests everything upon the logic emerging from "the original position." Again we encounter, although in new and intriguing form, the Myth of the Return. If only we can get back behind history, if only we can abrogate the particularistic distortions caused by experience in time, we will somehow get in touch with the really real. We will leave it to the psychologists and sociologists of knowledge to discuss whether it is meaningful to talk about moral reasoning or, for that matter, any kind of reasoning when the reasoners have been stripped of personal and social experience. Rawls insists that we can, for purposes of discovering first principles, put ourselves into the original position. I find it highly implausible. The more pressing argument, however, is with the notion that history is the opponent rather than the agent of the discovery of truth.

As with almost all who would discover truth in Nature and, so incidentally, Nature's God, Rawls would argue from a static and, in his case, highly mechanistic universe. Reality is not going anywhere, it is already "in place." Like Bacon, he would have us play hide-and-seek with a reality that has been hidden by history and is to be sought in nature, including "human nature." As to the set, mechanistic character of reality, one recalls Rawls on moral geometry. He acknowledges that his own reasoning falls short of the desired geometrical precision, "Yet it is essential to have in mind the ideal one would like to achieve."[8] Elsewhere he makes clear that he believes such exactitude is achievable, if we are only "rational" enough in its pursuit. This assumption, so clearly incompatible with the understanding of reality as an unfulfilled, still-provisional project, permeates contract theory.

Rawls asumes the rationality of the native order. He acknowledges that "the contract doctrine is purely hypothetical." But he insists, "If a conception of justice would be agreed to in the original position, its principles are the right ones to apply."[9] Of course, particular contingencies might arise in which the principles emerging from the original position would not seem to be applicable. The only way to refute a contrary principle that might be proposed, however, is to "show that the principle . . . would be rejected in the original position."[10] There is a dogmatic and definitive character to the revelations of the original position.

The religious parallel, as noted earlier, is what Robert Wilken describes as Eusebianism; certitude requires that the revelation once given is changeless and unchangeable. It may be reinterpreted but there can be nothing new; it is history without history. "Since the original agreement is final," Rawls writes, "and made in perpetuity, there is no second chance. In view of the serious nature of the possible consequences, the question of the burden of commitment is especially acute. . . . When we enter an agreement we must be able to honor it even should the worst possibilities prove to be the case."[11] One must wonder whether "rational" people would choose such a world bereft of forgiveness, bereft of grace, even rational people deprived of experience by virtue of having their innocence protected behind the veil of ignorance.

But what kind of people are these decision makers in the original position? They are, we are told again and again, rational people. Ah, and what might constitute rationality? "The special assumption I make is that a rational individual does not suffer from envy."[12] An extraordinary assumption indeed. Whole theories of social behavior have, perhaps with some exaggeration, been constructed around the pervasiveness of envy in human affairs.[13] Its omission from Rawls' depiction of the original position is marvelously convenient. He says the omission of envy is a "special assumption." It is far from the only assumption he makes about human nature. He assumes, for example, that people will be somehow naturally fair, motivated by mutual disinterest. "The assumption of mutually disinterested motivation is not a demanding stipulation.[!] Not only does it enable us to base the theory upon a reasonably precise notion of rational choice, but it asks little of the parties: in this way the principles chosen can adjust wider and deeper conflicts, an obvious desideratum."[14] There is no doubt the assumption makes for greater precision; what it does for plausibility is yet another matter.

Envy is excluded from the original position. So also are propensities to gamble, to take risks, perhaps even to pursue a death wish. Rawls wants to take into account the evil person, the person who strives for excessive power, who desires to hurt and humiliate others, who would turn everything to his own gratification. "The evil man aspires to unjust rule precisely because it violates what independent persons would consent to in an original position of equality . . ."[15] The evil person is neither independent nor rational. In the final analysis, evil itself is not real because it is, quite simply and devastatingly, irrational.

In a realistic view of history and of our experience within history, Rawls' argument is, for all its rational fastidiousness, not so much an exercise in moral geometry as an indulgence of naturalistic fantasies about human nature. "Moreover the more someone experiences his own way of life as worth fulfilling, the more likely he is to welcome our attainments. One who is confident of himself is not grudging in the appreciation of others. Putting these remarks together, the conditions for persons respecting themselves and one another would seem to require that their common plans be both rational and complementary: they call upon their educated endowments and arouse in each a sense of mastery, and they fit together into one scheme of activity that all can appreciate and enjoy."[16] One need not belong to the "realist" school of ethics, associated with the name of Reinhold Niebuhr, to be repulsed by such liberal seepage of irresponsible sentimentality. It is an illusory escape from history's horrors, from both the Gargantuan horrors such as Auschwitz and the quotidian horrors of the jealousies, fears, compulsive pettinesses and cruelties that are our lot. This is not to suggest, against Rawls' illusions, that the horrors have the last word. It is to suggest that we counter the horrors by appeal to what may yet be, not by seeking refuge in an idealized past or in a fantastical notion of human nature.[17]

Most disturbing, however, is the reappearance of the by now ancient Enlightenment myth of the relation between nature, reason and truth. What we disapprove of in ourselves and in our world is irrational and can be demonstrated to be untrue by recourse to nature. In a sense, it is a protest against the "givenness" of historical fact, and, God knows, much that is historical fact should be protested. It is a protest, however, not from an open and promising future but from an illusory and idealized past where our true nature is revealed, or, more accurately, where it is unlocked by the magical key of reason.

On a practical level, Rawls acknowledges that even in the most just society there would still be inequities. He assumes that the less favored will have agreed to the principles, and therefore to the consequences. "For all these reasons the less fortunate have no cause to consider themselves inferior and the public principles generally accepted underwrite their self-assurance. The disparities between themselves and others, whether absolute or relative, should be easier for them to accept than in other forms of polity."[18] It would seem that our experience suggests just the opposite. The less favored may find their lot easier to accept by appealing to "rotten luck" or unfairness "in the system." "Life is unfair," John Kennedy used to say, and millions took comfort.

If you are among the less favored, it is intolerable to believe your placement is entirely and unequivocally just. The arbitrary and serendipitous character of history is essential to human self-respect, as well as, for the more favored, to modesty. Michael Young's fable, *The Rise of the Meritocracy, 1870–2033,* spells out with great force how intolerable it would be to live in a society in which every inequality was demonstrably and absolutely just. In such a society, the less favored would have no more excuses for their failures, they would bear the stigma of rejection, they would have no reasonable complaint against their inferior placement. They would, and they do, rebel. Young's acknowledged fable would seem much closer to the human truth than Rawls' meticulously ratiocinated assumptions. If the choice is between a perfectly just order, which we cannot achieve, and a grossly unjust leveling, which we should not desire, we are in a rather dreadful predicament. We live by hope for yet another alternative, a genuinely new alternative.

Rawls, along with many other contemporary theorists, has little but disdain for an ethics that reaches toward the future. Teleology, as it is called, is out of favor. "The liberties of equal citizenship are insecure when founded upon teleological principles," Rawls writes. And then, most remarkably considering his own calculations and premises, "The argument for them [teleological principles] relies upon precarious calculations as well as controversial and uncertain premises."[19] In fact, operating by any notion of the good other than what would be agreed upon by rational people in the original position (as Rawls defines both) is to be excluded. Taking issue with Thomas Aquinas on a particular judgment, for example, Rawls concludes, "But the premises on which Aquinas relies cannot be established by modes of reasoning commonly recognized."[20]

As a rational being, Rawls would seek all of his guidelines and warrants from a dehistoricized myth of the past. This, as we have seen, leads him to say some things that exclude the possibility of living by grace, by forgiveness, with the hope of new beginnings. "Now one feature of a rational plan is that in carrying it out the individual does not change his mind and wish that he had done something else instead. A rational person does not come to feel an aversion for the foreseen consequences so great that he regrets following the plan he has adopted."[21] Rational people do not sin.

Such a vision is both dismal and frightening. Sterile, aseptic, static, disinfected of change and devoid of drama. But there is, one suspects, another John Rawls of whom we are given only a glimpse in these pages.

Uncertainty, if not repentance, may be admitted. "This principle will not certainly prevent us from taking steps that lead to misadventure. Nothing can protect us from the ambiguities and limitations of our knowledge, or guarantee that we find the best alternative open to us." And when we discover we have made the wrong decision? The response is stoic: "Acting with deliberative rationality can only insure that our conduct is above reproach, and that we are responsible to ourselves as one person over time." Only reluctantly does he admit a point of reference that until now has been carefully secured in the closet. "We should indeed be surprised if someone said that he did not care about how he will view his present actions later. . . . One who rejects . . . the claims of his future self . . . is irresponsible . . . to his own person. He does not see himself as one enduring individual."[22] As human beings we end up where as rational beings we should have started, with concern for the judgment of the future.

Rawls concludes his monumental essay with a passage that so beautifully and so painfully illustrates our common yearning for eternity:

Thus to see our place in society from the perspective of this position is to see it *sub specia aeternitatis:* it is to regard the human situation not only from all social but also from all temporal points of view. The perspective of eternity is not a perspective from a certain place beyond the world, nor the point of view of a transcendent being; rather it is a certain form of thought and feeling that rational persons can adopt within the world. And, having done so, they can, whatever their generation, bring together into one scheme all individual perspectives and arrive together at regulative principles that can be affirmed by everyone as he lives by them, each from his own standpoint. Purity of heart, if one could attain it, would be to see clearly and to act with grace and self-command from this point of view.[23]

The yearning is for the Kingdom. The answer offered is the siren song of a premature synthesis. Things cannot be "brought together into one scheme," for the world is not finished yet. Reason is not only the analysis of what is, but the reaching for what is yet to be. The good life now is not that of moral geometry but that of the moral drama that is hope.

15

Speaking of Home
in Public

In searching for an approach or framework that will bestow some kind of ultimate meaning upon our lives and provide a degree of moral guidance, we human beings are inclined to resort to some rather desperate measures. We have discussed in some detail the regression to a Golden Age. It is, in one form or another, perhaps the dominant device in contemporary culture's quest for an Archimedean point from which to understand the whole of reality and where it might be going. All our structures, institutions, taboos, rewards and sanctions—in short, all that we call civilization—must be destroyed if we are to be liberated to be our true selves. As the contemporary novelist William S. Burroughs has written, "When nobody cares, then shame ceases to exist and we can all return to the Garden of Eden without God prowling around like a house dick with a tape recorder."[1]

We have also considered much more subtle and sophisticated appeals to nature, from Francis Bacon to John Rawls, that locate the ultimate truth either in our origins or in the discernible plans and processes of the natural order. Much of the writing of Teilhard de Chardin, whose thought so pervades the overcast of consciousness that is our moment in the noosphere, is supportive of this approach. He is understood by many to imply there is a divine plan in the evolutionary process that leads inevitably to that Omega Point in which reality is finally fulfilled. The emphasis, unlike that of covenantal thought, is on evolutionary purpose more than divine promise, upon a past unfolding more than a future arriving. And, of course, there is the more conventional religious vision that invests certitude in a past revelation that is entire, complete and unchangeable. In that case, subsequent history is an embarrassment of more or less inexplicable divine delay.

Some of these world views are more plausible than others, some more winsome than others, but all have in common the discovery of the ultimate in already existent reality, whether past or present. None is consonant with that radically covenantal faith that is "the assurance of things hoped for, the conviction of things not seen" (Heb. 11).

It is true, of course, that there are those who say they can get along quite well without ultimate meanings. This is frequently styled as the secular approach to life, and for many who felt their childhood religion to be oppressive it presumably represents a form of liberation. According to the conventional wisdom, it is very much on the increase. Yet even here, Karl Popper has argued, modern secular thought does not quite come clean about itself. That is, even those who eschew theological or metaphysical explanations of reality assume that there is a rock-bottom foundation upon which our knowledge, limited though it may be, can be secured. There is no such foundation, says Popper, neither in the data of our senses nor in the integrity of ideas. Knowledge, he writes, "does not rest upon rock-bottom. The bold structure of its theories rises, as it were, above a swamp. It is like a building erected on piles. The piles are driven down from above into the swamp, but not down to any natural or 'given' base; and when we cease our attempts to drive our piles into a deeper layer, it is not because we have reached firm ground. We simply stop when we are satisfied that they are firm enough to carry the structure, at least for the time being."[2]

At another point he suggests that knowledge is like a ship that must be constantly repaired while it is afloat. The fact that we cannot make it unsinkable may seem lamentable, but unsinkable boats are like uncrashable airplanes—they cannot move.[3] This sense of high risk, improvisation and uncertainty is compatible with the Christian view of covenantal existence. Except the distinctiveness of the Christian claim has to do with the ship's destination, namely, the Kingdom of God. The issue is not one of our survival but of vindication, the vindication of the glory of God. It is not a question of what we can get by on, but of the revelation of history's meaning, without which existence is intolerable, without which the only alternatives are suicide or heroic despair.

Nowhere is the quest for abolute certainty so pressing as in the realm of ethics, both personal and public. Here, it is thought, the "oughtness" of life should be logically inferred from what we know for sure about the "isness" of reality. There must be an Archimedean point, a rock-bottomed foundation; the center must hold, or everything will fall apart. As we have noted, this insistence marks not only the Apollonians among us —the supposedly uptight lovers of law and order—but also the Dionysians who can risk the chaos of decadence precisely because they are convinced that, beneath the artificialities of civilization's distortions, there lies a true humanity awaiting liberation.

The ethos of a covenantal community, on the other hand, readily admits that it is not secured by sure knowledge. Rather, it is attuned to a hope that is not yet *known* in the ordinary sense of that word. To be sure, it is a "reasonable" hope, supported and reinforced by its own kind of evidence, even as there is much evidence to the contrary. Whether the hope is *true* or not, however, is entirely and by definition dependent upon the future. We are saying, then, that for a covenantal community ethics must not begin at the beginning but begin at the end. Unscrambling that statement, which at first may seem puzzling or even nonsensical, calls for a brief survey of the various ways in which people have tried to locate the primary point of reference by which ethics is to be shaped.[4]

It comes as no news that ours is viewed as a time of radical ethical relativity. Nietzsche is cast as the villain (or the hero, depending on one's viewpoint) who proclaimed the revaluation of all values. Values, he said, are what we determine to be values, they are the product of the evaluating will. The consequence, not surprisingly, is a host of "situational" ethical systems reflecting, in many cases, an utter arbitrariness in value decisions, including the decision—Why not?—to declare the death of ethics. Of one thing everyone seems quite sure; there are no fixed points of reference for ethical judgment, except the fixed point of reference that there are no fixed points of reference.

A less remarked consequence of pervasive ethical relativity is the growth of conformity. Contrary to most preachers, the absence of ethical standards does not mean that most people are living in a riot of immorality. As Frank Sheed once remarked, "Most of them do not have the constitution for it, they would be dead in a week if they tried." No, the more common result is a quiet and stifling conformity. It is not moral obedience, and certainly it bears little similarity to anything associated with righteousness. It is rather a superficial adherence to conventions. One "goes along," brings behavior "into line," but without any real conviction about the rightness or wrongness of things.

Undoubtedly there are many people who see ethics as a matter of obeying a divine authority. They do not lie, fornicate or cheat on their taxes because God has forbidden such behavior, and that is that. Contrary to the prophets of secularization, it is not at all clear that those who believe this represent simply a residual element of leftover religiosity. The growth of authoritarian religious movements, especially among the young, may be confounding yesteryear's predictions of inexorable secularization. Indeed it may be that, with the greater secularization of society, individuals are more disposed than ever to the *fanum,* to the self-enclosed religious explanation of reality, at least in their private lives. In any case, most of us are not ready to obey an imperative simply because some authority tells us it is God's will. We ask for reasons. We are persuaded that our asking is not an instance of rebellion but of faithfulness to ourselves and to whatever larger meaning our lives may have. We resist conforming in order that we may obey.

Nor are we persuaded that ethical dilemmas can be resolved by appeal to conscience. We know conscience to be culturally conditioned, reflecting the beliefs and values of our very limited place in the scheme of things. Then too, we know ourselves too well; we know how successfully the conscience can be trained to be an amiable companion, and how easily it can be bribed to withdraw objections to what we really want to do. Of course when conscience persists in its protest, it is never to be crossed, but it is more brake than guide. In any case, individual conscience is of limited use in communal decisions.

We sometimes speak of a communal conscience. We say a certain person or event may prick the "conscience of the nation," for example. But we are then speaking of the communal values that make up the public piety or civil religion of the group. These values are established not by an ongoing referendum of individual consciences but by traditions and institutions of agreed purpose and shared hope. In a viable society there is a general, most-of-the-time concurrence between communal values and what individual consciences suggest is right. When significant numbers "conscientiously object" there must be a redefinition of communal values (even the repression of the objection is, in American society, a redefinition of values). But the conscientious objection itself appeals to values beyond the dictates of individual conscience, to socially constructed and sustained values that are, or should be, shared by other members of society. Our question has to do with the point of reference by which such communal values are shaped in a covenantal community.

In addition to appeals to authority or to conscience, there have of course been many other efforts to find some objective standard for ethical decision making. Monumental among these efforts is Kant's attempt to base ethics upon the formal imperative of action according to reason. As an exercise in the rigor and elegance of human reasoning, Kant's argumentation has few equals. All the more distressing, then, to discover Adolf Eichmann, in the dock in Jerusalem, solemnly affirming that he acted always according to Kant's imperative. Who is to deny that he believed the extermination of Jews to be a universal law to be universally followed? Kant's house of formal imperatives is large enough to accommodate sundry fanatics and scoundrels. Equally important, if an action is moral only if it lends itself to being a principle of universal law, there is an inevitable denial of that individuality which is essential to moral behavior in this provisional moment of history. There are things that one can do, things one should do, that cannot be formulated as universally applicable principles. To be sure, orthodox Kantians engage in Talmudic and seemingly infinite refinements of principle in order to cover every real and conceivable contingency. But in fitting possibilities to their Procrustean bed, they either have to chop off too much real life or else expand the bed to accommodate limitless original positions, to abuse John Rawls' term. As with Rawls, the notion of formal imperatives of action based on reason assumes the possibility of a "moral geometry" that ignores the "not yetness" of an incomplete world.

There are numerous ways in which people who think about the nature of ethics have tried to confine ethical discussion to the sandbox of subjectivity. Some of the more exotic theories have to do with the analysis of language. It is said, for example, that a great gap is fixed between value statements and being (or fact) statements. If I say, "This is a bar of steel," that is a statement of fact. "Steel is very strong," is, we are told, a quite different kind of statement. This distinction is reflected in our everyday talk. In arguing some point, whether trivial or momentous, one person will frequently object to another's statement by saying, "Ah, now you're making a value judgment." It is implied that the rules of the game require sticking to the facts. Values, it is suggested, may be attached to certain realities, but they have no reality in their own right. What is good or bad, right or wrong, is finally dependent upon the person doing the evaluating. Here again, we encounter an intolerable restriction upon the role of reason, a cramped and confined notion of what is valid in public discourse.

Such a restriction, confining value judgments to the realm of subjectivity, makes the discussion of *public* ethics almost impossible. It nurtures that moral abdication that is so rightly condemned in the "intellectual mandarins" who sell their technical skills to the Pentagon or to the corporation while refusing to ask the moral question about the purposes for which their skills are employed. That same bifurcation between value and fact is evident in the Kissinger style that envisions foreign affairs as a mechanistic "system" or "structure for peace" from which meddlesome moral questions must be rigorously excluded.

In early 1969 a small delegation met with Dr. Kissinger for two hours at the White House to discuss our frankly moral concern about U.S. policies in Indochina. Rabbi Abraham Heschel in particular tried to evoke from Kissinger some articulation of moral principles that, he hoped, might have remained from Kissinger's early religious training. He received for his troubles a demeaning little homily on the ethical insights of Reinhold Niebuhr, the chief point of which Kissinger misunderstood to mean that moral judgments had little or no place in the real world of power relationships. Reinhold Niebuhr lived long enough to witness the tragedy of the Vietnam war and to be outraged by the way in which the best and the brightest of his professed students perverted his thought into a moral carte blanche for whatever was prompted by the impulse to power. Journalists whose last contact with the subject was Introduction to Western Philosophy I regularly make adulatory sounds about Dr. Kissinger's "philosophical approach" to international relations. So enamored are they by the aura of Harvard and the accent of Middle Europe, that they fail to see that Mr. Kissinger's philosophy, so to speak, consists in his repudiation of most of the philosophical questions without which "being philosophical" is no more than a media image and pretense to profundity. Careful examination of his own writings, and most especially of his record in office, gives dismal evidence that Dr. Kissinger is the archetype of the technocrat bewitched by the exercise of power. In short, his is precisely the style of the "mandarins" who were presumably exposed and repudiated by the Vietnam tragedy.

I single out the Kissinger style only because it is such an obvious instance of the divorce between value and fact that is so endemic to our culture. It is by no means a singular instance. The debate of the last few years over abortion on demand is another glaring example of the same problem. Quite apart from how one feels about the rights and wrongs of abortion, the thoughtful person must deplore the widespread dismissal of frankly ethical concerns. People who believe abortion on demand to be immoral are accused of "trying to impose their private religious beliefs on the public." Moral judgments are confined to the realms of the "private" and the "religious"; consigned to the sandbox of subjectivity, they have no legitimate place in public discourse. Again, quite apart from our views on the rights or wrongs of abortion, it should be obvious that the abortion issue poses ominous questions about the definition of human life and what forms of human life are to be afforded society's protection. It is hard to imagine issues of greater public moment. The mindless argument that, since the 1973 Supreme Court ruling, abortion (for all practical purposes) on demand is the "law of the land" should carry as much weight with us as the Dred Scott decision of 1857 apparently carried with the Abolitionists. It is a sad comment on the quality of moral discourse in our society that enlightened liberal opinion has superstitiously elevated the Supreme Court into the role of Delphic Oracle whereby the discussion of the difficult is conveniently terminated. It reflects a communal failure of nerve, a loss of confidence in the democratic experiment in which we exercise the office of citizenship in determining—always in a provisional and unsatisfactory way, of course—the values and policies by which we will live together.

In a similar vein, there is much discussion today about "decriminalizing" so-called victimless crimes. One may be personally sympathetic, as I am, to minimizing and, when possible, eliminating public control over essentially private behavior. The arguments we hear, however, are frequently thoughtless and further debilitating to democratic discourse. It is said, for example, that you cannot legislate morality. Presumably you can legislate aesthetics (which is by nature subjective and socially tenuous), as, for example, in admirable laws protecting certain urban streets as "historical landmarks." But you cannot legislate morality. Those who make this argument forget it is precisely the case made by President Eisenhower and others in their opposition to civil rights legislation in the 1950s. They forget there is an inseparable relationship between values, behavior and laws. Laws do not drop from heaven, nor do they emerge with inexorable logic from a book of precedents. Laws, if they are to have any life, exist in symbiotic connection with the values, aspirations and fears of a community. If explicitly moral questions are omitted from the formulation of law, it does not mean that we will no longer be legislating morality; it simply makes it more likely that we will legislate bad, or at least unreflective, morality.

The isolation of values from our public discourse is as endemic to the political right as it is to the left. It is evident in the economic Darwinism of conservatives who believe that the free interplay of market forces will automatically result in as close as we can get to an approximation of social justice. They rule out of bounds the moral questions raised about the intolerable plight of the poor who are left out of their mechanistic universe. The divorce of value and fact is, as we have seen, evident in the technocrat's insistence that his job is merely to devise and implement policy, not to make moral judgments—whether such technocrats are right or left, conservative or liberal, depends merely upon which administration is handing out the grants in Washington. And the divorce is evident in current public discourse about subjects such as abortion, the right to "death with dignity," victimless crimes and a host of other issues. For intellectuals to go along with this divorce is finally suicidal, for the divorce is self-liquidating of the intellectual vocation itself, which is, to use Hans Morganthau's phrase, to "speak truth to power." If the American democratic experiment is to be revitalized, moral judgment must be liberated from the sandbox of subjectivity.

It is to the credit of people like John Rawls that they are committed to that liberation. Our dissent from such enterprises comes at the point where they attempt to locate in existent reality the "objective" (however imperfectly perceived) point of reference for moral judgment. Values do have their own integrity, their own reality, their own "objectivity." That reality is derived from "the good" to which they point. From a Christian perspective, that good is the coming Kingdom of God, which is to say God himself. As it relates to public secular discourse, that reality is to be located in the aspirations and hopes implicit in the American experiment. There is a complicated interaction between the explicitly Christian hope and the public piety of the American experiment, and we will come back to an examination of that interaction. For the moment, we want to survey briefly the development of ethical thought as it relates to the gospel of the coming Kingdom and consider that gospel's potential for liberating moral discourse from the swamp of subjectivity and the impotence of its present privatization.

16

A Contract
for the Duration

It is frequently noted that the American constitutional theory is largely focused upon *procedure* rather than *content*. A contractual view of society assumed, more or less, that if people could agree on the rules of the game it was not necessary to agree on the goal of the game. I say "more or less" advisedly, since it was thought that there were some self-evident goals—of the "life, liberty and pursuit of happiness" variety—to which the rules must be subject. But in contractual thinking there was no conflict between rules and goals. In a rational universe rational people would pursue rational goals; the task was to structure the rules of the game in such a way as to assure that reason would have its way.

The constitutional fathers had good reason to fear the impact of religious dogmatism on public affairs. At the same time, however, there are numerous statements from Franklin, Jefferson, Madison and others indicating that they did not rely entirely upon procedural structures to assure the society's health. They assumed there was a reservoir of religious-ethical conviction in the populace and they spoke appreciatively of the role of the churches in keeping that reservoir filled. Nor were they so cynical as to think such convictions, while useful for keeping the masses in line, were unimportant for themselves. Their devotion to the goddess of reason did not entirely displace their own, often explicitly religious, judgments about right and wrong. In order to avoid the divisiveness of the past and to form a more perfect union, however, it was thought necessary to focus on that on which people could agree, namely, the procedures whereby it was possible to live and plan together while agreeing to disagree about more ultimate purposes. The subordination of substantive issues to procedural structures, in the confidence that through right process reason will lead to truth, is quintessential liberalism. In fact the substantive has been regularly surfaced in the history of American public discourse, although usually within the contractual bounds of the procedural. There are troubling signs that this has changed in the last several decades.

From the beginning there have been those who did not embrace the liberal creed. The historian Robert Handy has traced the theme of a "Christian America" as that goal has been perennially pursued by some, often conservative, forces that would bend the rules to accommodate a more substantive definition of the society's goal.[1] Radicalisms of various sorts have also dissented from the liberal confidence in "mere" procedural justice. Obviously, both abolitionists and Southern defenders of slavery were prepared to terminate the procedural experiment when it could not accommodate their conflicting convictions about the demands of righteousness. In this century, radical labor movements such as the Wobblies and sundry Marxisms have challenged the terms of the contract, insisting that the procedural provisions were in fact loaded dice designed to roll in such a way as to evade issues of substance. During the Vietnam war, protestors were frustrated by the administration's habit of congratulating itself upon permitting free protest while refusing to take seriously the *content* of the protest. At one point of high irony, the United States Information Agency was showing abroad films in defense of U.S. policy in Indochina which included clips of domestic protest demonstrations in order to illustrate America's devotion to freedom. That was the context in which, quite understandably, Herbert Marcuse's notion of "repressive tolerance" gained a certain currency.

A covenantal view of the American experiment focuses on the *what* as well as the *how,* on the goal as well as the rules, on substance as well as procedure. It is not opposed to the procedures devised through contractual thinking. To the contrary, the procedures agreed upon in the contract are essential in view of our distance from history's definitive fulfillment and the consequent pervasiveness of human wickedness. But the contract and its procedures are not the last word; they are provisional, they are designed to accommodate the pursuit of goals for which the experiment was launched. Even a cursory reading of American history makes it obvious that explicit moral judgments, visions of the good toward which we strive, and the religious values to which the nation was accountable, all surfaced more freely and less self-consciously in the past than at the present time.

There are no doubt many reasons for this change. Until the late nineteenth century, America was more religiously homogeneous. Well into the twentieth, it was assumed that the ethos of the much-maligned WASP constituted the "common culture" of American society. As the heterogeneity and radical pluralism of American life has become more evident, the dangers of divisiveness seem to loom larger. In order to avoid inflammatory divisions, the trend has been to ever more narrowly restrict the bounds of public discourse. We use only the points of reference on which we can all agree and since we agree on less and less, we are finally left with a procedural skeleton stripped of the flesh of common dreams.

Then too, those in charge of the British-American-Protestant moral hegemony seemed discredited—along with most everybody else—following the post-1914 shattering of their optimistically progressive world view. Since then American protestantism has produced very few culture-forming influences, except for Reinhold Niebuhr, who, in the opinion of many, cleaned out the social ethicists' account. Those who claimed to have learned most from him seem to have learned chiefly that they need no longer bother about questions of moral judgment. Two of the more vital sectors of American religion, Roman Catholicism and the evangelicals (the impolite word is fundamentalists), have not helped the situation very much. The antiworld, antihistorical proclivities of most evangelicals prevent, indeed forbid, their taking with religious seriousness the task of shaping an ethic for this society which, after all, is going up in flames as soon as Jesus gets around to coming back. To be sure, there are promising signs among what are called the "young evangelicals." One thinks, for example, of the witness of Sen. Mark Hatfield or of the "Chicago Declaration" adopted by forty evangelicals in the fall of 1973 and proposing a vigorous reappropriation of the culture-forming tasks that once marked revivalism in America. Yet these young evangelicals are small in number and, while wishing them the best, one acknowledges that the odds against their turning around the forty million Americans who call themselves evangelicals are long indeed.

As for Roman Catholics, they have only recently worked through the theory of being simultaneously Roman Catholics *and* Americans. The importance of the achievement of John Courtney Murray can hardly be overestimated. Yet the truths that Murray held to be self-evident represented Roman Catholicism's finally entering the American liberal mainstream. Murray, and subsequently Vatican II, dismantled notions such as the State's obligation to establish Catholicism or to heed the assertion that "error has no rights." Thus the chief impediments were removed to Catholicism's admission to the communion of American liberal orthodoxy. The election of John F. Kennedy was but the political sign of that admission. Now we listen for those new voices from American Catholicism that will be content neither to bask in the still fresh sense of respectability nor to form a Catholic Club within the company of alienated intellectuals, as some "radical Catholics" seem intent upon doing. The quality of moral discourse in American public life depends, I believe, in large measure upon the nerve with which American Catholics join in the struggle to revitalize and redefine the terms of our common covenant.

In tracing the way in which public discourse has sacrificed the substantive in favor of the procedural, some commentators would place heavy emphasis on the ascendancy, especially since the 1930s, of Jews in

American intellectual life. Obviously, the mention of this factor touches upon a mare's nest of issues and sensitivities, not the least troubling of which are the perduring and insidious forms of anti-Semitism also in American life. But the phenomenon itself cannot be evaded in any discussion of moral discourse and public purpose. The "disproportionate" number of Jews in positions of intellectual influence, especially in the academy, is a disproportion in relation to numbers but hardly in relation to talent. Whether the talent is to be attributed to genetic superiority, as C. P. Snow and some others suggest, or to sociocultural factors is best considered a moot issue. The fact is that many of the participants in the community that Irving Howe described as the "New York Intellectuals" felt, as Jews, that they had every reason to fear the impingement of religious particularism upon the rules of public life. Sticking to the procedural terms of the contract was viewed as protection against the substantive visions of the covenant in a nation overwhelmingly Christian in population.

One must quickly add that the phenomenon alluded to here was chiefly characteristic of "emancipated" or secularized Jews who de-emphasized their religious and cultural particularity as Jews and sought safety in the procedural terms of the liberal contract. They endorsed a style of public discourse in which participants should check at the door the covenantal dreams shaped by religious and cultural particularism. Thus statements of more or less explicit religious values were deemed sectarian and therefore inappropriate in the public discussion of our common purpose. Respectable public discourse is, in this view, deracinated public discourse. While religion may have its place in private life and in smaller natural communities, as public persons liberals in good standing join on the basis of procedure rather than substance, of contract rather than covenant.

Many Jewish intellectuals have had quite a different view of what is prudent and desirable, both for the survival and integrity of Judaism and for the Jewish contribution to the American experiment. They have fewer illusions about the protections afforded by secular liberalism, remembering the false sense of security "emancipated" German Jews felt during the years of the Weimar Republic. In recent years there has been a strong, and I believe hopeful, resurgence of Jewish cultural and religious particularity. This is in part a defensive response to some of the confrontational and even violent politics of the 1960s in which it seemed nobody was following the rules, the contract seemed almost rescinded. It was also in response to Israel's, and therefore Judaism's sense of isolation following the 1967 war. Some intellectuals associated with, for example, *Commentary* magazine suggested it was time to ask without apology, "What is good for the Jews?" This seemingly sectarian and parochial approach to public policy appeared necessary in a time of apparent fragmentation when every group—racial, ethnic and ideological—seemed to be out to advance only its own ends. The question was the intellectual's version of the more vulgar Jewish Defense League that for a short time seemed determined to prove that Jews could be as mindlessly violent and generally unpleasant as any other group in American society.

On a more positive note, the reaffirmation of Jewish particularity may reflect an understanding that the chances of all of us surviving together are enhanced by a more religious, less secularized, ethos. The fragile terms of the contract were never meant to stand alone in isolation from the values and belief systems that are rooted in particular communal and religious traditions. The religious sense of America as a covenanted community requires a reappropriation, by Christians and Jews alike, of the essentially Jewish understanding of the historical purpose implicit in the messianic promise.

The style of American public discourse is again in a state of great transition, away from the deracinated and religiously antiseptic, moving toward a liberation of the covenantal hopes and imagination of the American people. There are of course other forces and tendencies. The transition I suggest and desire is by no means inevitable. There may be a collapse of the contractual without any replacement by the covenantal. That is, we may end up both believing less and less in public and becoming more and more bereft of any procedures for living together in our unbelief. There is, however, some evidence supporting a more promising prospect.

I have already mentioned the growing Jewish reaffirmation of cultural and religious particularity. Another promising sign is the style of black intellectual engagement in recent years. As Harold Cruse and others have described, black intellectuals of a prior time were forced to conform to the secularist, white-washed ways of the dominant intellectual elite. There is strong reason to believe that the black intellectual now joining the discussion of America's meaning and purpose will refuse to surrender the particularity of his vision. Especially vital is the insistence upon the importance of religion in shaping the black experience, past, present and future. One hopes that the ethnic counterpart to the black insurgency will find increasing numbers of Polish, Italian, Slovak and other intellectuals resisting the demand to abandon or sublimate their particularity, including their religious particularity, in order to be admitted to the *agora* of respectable public debate. (Since the "ethnic renaissance" is so closely tied to Roman Catholicism in this country, this last development is symbiotically related to the future of Catholicism, as mentioned earlier.)

The revival of covenantal thinking in our public conversation also touches upon the alienation of the intellectual in American society. Although Vietnam, and various instances of racism, sexism, imperialism and general dreariness are commonly cited as the reasons for the intellectual's disenchantment with the American experiment, alienation as such is hardly of recent vintage. There is a sense, of course, in which the intellectual is by definition alienated, that is, he or she must maintain some distance from the society in order to offer a critique of it. But there is a less happy, and less necessary, style of alienation which is a lack of sympathy or even hostility toward everything America is and represents. Richard Hofstadter cites evidence in support of his thesis that it was around 1890 that "it became possible for the first time to speak of intellectuals as a class."[2] Here "class" means not so much economic class as an identifiable group somehow apart from the mainstream of American experience.

Today when one speaks of anti-Americanism among intellectuals we think immediately of some of the more prominent spokesmen of the more recent New Left. But what is now called alienation among intellectuals goes back to the polished disdain of Henry James for all things American and reached a kind of vitriolic height in the writings of H. L. Mencken who is still much celebrated in some intellectual circles (apparently anthologies of his writings still sell, although they usually omit some of his less tasteful assaults upon liberals still in good standing). Mencken was nothing if not thorough in his condemnation of Americans as "the most timorous, sniveling, poltroonish, ignominious mob of serfs and goose-steppers ever gathered under one flag in Christendom since the end of the Middle Ages."[3] (When Hitler arrived on the scene with the real goose-steppers, Mencken was not so quick to register his objection.) If Mencken strikes us as outrageous, his "alienation" is not that different from that of the urbane and prestigious *Partisan Review* which describes the dangers of right-wing politics as appealing to the "neanderthalism lurking in the so-called average man."[4]

Religious belief is part of what "lurks" in most Americans. To the extent that religious belief is anti-intellectual, obscurantist and indifferent to the common good, it is that way in part because many intellectuals proclaim the dogma that religious belief is inherently anti-intellectual, obscurantist and indifferent to the common good. The cognate dogma is that one must choose between liberation (emancipation) and religious tradition, between reason and faith, between the universal and the particular, between public discourse and private belief. But as we have emphasized these are all false choices and must be refused. The challenge is to think out loud, in public, about the nature of the American experiment, and to do so in a way that is informed and enriched by the diverse, sometimes contradictory, usually complementary, beliefs we hold about the good, about God, about the possible meanings of history. This is what is required if covenantal consciousness is to be renewed. Of course there is the danger of divisiveness. That is why we needed the social contract to begin with. The contract is designed to facilitate, not to preclude or to replace, the public discussion of what we believe and hope.

The social contract itself is always the object of examination and lively discussion, yet the good that we seek in common cannot be realized through merely redefining or renegotiating the terms of the contract. That which human beings seek, individually and collectively, goes beyond the rules and touches upon the goals of the game. It is an unabashedly utopian dream. It is neither return to Eden nor the discovery of the perfectly calibrated social system established by geometrically precise moral rules. It goes beyond anything that has been and anything now existent, pointing toward the promise of future vindication.

That for which we hope is political in the sense that it is promised in the form of the *polis* of the New Jerusalem, yet the possibilities of experiencing it, in part, now are not exclusively, nor even primarily, in the realm we call political. In this very provisional moment of history, the End Time may be better glimpsed in the realms of the aesthetic and the sacramental. In worship, in the arts, in music, in mystical experience, in the anguish of love—in all these ways we may apprehend, more than in political action, that for which we yearn. Indeed, short of the Kingdom's coming, politics in the apocalyptic mode is illusory and degenerates into psychodrama and elitist self-indulgence. It is the perennial source of phantom revolutions and of radicalisms in search of the sensation of being radical.

Yet the political tasks of determining public purpose and policy are part of the reality for which we seek redemption. What we do in this realm is to be a form of obedience, albeit imperfect, to God's command to seek the beloved community. Political measures can either welcome or resist the coming of the Kingdom which transcends our every political design. Believing Christians and Jews must seek a *public ethic* that is consonant with their understanding of the whole of reality. Otherwise there is an artificial bifurcation of the religious, essentially private, construction of reality and the political, essentially public, construction of reality. This division cannot help but be to the great detriment both of true religion and of our life together in society.

To say that the public ethic must be consonant with biblical belief is not to say that we should engage in a wholesale scramble to impose our several belief systems on the whole society. The provisions of the contract, as embodied, for example, in the First Amendment to the Constitution, are designed precisely to avoid that. The so-called doctrine of the separation of Church and State was not designed to hermetically seal off our public life from the influence of religion, although, as Richard E.

Morgan and others have pointed out, this is how it has often been interpreted by the courts.[5] Were this the purpose of the First Amendment, believers would find themselves in in a very difficult position. If they believed that God's redemptive purposes have nothing to do with the political or public sphere, they could readily support the bifurcation of the political from the religious, since the political would then be a matter of indifference to what they really cared about as believers. If, on the other hand, one believes the promise of redemption encompasses the whole of reality, including the political, any provision that would exclude this belief from the political realm would have to be conscientiously resisted.

Fortunately, there is a quite different way of understanding the wisdom of the contract on this point. The First Amendment, far from suggesting a wall or unbridgeable gap between religious belief and the business of the *polis*, reflects the most profound of biblical insights, namely that we are still a long way from the Kingdom. The final truth has not yet been revealed, no one should be permitted to impose their premature synthesis upon the body politic. As many constitutional scholars have argued, the First Amendment is misunderstood if it is seen exclusively as a negative restriction upon religion. It was that, of course, but it was also designed to maximize the free flow and interaction of the variety of visions by which people articulate their hopes. The notion of separation of Church and State aims at preventing the State from becoming captive to any one religious vision or restricting any religious vision, except, in the latter instance, insofar as the liberty of some must be restrained in order to protect the liberty of all.

Understood properly, then, the wisdom embodied in the First Amendment is consonant with, indeed it can be seen as an imperative derived from, the biblical promise of the coming Kingdom. It must be honored as an abiding part of the social contract. It is, of course, like every human arrangement, provisionally abiding. That is, when the Kingdom comes in its fulness, neither the First Amendment nor any other terms of the contract will be able to resist the Kingdom's imposing its truth upon the whole of reality, vindicating some visions and discrediting others. The objection that a procedural concern for maintaining pluralism may get in the way of acting decisively upon the definitive moment of truth is a spurious objection. If the First Amendment to the U.S. Constitution or any other such human contrivance can prevent its coming, what's coming is not the Kingdom of God. And there are no other "definitive moments of truth" short of the Kingdom of God that are worth the sacrifice of the freedoms protected by the First Amendment and similar provisions of our social contract.

Against the fanaticism of both left and right, religious and secular, we must insist that error has rights. (If someone wants to distinguish between the error and the erring, we have no quarrel; although it is a little like the business of hating the sin but loving the sinner—the distinction tends to be lost on the person for whom it is devised.) If and when the Kingdom comes, the truth will need no constitutional protections. Until then, the protection of the truth requires the protection of much that is untrue.

The present argument does not propose an establishment of religion; it does propose that the revitalization of a public ethic requires a more natural, less inhibited, conversation between public values and the traditions, including religious traditions, from which those values emerge. That conversation has been muted and even throttled by a regnant and quasi-religious secularism. We have been increasingly fearful to admit in public the obvious fact that we are a Western society whose values cannot be explained apart from the Jewish-Christian religious tradition. To be sure, most thinkers are prepared to acknowledge that in order to explain the rise of democracy and capitalism, and their sundry reactions such as Marxism, it is necessary to resort to the religious history of our Western world. But, it is implied, that is all a thing of the past. It is as though the wisdom distilled from the admittedly religious past can now stand on its own merits.

For millions of Americans, however, the primary definition of what the world is all about is consciously derived from, and asserted in, the terms of explicit religion. For all practical purposes, this means some form of Christianity or Judaism. By their virtual monopoly of intellectually respectable public discourse, the religiously "emancipated" have alienated these millions of Americans from participating with religious seriousness in the political process. Their primary, that is, religious, definition of reality has been forced more and more into the realm of the private, becoming increasingly apolitical or even antipolitical.

Conversely, and not unexpectedly, discussion of public policy has been enfeebled by a dishonesty that refuses to be explicit about the religious dimensions that are in fact in play. So, for example, we debate national priorities without admitting that *priorities* is simply another word for *values,* an explicitly ethical term that invokes our ultimate, that is, religious, understanding of reality. So also, Justice Blackmun, in writing the majority opinion in the aforementioned abortion cases, can say he will not make moral or metaphysical judgments since philosophers and theologians have not been able to agree on the complex issues involved, and then goes on to make breathtakingly sweeping judgments, even implying a legal definition of what constitutes "meaningful human life."

Public discourse in American life is presently floundering in moral evasiveness and mendacity. There is enough blame to go around for everyone to have a generous share. The result of bifurcating religion from political vision is unhealthy, unnatural and possibly lethal to our hopes for a common purpose as a people; it may even be lethal to our hopes for continued life together. The most religiously intense sectors of society are being forced into intellectual atrophy and antipolitical privatism. Conversely, a quasi-established secularism, cut off from the historical restraints implicit in the gospel of the Kingdom, approaches the political task in salvational and sometimes apocalyptic ways that lead inevitably to the disillusionment that now so bitterly afflicts American public life. Apocalyptic revolutionism and Enlightenment liberalism both set us up for disappointment. The laws of dialectical materialism and the moral geometry of a restricted rationalism both defy the key Jewish-Christian insight that ours is a provisional moment in the unfolding revelation of history's purpose.

The necessary change is that the terms of the contract and the hopes of the covenant will again be on speaking terms in public. On the side of the regnant secularists, it means an end to evasiveness. The talk about national priorities and purposes must be acknowledged for what it is, a search for a transcendent ethic. On the side of the religionists, it means refusing to pander to a religious construction of reality that makes the tasks of history, including the American experiment, a matter of indifference in the scheme of redemption.

Both "sides" have their work cut out for them. In the secular sphere there is a growing awareness, one hopes, of the impossibility of value-free reasoning about the great issues facing our society, of the need for greater candor and depth about the moral and religious dimensions of public discourse. That awareness should be encouraged. In the religious community there is a growing awareness, one hopes, that faithfulness to the messianic vision has vast implications for "building the earth," here and now. That awareness should be encouraged.

It is not enough, however, to trace the various historical reasons for the parting of the ways between contractual and covenantal thinking. Nor is it enough to express a hope for *rapprochement* between contract and covenant, procedure and substance, emancipated liberalism and committed religion. Whatever the nonintellectual factors that have brought us to the present sorry pass, we began with an acknowledgment that there is a very real problem in the realm of ideas as such, namely, where do we begin reconstructing an ethic that is serviceable in public discourse? We suggested that we begin at the end, finding our primary point of reference in the hopes associated with the promised coming of the Kingdom.

In the next few pages I will try to at least sketch the outlines of such a reconstructed ethic. The hope is that theologians and ethicists within the religious community might challenge, modify or elaborate what is proposed. Thus the religious community might be emboldened to make a new and distinctive contribution to the way in which Americans debate the rights and wrongs, hopes and fears, of our life together. At the same time, I would like to think the outline might be suggestive for people who are not entirely comfortable with the theological language it employs. The ethics of beginning at the end should threaten nobody's emancipation from whatever religious orthodoxy. The intention is to suggest a way of escape from our present unhappy encavement, an alternative to premature syntheses, an emancipation from the various Myths of Return and of moral geometry. The hope is to find a way of rethinking the American covenant within the covenantal interdependence of the whole of humanity.

17

Destination Ethics

Hope is the form that faith takes in relation to the future. Human hope is the point from which we can begin to build a new ethic, personal and public. To be more precise, the starting point is not human hope as such but that to which hope points and from which hope lives. Hope is related to the good, great hope to the ultimate good. Obviously, our future in time is not all good. This is painfully evident from our experience of past and present, which were once future. Therefore hope is not our only posture toward the future. Despair is the form that unfaith takes in relation to the future.

The enterprise we call ethics is always posited against despair. Ethics is the hope for meaning, despair the logical conclusion to be drawn from meaninglessness. We speak ethically in the hope that there is some ontological support system for the "oughtness" we posit against "wasness" and "isness." Serious ethics can only be done in the hope that we are not spitting against the wind. That hope has yet to be vindicated, otherwise it would not be hope. As we have seen, the hope is not vindicated by reference to some mythical state of nature, nor by the logic of categorical imperatives, nor by the calculus of utilitarianism, nor by conscience, nor by act of will. As is the way with hope, it can only be vindicated by the future.

Thus ethics is teleological. The most elementary assertion in such an approach, contrary to popular opinion, is that the end *does* justify the means. Nothing else can justify, or vindicate, the means. But the end does not justify *any* means. It vindicates those means that turn out to be instrumental to the end. By "end" we of course mean the End beyond our ends, the Purpose beyond our purposes.

The connection between ends and means has been discussed, and will be discussed, without end, or at least until the definitive End. It is what moral discourse is all about. It is sometimes said that the distinction between ends and means is misleading. The means, it is said, is the end in the process of becoming. Thus, for example, "There is no way to peace; peace is the way." There is much wisdom in this insight. The problem is that we do not know, except in retrospect, what means were instrumental to what ends. Only the result reveals what was in the process of becoming. This is as true in resolving personal ethical problems as it is in constructing a moral system appropriate to the destiny of the whole cosmos. Was I right in being cool, perhaps even unkind, to him in order to break a dependency pattern and force him to stand on his own two feet? Only time will tell. That is, it will be revealed by the future. My action, no matter how "moral" in motivation, will be vindicated or repudiated.

Ordinarily, we choose those means that look like a good end in the process of becoming. But, while history is not capricious, neither is it devoid of serendipity. There are ironies and discontinuities that make our predictive abilities imperfect at best; and they are seldom at their best in any case. The term *teleological* might therefore be somewhat misleading. It suggests to many a more continuous relationship between past, present, and future than our experience of reality would warrant. From A to B to C frequently turns out to be from C to A to B. We must therefore also speak of ethics as being eschatological. Our provisional ends, and the means used to reach them, stand under the judgment of the Eschaton, which is the ultimate destiny of all things. As Jesus' many parables of the judgment make clear, there are surprises in store.

Teleological ethics suggests a projectory, from *this* means to *that* end. Eschatological ethics is anticipatory, embracing and acting upon a promised end, even when the means to reach that end are not apparent. The cause-effect hypothesis is, as we discussed in an earlier chapter, the assumption acted upon in our everyday world. The hypothesis of the "ontological priority of the future" is the reason for the hope that is within us. Therefore ethical behavior is provisionally teleological and ultimately eschatological. The classic ethical dilemma is Abraham's readiness to sacrifice his son Isaac. Isaac was the means by which God was to fulfill his promise to Abraham that he would make a great nation of his descendants. In his readiness to kill Isaac, Abraham was "hoping against hope," acting against promise in obedience to the Promiser. It is commonly cited as an example of the "teleological suspension of the ethical." It is more accurately described as an eschatological suspension of the ordinarily ethical.

An eschatological ethics also comprehends that, in the present unfinished state of reality, there are some ethical dilemmas that are insoluble. There are situations in which we do not know and have no way of finding out what is the "right" thing to do. Professional ethicists seem to enjoy tinkering with a case called "the prisoners' dilemma." Without going into all the details, it has to do with two people arrested and interrogated separately. They both know that if neither confesses, they will receive a sentence of one year for a lesser offense. If one confesses, he will be released but his partner will be sentenced to ten years. If both confess each gets five years.[1] Without knowing what the other will do, the most "rational" decision each could make would result in both being worse off. It is even less helpful to suggest, as some proponents of "situational ethics" might, that each should do the "loving" thing.

It is not simply that if we were more reasonable, or more able to act in accord with our reason, we would then do the right thing. Sometimes there is no right thing. For Brutus and for all of us, the fault is indeed within ourselves. But it is also in the stars, that is, in the whole of a creation still in labor. To know this is to live by the ineffable mystery that is grace. Martin Luther said to Melanchthon, "Sin boldly," and Lutherans have never heard the end of it. It is too often forgotten that Luther added, "And believe yet more boldly."

Hope is the form that faith takes in relation to the future. Ethics reaches toward the good, the hoped-for good, the good that is not yet but may become. It is our hope for hope that our hoping may be instrumental to the becoming of the good for which we hope. (That rather complicated sentence is in fact a partial definition of prayer, which is the petition of faith reaching forward to anticipate, and thus play a part in effecting, the good desired. The good desired, ultimately, is the rule of God, as in "Thy Kingdom come.")

The idea that ethics has to do with reaching beyond what presently exists is no novelty. Toward the end of the *Republic,* Socrates is forced to confess that the supreme metaphysical principle that informs ethics, the good, can only be anticipated by analogy. The analogy is with the sun's relationship to the whole system of visible things; it is at the same time the source of their existence and of the light by which they are apprehended. The good is thus a transcendent reality which can be apprehended but never comprehended. Although our eschatological model of time is obviously foreign to Plato's thought, he too sees the good as the supreme beauty that only dawns upon the pilgrim as he draws near to the end of his journey. When he perceives the supreme beauty, when it enters into his everyday reality, the pilgrim recognizes it was always there.

So also in the Christian vision of the Eschaton, the vindication of our hope is also the confirmation that that which we hoped is indeed true not only at the End but all along our pilgrim way. Thus the dialectic between the "now" and the "not yet"; thus we pray and sing God's present omnipotent rule over all things, all the while pleading "Thy Kingdom come!"

Clearly there are many differences between the Socratic and Platonic ethics of the good and the biblical hope for the Kingdom. The point of similarity is that ethics is striving for the good. The good, said Plato, "is beyond being." The problem, of course, is that since the good is so elusive people are forever mistaking it. We need some sort of criterion for the good. The search for a criterion led to what subsequent thinkers have criticized as the "eudaemonism" in Socratic ethics, namely, the notion that that is good which contributes to happiness or a sense of well-being. Immanuel Kant, for example, was withering in his criticism of Socratic ethics because it failed to take seriously the rigorous claim of the ethical principle. What is true of Socrates and Plato is, of course, also true of Aristotle, who finally arrived at the conclusion that true happiness consists in virtue, and ethics is therefore a doctrine of the virtues.

Eudaemonism in whatever form is of little help in our searching for an "objective" point of reference in ethical discourse. If striving for the good and striving for happiness are the same thing, then the question must be limited to what is "good for" this person or that person. If the criterion of the good is related only to satisfaction and happiness, then we are still trapped in the sandbox of subjectivity.

Much conventional religious ethics is heteronomous, that is, it proposes that we are devising our own rules but are subject to the law of another, namely, the revealed law of God. Since it is commonly thought that living in line with this law will bring rewards, either here on earth or later in heaven, this approach too suggests that the good is the same thing as what is "good for" us. The good is not sought for its own sake. Now in fact, as we discussed earlier in connection with the story of Job, there is a felicitous coincidence between the pursuit of the good and the realization of what is good for us. At least that is the promise on which our hope rests. But what is good for us is realized only as we pursue the good for its own sake.

We noted above that we must resist conforming in order that we may obey. By conformity is meant mere compliance, getting into line with, an order external to ourselves. Obedience, as it is used here, means entering into, participating in, the source of the order which can then be no longer external to ourselves. The heteronomous ethic commonly inculcated under religious auspices encourages conformity rather than obedience. Pannenberg goes so far as to say, "Conformity is conducive to reaching certain goals, whether they be forms of earthly blessedness or heavenly reward. This is the hypocrisy inherent in every heteronomous morality." Then, somewhat harshly perhaps, "Such morality is a second-rate eudaemonism because it does not even engage the critical faculties of its adherents."[2]

Augustine took a giant step forward in establishing the priority of the good over subjective notions of happiness. It may strike the reader as strange that one should have a good word for Augustine in the context of this book's argument. His thoroughly pessimistic view of history's possibilities and his conviction that the City of God is the City of God and the City of Man is the City of Man and never the twain shall meet would seem entirely incompatible with the approach suggested here. Indeed I am not entirely unsympathetic to the hyperbole of F. D. Maurice, the nineteenth-century English theologian of the social gospel movement, who declared, "the greatest progress in these stirring times has been the exposure of the Augustinian idea of the City of God."[3]

Yet it was Augustine who made the conceptual breakthrough out of the cirle of eudaemonism. Augustine was convinced that true happiness could not be found in this present life; therefore presently attainable satisfaction could not be the criterion of the good. Aristotle's proposed goal of existence, happiness, was, for Augustine, precisely the definition of human sinfulness. The goal of existence, he said, is God. Augustine did not come up with his doctrine of God from nowhere, so to speak. He was solidly within the philosophical tradition. Plato, as many commentators have noted, already had a rather esoteric idea of God as the good that is good in itself, the good that is beyond every existence and even beyond being. The good is the future, yet to be realized in history. Again Pannenberg: "The good then asserts an ontological priority over against everything extant. . . . If not only all men but all things strive for the good, as in Plato's vision, we have reason to think of the good as the divine that rules over everything."[4]

Augustine, in agreement with biblical thought, conceived God in terms both personal and voluntaristic. God is the God of contingent events, the God who acts. Less happily, mixed with this were residual and nonbiblical, elements of the idea of a realm of the gods, far removed from the grubby business of history. Augustine's pessimism about life encouraged an otherworldly piety that longed for union with a God safely ensconced in splendid self-isolation, eternally enjoying his utter transcendence. It is this caricature of a static and immutable divine being that led F. D. Maurice, and many before and since him, to a wholesale condemnation of "Augustinianism." (Whether or not this *is* a caricature of Augustine's doctrine of God is for others more qualified than I to say.) There is no doubt, however, that over many centuries it is the way Augustine's idea of God has been used, or abused, as the case may be.

The great achievement, then, was to identify Plato's idea of the good with the biblical understanding of God. In distinction from Augustine, we see the key to the biblical message in the promised coming of God's rule over all things. God does not call us to escape from time and from this world in order to join him in his eternal transcendence, but he himself affirms the world, relating to it both as its creator and as its future. He is engaged in the divine pathos, indeed he is the pathos at the heart of all things seeking their fulfillment in him. *Time is not the enemy but the way toward the home for which all creation yearns.*

For Plato, the good was not something that we ever completely possessed. We are always striving for the good. In other words, the good is transcendent. Augustine escalated, so to speak, the idea of the good, so that the good was seen as what Christians mean by God. If we cast this insight in the model of history, of experience in time, we see that the good is the Absolute Future. As we have been saying all along, the rule of God is not yet fully established. Since God's rule cannot be separated from his existence, it is true to say that his existence has not yet been fully revealed. Thus the good is still future, it is still the object of our striving. The Kingdom of God for which we hope is the concrete, historical realization of the good. This good has priority over all human striving for the good; although, by the grace of God, our striving can participate in the coming of the promised good. To live morally is to live in the obedient hope that what we do and what we are may be instrumental to the realization of the Kingdom we seek. Thus it can be said that "the Kingdom of God defines the ultimate horizon for all ethical statements."[5]

The love of God is seen in that he has related himself to the world as its promised future. We therefore cannot seek the Kingdom of God apart from the world. If we seek God apart from his groaning creation, we miss the appointment he has made with us in history. Much conventional Christian piety suggests that we must leave the world behind for God's sake. The gospel of the Kingdom, on the other hand, demands a conversion to the world. We do God no favors by refusing to join him in his project, which is the history of the world.

Several distinctions are in order. Our commitment is to the Kingdom of God, that is, to the world that *is to be.* But that means that our commitment in our particular moment of time is to this present world, which is the world that is to be in progress of becoming. Therefore, while we say our commitment is to this world *transformed,* we at the same time underscore that it is *this* world that is to be transformed. There is a sense in which we "leave the world behind" in order to seek the Kingdom of God. There is weighty and venerable precedent, for example, in the tradition of Christian asceticism. In both word and example, Jesus asserted a radical freedom from the structures and securities of the present world order. What he said against the world, however, was precisely for the sake of the world. In the name of the world's future (the Kingdom of God), he condemned everything in the present that resisted that future. Thus his persistent return to the theme of the dangerous illusions of security in riches, status and power.

Although today our hope is attuned to a different time schedule than the one Jesus had in mind, there is still a need for Christians who radically assert their freedom from the structures and securities of the present time. Experiments in communal living today can be as revolutionary in their impact as was monasticism at various times in the Middle Ages. Paradoxically, such an abandonment of the world's ways can be the highest form of conversion to the world—if, that is, one abandons the world for the sake of the world. Such communities of radical freedom serve the world by keeping the present order under judgment, by giving dramatic witness to the new community that is the future, not just of the few who are called, but of the whole world.

Today we are witnessing a hopeful revival of experiments in Christian communal living. If such experiments are undertaken merely to find a more satisfactory or fulfilling life-style, there is no real objection to them but neither do they have much claim upon the world's attention. Such experiments can be comprehended under the cultural commandment that everyone should "do their own thing." If such experiments are undertaken on the assumption that it is possible to live now in the full enjoyment of the Kingdom Come, then we have more severe problems. Such a working assumption is illusory, and in order to sustain the illusion such experiments quickly degenerate into self-righteous isolation from the realities that witness so painfully and overwhelmingly to the incompleteness of our moment in history. The desire that I as an individual, or that we as the chosen few, should be saved apart from the salvation of the world is a self-serving conceit. It is the most sickly, because self-serving, refusal to enter into the divine pathos.

Christian ascetism is, at its best, a leaving of the world in order to alert the world to its future. By saying no to those structures and securities in which most people trust, such Christian communities are saying yes to their radical trust in the world that is to be. Such communal experiments are like the Eucharist. The liturgy of Christian worship is, among other things, an acting out in present time the meaning of the future for which we hope. In the symbolic play-acting of ritual and ceremony, we posit against all present definitions of reality a reality that, we believe, is yet more really real. The liturgy is thus an eschatological sign that places the existing order in the perspective of the Kingdom. In liturgy we celebrate the triumph of good over evil, the realization of perfect community, the defeat of suffering and death.

For most of us, liturgy is time in parenthesis, a blocked-out time. We return to the tasks of a world in which the glorious truths we had celebrated in liturgy seem at best ambiguous and partial, at times even preposterous. All Christians are called to be "in the world yet not of the world," that is, in the present order, yet firmly attached to the promised reality of the future. Even the action of the liturgy is very much "in the world." The very "as ifness" of the liturgy is possible only because of the "not yetness" of the present time. When the Kingdom comes in its fullness, there will be no further need of liturgy as eschatological sign. Until then, every Christian life is to be a signal alerting the world to its future. Most of us attempt to send our signals in the course of our everyday duties, fulfilling the tasks to which we feel "called." Some among us are called to the task of communal model-building, of a kind of full-time liturgy, of a sustained symbolization of alternative possibilities. Those who join such an enterprise may abandon the world in order better to serve the world by symbolizing the world that is to be.

These brief remarks on asceticism and Christian community are necessary to avoid misunderstanding what is meant by "conversion to the world." Conversion to the world is by no means to be confused with the "secular Christianity" so much in vogue a few years ago. Much of what was called secular Christianity was no more than capitulation to the world as it is. Far from being radical, it destroyed the dialectic between what is and what is to be, between present and future, between existing reality and the Kingdom of God. It was radical only in the sense that it brazenly celebrated the fact that the salt had lost its savor. It was but another instance of resignation to the cave, of loss of nerve in the face of the future. To the extent that it was superficially optimistic (it was, remember, the religious version of Camelot) it reinforced blind trust in the very principalities and powers which the gospel of the Kingdom would bring under judgment. True conversion to the world is a love for the world so relentless that it cannot help but protest a present order that falls so short of its Creator's promise.

Such a conversion to the world surpasses eudaemonism of every sort. Far from seeking personal happiness and a sense of well-being, this ethic calls us to the way of the cross. The cross is perceived not as resignation to things as they are but as the stern and, in view of the resurrection, promising struggle for what is to be. The individual's joy and hope for personal fulfillment is comprehended in the larger love that is God's affirmation of the world. To participate in the love that is the divine pathos is already to be in communion with God himself; it is the only possible communion with God. "God is love, and he who abides in love abides in God, and God abides in him" (1 John 4).

It is this conversion to the world that makes it possible to take the human struggle, including all our human hopes and covenants, with religious seriousness. To surrender ourselves to the fulfillment of the human enterprise is to participate in the love of God; it is to have a part in the coming of his Kingdom. It is not as though there were two loves: a love for God that then generates a love for humankind. There is, contrary to much pious literature, no "vertical" love for God that takes off for heaven and then a "horizontal" love to be exercised here on earth. There is but one love and that is the love of God. We participate in that love as we love God in our loving others.

The ethic of the coming Kingdom has wide-ranging implications for both personal and public life—for example, the relationship between love and justice. Christian thinkers in the Augustinian tradition have sometimes suggested that love has little or no place in a public ethic. That is, love is conceived as a peculiarly personal gift of grace. It is exercised in personal relations, but its social significance is limited, at most, to the church, the community of the redeemed. Justice, it is said, is the appropriate metaphor for the public sphere. Without belittling the importance of justice, we must reject this conventional dichotomy. It smacks too much of the various notions of "two kingdoms" that would separate the sacred from the secular, the realm of grace from the realm of the law, the realm of redemption from the realm of creation. All of history is redemptive history or none of history is redeemed.

It is love that has put the world on alert to its future. That is, the Kingdom is announced beforehand so that we might be prepared to welcome its coming. For some it will come as "a thief in the night," not because God delights in sneaking up on people and taking them by surprise, but because they refuse to heed the advance warning and promise. For those who do heed the alert, it is possible now to anticipate, to enter into communion with, the Power of the Future. This communion with future time explains, for instance, Jesus' authority to forgive sins. Faith cracks the wall of fear's resistance to the future and permits such "future flashes" to break into present time.

The love that puts the world on alert is a universal love. That is, God is no respecter of persons, nations, economic classes, or of any other divisions we devise for his creation. This is not to say he does not have special uses or designs for particular persons and groups. It is to say that the dynamic of love is universal in its intent. We are uncomfortable today with the idea of universal mission, whether it be proclaimed by an individual or by a country such as America. It strikes us as pretentious, grandiose, and downright dangerous. And indeed it is all these things if it means we try to impose our present reality upon others. One social order may in many respects be superior to another, but all existing orders are promising only to the extent they signal a new and more universal unity. In such unity, the particular is not destroyed but fulfilled in the universal. The ethical thrust toward the unity of humankind is not made necessary by some notion we have of justice, it is rather inherent in the dynamic love of the one God who is, whether the world knows it or not, the future of all.

In personal relations, true love does not seek to control the beloved. Love rather senses a "solidarity in incompleteness" with the beloved. It perceives the beloved as being more than he or she appears to be, in the light of future realization. From this solidarity in the face of the future emerges our social ethic of equality. Equality is not a system to be imposed in accord with a notion of justice derived from a state of nature, or distributive calculus or original position of choice. Equality is rather the process of maximizing respect for the diversity of ways in which human life is to be realized. There is finally an "equality of result," and that is the equality of the destiny we all share. In this provisional moment, far short of that destiny's realization, the moral mandate is to open the path of self-realization as much as possible, so that each may anticipate in his or her own way the realization of the future we face in common.

In this connection, not so incidentally, we must take with utmost seriousness the Marxist critique of "formal freedoms" that ignore the inability of many to avail themselves of those freedoms. Anatole France's sardonic observation remains bitterly pertinent: "The law, in its majestic equality, forbids the rich as well as the poor to sleep under bridges, to beg in the streets, and to steal bread." In American society we have only recently begun to undertake those compensatory actions that make rights in law "rights in life" for the poor.

The concern for equality of process derives from the promise of equality of destiny. Equality cannot be determined by a notion of distributive justice that assumes we live in a basically static world where the task is to divide up the goods "equally." There is no point of reference in existing reality, nor in the higher mathematics of moral geometry, by which such a division can be justly determined. Rather our very notion of justice is derived from love. That is, the "sense of fairness" is itself an intuition about the future. It is one manifestation of that respect we have for one another in the solidarity of our facing a common future. There is, let it be admitted, an element of fear in this sense of fairness. To the extent that we can speak of distributive justice, it is a corollary of retributive justice. We intuit that there is to be a day of reckoning, that somehow our destinies are interlocked. What fear finds intimidating in this prospect, faith anticipates with earnest longing.

This has very practical implications for American life and for America's role in the world. Why should rich Americans care about Americans, or why should we all care about several hundred million people who daily teeter on the edge of death by starvation? Some say we should care because it is in our self-interest to care, because it is impossible for the world to survive half hungry and half overweight. It is a fetching argument, lacking only a basis in common sense. The world has persisted with spectacular injustices for centuries and there is no way of proving that the privileged could not secure their privilege, at whatever cost to the poor, for centuries to come. The United States is singularly positioned to embark upon a course of almost perfect autarky.[6] As for the argument that we should be concerned for the poor because of the threat of ecotastrophe, running out of resources, and all that; well, it is quite clear this is a game in which any number can play, and play with almost any numbers. Others have rushed to their pocket calculators to discover that, given the continued growth of advanced industrialized societies, planet earth shows every readiness to be host to a happier, if not happy, twenty billion or so people.[7]

A few years ago, enlightened lapels were sprouting little buttons, distributed by the Urban League, exhorting all of us to "Give a Damn." The buttons failed to say why we should give a damn. In truth there is no reason why we should give a damn. Perhaps the revolutionary rage of the wretched of the earth, both domestic and foreign. But the Pentagon and associated agencies seem to have that problem well in hand. No reason at all, really, unless—unless it is more than poetic whimsy that "no man is an island." Unless our sense of solidarity and consequent sense of fairness has some ontological base in the way things really are. Unless, knowing we are all together in this project, certain inequities are simply intolerable. Unless, minimally, we fear a judgment to come. Unless, better and by grace, we have glimpsed the possibility of a new order. Unless love.

18

Hope Active in Love

Because its supposedly objective points of reference are illusory, the definition of justice is subject to the whims of whomever invokes it. "Justice" is the greed of the poor and the self-protection of the rich. Those who say that concern for the poor must "move from compassion to justice" (it is commonplace in some circles today) begin to stammer when challenged to produce a definition of justice. Finally, and frequently moved by feelings of guilt, they pass on the definition of justice that is the greed of the poor, a definition that carries little weight with their fellow rich who are less burdened with guilt feelings or inclined toward masochism. If we give a damn, it is because we know the initiative lies with love, and that the love has a purpose, and that purpose implies judgment. We give a damn because we wish, quite understandably, not to be damned.

Justice has no independent existence. It is the sense of fairness born from our sense of solidarity in the face of common judgment. And that judgment is the dynamic of love relating in time to open our present to a better future. "For still the vision awaits its time; it hastens to the end— it does not lie. If it seem slow, wait for it; it will surely come, it will not delay. Behold, he whose soul is not upright in him shall fail, but the righteous shall live by faith" (Hab. 2).

Hope is the form that faith takes in relation to the future, and this hope or future-directed faith is essential to the life of covenantal community. The new order for which we hope is anticipated by those who now enter into communion with the promised future of the Kingdom. That anticipation is corporately acted out, articulated and sustained in the life of the Church. In this believing community of rich and deep covenantal experience, we can and do hail the presence of the future in Jesus the Christ. In this community we make absolute commitments, commitments that are ultimately definitive for who we are and who we hope to be. Outside this community, in the larger society, convenantal existence must of necessity be much attenuated and commitments to particulars must be deliberately restrained.

In other words, while there is only one covenant, which is finally God's promise and project in creation, it is celebrated quite differently in different communities. Christians believe, for example, that the preaching of the gospel and the celebration of Christ's presence in worship will continue until the End Time. That proclamation and sharing therefore warrant the kind of reckless abandonment and total commitment to which disciples are called. The same thing cannot be said of commitment to any other activity or structure. There is not, for instance, any promise that any facet of the American social system, or even the American experiment as such, will continue to the End Time. The American experiment is at its best a signal or prolepsis of future possibilities which, if realized, must of necessity transcend the American experiment. Like any other social experiment, it is at its worst a barrier that will be shattered by the future's coming.

It is necessary to stress the conditional character of America as a covenanted community because of the tendency in social structures to absolutize themselves. This tendency is nowhere so evident as in the modern state. In American history this tendency has sometimes been manifest in the society's notion of itself as the New Israel, presided over by a president who is a veritable priest-king, whose perceived interests automatically coincide with divine purpose. The conditional character of America's covenantal existence is understood as we accent the element of contingency that is inherent in the very concept of covenant. Covenant does not confirm us in our righteousness or chosenness but calls us to accountability, keeps us ever under judgment. This is the conceptual check that the idea of covenant places upon national hubris.

The formal or structural check is the social contract that makes constitutional democracy possible. *The covenant makes possible the vision without which the people perish. The contract keeps the vision always vulnerable to challenge and revision.* Resistance to the apotheosis of any social structure, especially that of the State, is the theological and moral foundation for pluralism, voluntarism and individual rights. We have said that the contract is for the sake of the covenant. Conversely, it is not too much to say that part of the covenant is to preserve the contract. From this dialectic between covenant and contract emerges what must be deemed one of the great achievements—maybe the great achievement—of the modern era, our understanding of democratic freedom. While the idea of the "defense of freedom" has been frequently prostituted for unworthy purposes, it is an idea worth living for and, if required, worth dying for.

On the face of it, we seem to be caught in a contradiction. Is not the notion of democratic freedom a peculiarly American, or at least modern Western, development? If so, is it not an intrinsic part of those systems and structures which we have said must never be absolutized but be kept under constant judgment? Yet now we seem to be attributing a degree of ultimacy to a system of formal checks that preserves the exercise of democratic freedom.

Our understanding of democratic freedom is, of course, the development of a particular history. Some would say that the concept of democratic freedom is ethnocentric, and would thereby sharply relativize its significance. To this it must be answered that certainly our understanding of democratic freedom is undergoing constant change. Obviously it is implemented very imperfectly. Unquestionably it is the product of a particular history. However, the fact that it needs extensive refinement in both theory and practice does not detract from the ultimate significance of the idea itself. As to its ethnocentricity or historical particularity, we are again reminded of H. Richard Niebuhr's observation that, while our idea of the universal may not be universal, that does not mean there is nothing of the universal in it. In this light, we can say that the intuitions that inform democracy and its ideal of freedom are universally valid and of revelatory significance. That is, they are part of the future that God intends for all people.

Obviously, that does not mean the United States or anyone else should undertake the task of imposing that future upon other people. Our attempts along that line have been singularly disastrous. More important, our own imperfect realization of freedom gives us no warrant to force our version upon others. Yet to the extent that democratic freedom is instrumental to signaling the universal future, we must indeed hope it will be more widely shared. America's responsibility in that process is primarily one of more fully signaling the promise of freedom in her own life.

Speaking of freedom in terms of revelatory ultimacy may at first seem somewhat extravagant. We do not speak, however, this way of democracy and freedom simply because we are enthusiastic about a particular kind of social order. After all, others may be equally enthusiastic about other social experiments that rigorously deny democratic freedom. They may even attribute ultimate and revelatory significance to such experiments. As we know too well, various totalitarianisms of the modern era have done precisely that. In such societies, the individual with his communities and associations are subordinated to the self-apotheosized state. Such societies represent an historical closure, a premature synthesis, that destroys the dialectic between present and future. In such a society, the state may say that it is not itself the absolute but is rather the only way and guide toward the new order in which the state will wither away, having served its purpose. This too must be rejected on theological grounds, for there is no basis in the gospel of the Kingdom for a claim to such a singular role in the revelation of history's purpose.

The gospel of the Kingdom inculcates rather an intense historical modesty. In the social order, that modesty is enforced by observance of the checks implicit in democratic freedom. The exercise of freedom that challenges and refines all social visions and structures is not then simply desirable but essential, if we are to prevent any vision or structure— especially those embodied in the state—from claiming the ultimate loyalty that is due the Kingdom of God alone. There is therefore a religious urgency in our commitment to democratic freedom. It is the biblical and prophetic urgency of protesting idolatry, which in our time is most seriously threatened by the modern state. Paradoxically, it means that we must with the same religious urgency nurture and develop whatever elements of democratic freedom are contained within this present social system. Our very protest against any threat of idolatry is part of that process of nurturing and developing.

It might be suggested that our absolute commitment to democratic freedom is itself a form of idolatry. That would be true if our absolute commitment was to any one way in which democratic freedom might be preserved and exercised, whether through party systems, parliamentary democracy or whatever. Clearly there is no existing way that is deserving of such unlimited confidence. But our commitment to democratic freedom as such can be absolute because it is implicit in the very gospel of the Kingdom. That is, in view of the coming Kingdom, every existing and proposed order must be relativized. What we today call democratic freedom is such a relativizing instrument. Perhaps we will one day have a better instrument called by a different name. But the value of the relativizing function itself cannot be relativized. It is absolute. It is revealed.

The gospel of the Kingdom also informs the public ethic in our understanding of what is meant by the sovereignty of the people. The relationship between the idea of popular sovereignty and the good (the commonweal) we are to seek communally is admittedly a complex one. In the ancient world, democracy failed in part because it became preoccupied with buying off rival groups. The will of the people was not subordinated to the commonweal. It is by no means evident that the same fate does not await contemporary democratic experiments. Indeed, as we have noted, today, as in the 1930s, there is widespread anxiety about the future of democracy as one Western government after another seems captive to a mare's nest of economic crisis and failure of political nerve.

Contrary to the liberal optimists, we can have no confidence that there is some kind of automatic balance built into the nature of things. The notion that the free play of "countervailing forces" will in itself keep the democratic enterprise alive is rooted in an Enlightenment idea of reality as harmonious and self-balancing, rather than in the understanding of reality as an incomplete and embattled project. Unless there is a shared vision of the common good, society collapses under the force of contending interests. "The commonweal, the manifestation of God's sovereignty, must be elevated above the people's sovereignty. Sovereignty of the people can only be sustained where the commonweal is esteemed."[1]

The second sentence of this quotation from Pannenberg poses a seeming paradox. It seems natural to many to set the commonweal against the exercise of popular sovereignty. All authoritarian governments claim to know better than the people what the commonweal is, what is "best for the country." In countries ruled by party dictatorship, for example, there is no doubt that the party believes that the exercise of popular sovereignty must be subordinated to what the party perceives as the commonweal. This is as true of fascist as it is of communist regimes. Such regimes represent a structure of deliberate encavement. There is no good that transcends their own interests, they cannot be brought under judgment. They claim either to embody or to be the exclusive instrument for the realization of the commonweal.

If, however, the commonweal is understood in all ethical seriousness as "the good," as the Absolute Future that confronts our every present, then it is true that "sovereignty of the people can only be sustained where the commonweal is esteemed." Only where such an understanding of the commonweal is esteemed is there an ontological basis for popular sovereignty with its diversity and challenge that keeps the pretensions of all social structures in check. Without this ontological basis, popular sovereignty may seem a rather nice idea, perhaps strongly to be preferred, but finally something of a luxury that cannot be permitted to get in the way of the society's (the State's) pursuit of progress. Sad to say, this demeaning attitude toward democratic freedom marks most of the regimes in the world today, especially among newly independent Third World countries where regimes, both left and right, assert their societies cannot yet "afford" democracy.

Esteem of the commonweal that transcends our structures and plans is the strongest foundation for the exercise of popular sovereignty. Even that foundation, as we know from bitter experience, is frightfully fragile. Only esteem for that commonweal prevents any social structure, existent or proposed, from passing itself off as the Kingdom of God. For all that such mottos are vulgarized and exploited, this is the profound wisdom and rightness in having on our coins "In God We Trust," and in the pledge of allegiance, "One nation under God."

Liberal religion is especially critical of the hypocrisy often evident in the use of such expressions of public piety. And, of course, hypocrisy needs always to be exposed. But if hypocrisy is the tribute that vice pays to virtue, the only way of bringing the vice under judgment is by invoking the virtue to which it pretends. The way to the renewal of public ethics is not through the denigration of the ideals to which the society professes to aspire, but through taking those ideals more seriously than do people who merely mouth them in order to acquire the appearance of righteousness. As the commonweal is more genuinely and popularly esteemed, the dialectic between present and future is intensified; the existing order is brought under judgment and made vulnerable to the possibilities of a better future.

Admittedly the idea of fighting claims to transcendence by appeals to the transcendent is fraught with problems. It means that, at least until the Kingdom comes, we will be engaged in perpetual discourse and disagreement about the nature of the commonweal to which we are accountable. That ongoing discussion, which is both liberated and limited by the terms of the contract, is a large part of what democracy is about. Needless to say, limitation and liberation are symbiotically related in the democratic process. Without agreed-upon limits that check the power of some participants, the process would quickly collapse. And, of course, the limits we agree upon are themselves the subject of constant debate.

The question of social limits is, of course, at the heart of what we mean by law in society. In the Enlightenment notion of a balanced clockwork universe, it is thought that the law is simply the social codification of rules and principles built into the nature of things. To be sure, there are also religious versions of the same idea, appealing to presumably revealed and eternal verities. But if, as we are arguing, the universe is more contest than clockwork, more struggle than system, with the outcome being far from self-evident, then law and the whole subject of social limits must be derived from our covenantal understanding of the commonweal.

This is not the place to enter upon a philosophy of law, yet one cannot help but remark in passing the abysmal vacuity of current thinking on the subject, especially in the legal profession. Many of the most distinguished law schools in America do not have even one required course on the philosophy or ethics of law. There are courses on the ethics of legal behavior, but not on the ethical foundations of law. The schools turn out mechanics of legal tactics and precedents, and the rulings of even the highest courts, quite predictably, reflect too often the mechanic's mentality. Law is treated as though it had an autonomous existence, as though it were a thing in itself, instead of the ongoing quest for how best to order our common life in accountability to the values to which we aspire.[2]

Are we suggesting that the formulation and interpretation of law is in some sense a religious enterprise? Would we have our judges be theologians? Yes, of course, there is no way around it. This implies no change, it merely suggests that we become self-conscious about what we are in fact doing. For very good reasons having to do with the First Amendment to the U.S. Constitution, the religious dimension of law making and law interpreting is usually guised in nonreligious language. Unfortunately, it is now so systematically guised that most professionals involved in the process, as well as most of the public, have been thoroughly deceived by the disguise. They are victimized by the false consciousness of thinking of themselves as mechanics tinkering with precedents when the task calls for philosophers capable of comprehending the visions by which communities live or die. It is ironic that the medical profession, which is essentially mechanical, has wrapped itself in the vestments of religious mystique, while the judiciary, which is essentially religious and moral, has settled for the mechanic's smock.

Social limits, like the contractual terms in which they are embodied, are finally aimed not at limiting but at opening possibilities. The better society is one in which the transcendent commonweal can be invoked in the most unlikely and sometimes irreverent ways; irreverent, that is, toward existing structures and attitudes. This does not mean, I hasten to add, that everybody is participating in every discussion that touches upon the public weal. Such a notion of "participatory democracy," as it was called some years ago, suggests pure hell. It can have appeal only for those who dream of the new order in terms of cradle to grave committee meetings or find masochistic satisfaction in the prospect of referenda without end. A totally politicized society is an inoperable society, and a totally politicized personal life is a formula for the decimation of one's humanity.

A viable society is one that is always in the process of striking a balance between freedom and order, between decisions that truly touch upon the commonweal and the routine and trivia that are adequately covered by prior decisions. It is nonsense to think that a healthy society is one in which everybody has a say in every decision that touches upon their lives. I neither need nor desire to participate in the decision about whether or not to lay a new sewer line on Bushwick Avenue, two blocks away. Of course I hope somebody else is taking care of that, since the wrong decision could indeed have unpleasant consequences for my daily life.

Having set aside the stereotype of participatory democracy, however, it is urgent to insist that limits should be so designed as to protect the *right* and *ability* to intervene even in what seem to be the most routinized decisions. The incremental force of apparently routine decisions can impinge in major ways upon the vision of the commonweal. Thus "institutional racism," for example, does not exist by virtue of public policy debate and decision but by unreflected conformity to everyday patterns of attitude and behavior. Democratic limits must be so designed as to permit, and the democratic ethos must be so nurtured as to encourage, the challenging of the taken for granted. Only in this way can prior decisions or unconscious "decisions" that touch upon the commonweal be made vulnerable to reexamination. And, of course, this process can be sustained only as all our decisions are confronted by that transcendent commonweal which is always "not yet" in its realization.

Also in American society we have only imperfectly devised limits by which the debate is sustained that keeps existing reality under judgment of the transcendent. Having said that, it is necessary to add that some societies are less imperfect than others in this respect. The perception of the superiority of American and a handful of other societies on this score is no invitation to complacency. It is rather a trust to be vigorously guarded and developed. It is not too grandiose to say that the best in the American democratic design and ethos is a trust to be maintained on behalf of the world. Indeed it is necessary to say precisely that, if in fact democratic freedom is, as we have defined it earlier, an ultimate value that proleptically participates in the future confronting the whole of humankind.

The imperfections in our American design of limits are obvious enough. Without some notion of economic rights and a guaranteed economic "floor of decency," civil and political rights remain for millions a formal fiction. For the tens of thousands of elderly people in our cities who struggle to subsist on six dollars a day and end up eating dog food, involvement in the democratic discussion of the commonweal is virtually meaningless. And, of course, the aged poor are but one sector among the many effectively excluded, to the great detriment and danger of our covenantal life together. In many cases, especially with those of immigrant background, the covenant with the American future has been broken.

For many others, the covenant never existed, or at least their small and private covenants seemed unrelated to the quest for the commonweal. For them, covenant means no more than commitment to survival. To the extent that the mythology of the American Way of Life encourages people to believe that commitment to survival, even to survival with style, is an adequate participation in our societal hope, it represents a massive betrayal of the American destiny. It is assumed the reader is familiar with the abundant literature critical of compulsive consumerism and religious devotion to "standard of living," both of which, while more easily criticized by the affluent than by the poor, represent such a betrayal.

Materialsm in whatever form is not at the heart of what covenantal existence is about. Here one must oppose what appears to be the strange affinity between Marxist critic and capitalist corporate booster. One sees materialsm as the motor force of revolutionary change, while the other views it as the self-validating success of the Great American Way. Both are wrong. That said, it is necessary to add that, while materialism is not at the heart of covenantal existence, the economic deprivation of millions of Americans is among the chief imperfections blocking the way toward a revitalization of covenantal existence. There is an element of truth in the claim of some societies that they cannot "afford" democracy. While democracy does not require anything so grandiloquent as Marx's transition from the realm of necessity to the realm of freedom, it does require a certain relaxation of the rigors of necessity.

This is a fact not sufficiently pondered by some middle-class proponents of no-growth ideology who seem unmoved by the implications of a severe downturn in American consumption and productivity (one suspects they would be quickly sobered as soon as the aesthetics of the new asceticism impinged by necessity rather than by choice upon their own life-styles). The unedifying fact is that there is probably a necessary connection between democratic society and continued prosperity, or at least the "feeling" of prosperity. The narrow escape from the 1930s, thanks to war production, gives us little reason to be sanguine about the prospects for democracy in the face of economic collapse. The intolerable fact at present is that the American democratic experiment is severely crippled by the denial to millions of "rights in life as well as in law." As with everything, the degree to which the rigors of necessity must be relaxed is relative and constantly changing. But it seems clear that it is both morally necessary and materially feasible that they be relaxed a great deal more than they are at present for millions now subsisting in poverty.

Unlike other limits aimed at protecting and sustaining democratic discourse regarding our common future, economic deprivation is a purely negative limit. While perhaps the most important, it is certainly not the only negative limit. The corruption of electoral politics, together with its ideological captivity to the salesmanship of the mass media, the arrogation of what should be public decisions by government, corporate and union bureaucracies, the decline in the social potency of voluntary and intermediate structures—these are among the gross imperfections that severely limit the exercise of democratic limits designed to keep our present open to the new possibilities of the future. In the face of these continuing and, in some cases, growing threats, there is no cause for complacency.

Yet so long as we have not lost entirely the transcendent point of reference by which we are held accountable, there is reason for lively hope. Even when the various systems by which democratic discourse is supposed to be sustained seem rusty from underuse or worn out from overuse, or when the intervention that would challenge the taken-for-granted seems frustrated in its expression or impotent in its effect, the American "system" itself is not exhausted. From the Boston Tea Party through the abolitionist movement through feminist struggles through the early years of labor organizing through the civil rights and peace movements of more recent times, repressed transcendence has been asserted in civil disobedience. Although often asserted "against the system," civil disobedience is, unlike the option of violent revolution, a part of the system. One does not step out of the system in exercising civil disobedience but is rather using an available, albeit extraordinary, means to recall the system to its constituting vision, to return it to the pursuit of the commonweal. People who would contain the world within the contractual security of a clockwork universe must be frightened by civil disobedience. They see it as the sign of the system's collapse when in fact it is the more perfect obedience that, when exercised in covenantal responsibility to other members of the society and to the community's founding vision, is the harbinger of the rebirth of the lively experiment.

Nonetheless, many foolishly persist in attempting to exorcise the transcendent from our public life. The dull logic of secular liberalism would, in Freudian terms, reinforce the social superego that censors and represses our libidinous itch for destiny and for judgment. When unchecked by historical modesty, the itch can be fatal. It can and has shown itself in the arrogance of manifest destiny and in self-destructive politics of apocalypse. But much more surely and immediately fatal to our social experiment is the suppression of the knowledge that it is an experiment, that there are ends to which all our ends are means. A relentless secularism in the public realm is not the mark of a society "come of age" but of a society eviscerated.

The process of democratic discourse and decision would seem to be endless. Although it is beyond the range of the present discussion, it might be ventured that the democratic process will continue in the definitive coming of the Kingdom of God. There are theological problems, no doubt, with the idea of continuing "tasks" in the Kingdom since it may require the perdurance of evils to be combatted. Yet Thomas Jefferson's proposal that paradise will consist in the leisurely public discourse of an elevated constitutional convention may be more than whimsy. Certainly it is no more problematic than is Luther's expectation of drinking beer and talking theology with the Apostle Paul when presumably, in the Kingdom Come, all theological problems will have been resolved. Such perhaps fanciful projections of the future belong to the "lost hairs and fallen birds" school of eschatological hope. They do help us, however, to overcome our fear of—they help us even to welcome—the ongoing, unsettled and unsettling process of democratic experiment.

On a perhaps more serious level, those who would terminate the covenant by encaving it in the present operate basically from one of two assumptions: either the Kingdom has already come and we must only make the adjustments appropriate to its existence, or it is not coming and we must just go on naming names and meaning meanings in the sure knowledge of absurdity. That the Kingdom has come in its fullness is, I believe, obscene illusion. To live in the belief that it is not coming is the course of heroic despair. The second at least has the merit of honesty (if Jesus turns out to be wrong, that is). Neither is able to sustain democratic experiment with its reaching for the good of the commonweal that confronts in promise all existing reality.

Two examples may help illustrate the role of the transcendent in democratic process. The first instance may seem rather limited in significance, but it reflects a much more pervasive problem. It is the rationale invoked by Gerald Ford when, in September, 1974, he granted a full pardon to Richard Nixon. The second example is of more obviously far-ranging significance, touching upon issues with which our children's children will still be trying to cope. It is the role of transcendence in shaping and finally destroying American slavery.

In addressing the nation on Sunday morning, September 8, 1974, Mr. Ford declared, "I do believe with all my heart and mind and spirit that I, not as President, but as a humble servant of God, will receive justice without mercy if I fail to show mercy." Richard Nixon and countless other hypocrites have trained Americans to be suspicious of such pieties in the context of politics. Secular liberals have refined that suspicion into the high art of scorn.

I hold no brief for the form or timing of Mr. Ford's pardon of Mr. Nixon. The interesting thing is the reason given. It was an action taken, we are told, in accountability to the transcendent, in reverence for the judgment of God. On the face of it, the rationale does not seem that different from reasons offered by others, such as Thomas Jefferson who trembled for his country when he reflected that God is just. More significantly, Abraham Lincoln, rightly proclaimed as the greatest theologian of the American experience, spoke frequently of justice, love and forgiveness in light of the judgment to come.

The crucial difference in this connection is that Lincoln posited the intimations of the transcendent precisely in the public realm whereas Mr. Ford's statement is one of private motivation. *"Not as President,* but as a humble servant of God." Reference to the transcendent is for one a gimmick in support of personal credibility, for the other a call to communal accountability. Lincoln conversed with the "sentiments embodied in the Declaration of Independence" which he and others believed to be intimations of a commonweal offering hope "not alone to the people of this country, but hope to all the world, for all future time." Ford invokes the holy to sanction his use of public power to do a private favor for a friend. Lincoln knew his deeds and decisions were contingent upon the future: "If the end brings me out all right, what is said against me won't amount to anything. If the end brings me out wrong, ten angels swearing I was right would make no difference." Angels are now excluded from giving public witness. Mr. Ford is forced to rely on his presumably self-authenticating private visions. Lincoln invoked "the mystic chords of communal memory"; Ford produces his Sunday School attendance card.

The Lincolns speak of corporate destiny, the Fords of individual sincerity. In that decline the pessimist might trace the enervation of covenantal existence in American democracy.

Gerald Ford, let it be said, is hardly to blame. He is but another victim of the exorcism of transcendence from our public life, forcing its inevitable reappearance in private visions that escape public accountability. In the situation he faced, there were no clear precedents or principles to be followed. Indeed Ford was correct in thinking the issue involved weighty questions of justice, forgiveness and the nature of the society we seek. Since there was nothing readily at hand to provide an answer, he had to reach out in order to realize a possibility yet transcendent. Although his goal was, one hopes, communal healing, his search for the way toward the goal was essentially individualistic.

Thus the transcendent rationale offered by Mr. Ford compounded our difficulties in speaking in public of the commonweal we seek. A privatized religious rationale was linked with a public decision that was distinctly unpopular with the leaders of the liberal secularism now dominant in American public discourse. The decision was condemned and the rationale invoked was held up to scorn. This only assures that appeals to the transcendent will in the future be driven even farther on to the sidelines of subjectivity. Faced with problems for which positive law, contracts and precedents provide no answers, future Presidents will be increasingly hesitant to speak in public about their wrestlings with the Spirit in the Lincoln bedroom. Indeed it is not unreasonable to suspect that many mandarins of secularism would just as soon that public people not wrestle with the Spirit even in private. But the vast majority of Americans seem to want a President who is "religious," and so the compromise is struck of secularism in public and transcendence in private, and never the twain shall meet. The result is the worst of religion and the worst of public philosophy; both are emasculated. Intimations of transcendence are either deprived of public potency or unchecked by communal memory and hope. Public philosophy is deprived of the points of reference which offer resources for renewal and judgment in facing the ever-new problems of an ongoing social experiment.

In fact, of course, the compromise of secularism in public and transcendence in private is impossible to maintain. Transcendence repressed keeps popping up, but is called by different names. The irrepressibility of the transcendent may be taken to mean that the situation is not so bad after all. That is, it may be suggested that the vision of the commonweal and the resources for renewal and judgment that vision offers will, despite the efforts of secularism, nonetheless play a role in shaping our public discourse. The situation, unfortunately, is more complex than that.

Anonymous transcendence is the only kind permitted in the thoroughly secularist world. Anonymous transcendence cannot, by definition, be linked to the tradition and discipline of religious thought. Therein lies the danger in this deceit. It is pretended that the terms appealed to—justice, fairness, the right—are somehow contained within the existing order. In this view, it is simply a matter of setting the order in order. This implies a mechanistic, clockwork approach to society, an emphasis on contract to the exclusion of covenant, the death of of a sense of experiment in time.

The essence of sin, according to Martin Luther, is expressed in the words *incurvatus est,* man turned in upon himself. This has its societal correlate and is closely connected with what we have spoken of as the sense of encavement. The twist is that a society, like an individual, cannot help but appeal beyond itself, to that which transcends itself, when it speaks of its ordering values. If, however, it denies, as our society is prone to deny, that it is in fact appealing to the transcendent, it deceives itself into thinking that its ordering values are in some sense already contained within itself.

Anonymous transcendence is socially dangerous, then, because it is not made explicit and thereby subjected to disciplined public discourse. Matters of belief are disconnected from the discipline of belief systems because we deny they are matters of belief. We think we are discussing mere points of law when we are, unknowingly, discussing the nature and destiny of humankind. We are conscious of ourselves negotiating the terms of the contract, while all the while ignoring the covenant, the vision of "the good," which the contract is to serve. Caught in a process of forever turning existing reality in upon itself, we become possessed by an inflated self-importance that is finally impervious to both the judgment and the promise of the future.

There is yet another danger in anonymous transcendence. As the irrepressible dynamics of the transcendent in the public realm are deprived of the disciplined reflection of communal memory and hope, so also is the explicitly transcendent in the "religious realm" deprived of public potency. Not only is explicit religion deprived of public potency, it is in that case also unchecked by public accountability. That is, one can say anything "religiously," without regard to its public consequences. The "God" one talks about religiously has nothing to do with "the good" one talks about publicly. This has devastating consequences for religious thought, as witness the present popularity of "theologies of play," "Christian polytheism," "transactional sacramentalism" and myriad other entertainments.

The less bizarre and weightier consequence of this bifurcation is, of course, that there are millions of Christians who see no religiously serious connection between being Christian and being American. Not only do they see no need to take the American experiment with religious seriousness, the very idea strikes them as preposterous, if not blasphemous.

Citizenship is not a vocation inherent in their being Christians in this time
and place, it is at best an accidental obligation hermetically sealed off
from what constitutes the heart of Christian existence. For them,
Christian existence moves not in the linear mystery of time but in the
vertical mystery of space, their hope is not directed toward a Kingdom
ahead of us but toward a heaven above us. Their existence as Americans
is incidental, more or less an accident in the "realm of creation" which
is already condemned. It is not to be taken with religious seriousness.
Their existence as Christians, however, is a question of eternal consequence, a matter of faith, the salvific fact in the "realm of redemption"
which is alone the proper object of hope.

What we have described is the religious correlate to the secularist
hegemony in our public life. The transcendent could not have been
exorcised from our public discourse to the extent it has been were it not
for the collaboration of this kind of religious thought and piety. In their
important "Chicago Declaration" of 1973, forty evangelical leaders asserted: "As evangelical Christians committed to the Lord Jesus Christ
and the full authority of the Word of God, we affirm that God lays total
claim upon the lives of his people. We cannot, therefore, separate our lives
in Christ from the situation in which God has placed us in the United
States and the world."[3] It is not clear from the discussion to date what
such a statement may mean. It may mean no more than that Christians
should be more actively engaged as individuals in the public arena. A fine
sentiment, no doubt, but one that can be readily accommodated within
the secularist rules of the game. In the churches, the sentiment will appeal
to a minority that "goes in for that sort of thing" (issues of social justice).
If, on the other hand, the statement is the prelude to a reconstruction of
theology and piety that makes it impossible to separate "life in Christ"
from the historical situation which is the stuff of his suffering and of his
promise, then one may look to the "evangelical renaissance" for a strong
reassertion of the transcendent commonweal in our social experiment.
With approximately forty million Americans identifying themselves as
evangelicals, it is a provocative prospect.

Again, the point in discussing the Ford decision is not to berate this
President. He is but one victim of a process for which illustrations are
lamentably abundant. We might have focused, for example, on John
Kennedy's famed meeting with the Houston, Texas, Baptist ministerium
in 1960, where Kennedy assured the nation that his being a Christian and,
more particularly, a Roman Catholic would have no bearing on the
decisions he would make in public life. That this curious promise was
hailed by Roman Catholics, bishops and lay people alike, as a sign of
great progress says much about the imperious need to be accepted. It was
not so much the pinch of incense offered to the emperor's statue; it was
trading miter, crosier, thurible and all for the emperor's throne. That the

trade was presided over by a group of religious leaders says much about the baffling history of church-state questions in America. Only in America could determined secularists get fundamentalist clergy to act as their surrogates, and leave the clergy feeling they had won a victory.

President Ford's rationale for pardoning Richard Nixon is an example of intricate failure in the interaction between ethical judgment and the transcendent commonweal. A happier example of the dialectic is to be found at crucial moments in the history of American race relations. Although he uses different language, the argument being made here is similar to that advanced by Gunnar Myrdal in his *An American Dilemma* and subsequent writings. Reflecting on American race relations more than thirty-five years ago, Myrdal asked why slavery had been abolished and why America had moved—although with tortuous slowness intermittently spurrred by spasms of urgency—toward greater racial equality. Testing various determinist economic hypotheses frequently advanced, he found them wanting. It had, he contended, something to do with the "American creed." Slavery and racial oppression were somehow thought to be unworthy of a people who felt vaguely "called" to a destiny of communal justice.

Not economic necessity, nor legal logic, nor the force of rational consistency about distributive justice, but an unabashedly moral sense of the judgment implicit in being, as Lincoln called them, "an almost chosen people"—this is what precluded the American people from devising their own "final solution" to their racial problem. This is not to suggest that morality can operate in a vacuum, apart from all the other forces—economic, legal, social—that shape our public life. It is to say that, apart from some vision of the commonweal to which it aspires, no society can take itself in hand, accept responsibility for itself; in other words, without the covenantal posture of accountability toward the future, America cannot be moral.

Myrdal's argument, here paraphrased in a way with which he may not be happy, is strikingly complemented by Eugene Genovese's more recent *Roll, Jordan, Roll: The World the Slaves Made.* [4] Genovese documents the ways in which religion was the crucial factor in simultaneously legitimating, humanizing and destroying the institution of slavery. As a professed Marxist, Genovese needs no instruction on the conservatizing functions of religion in society. All the more remarkable is his conclusion, painfully forced by the evidence, that it was the Christian teachings about the sovereignty of God and the ontological equality of his children that enabled the slaves to imaginatively establish and develop their humanity under a fundamentally inhumane institution. The world the slaves made in the American South stands in sharp contrast to slavery in other places, such as the Caribbean and Brazil, where this dialectic between profession and practice, between hypocrisy and the virtue to which it pretended, was not allowed to operate. In short, the slaves hoisted the slaveholders on their own petard. The otherworldly commonweal which the slaveholders professed could, finally, not remain sealed off from its this-worldly antithesis.

As a Nobel Laureate *economist,* Myrdal's assertion of the primacy of politics and moral judgment over economics is the more striking. Even more striking is the witness of a Marxist to the revolutionary force of religion. Time and again in Christianity, the dehistoricized heaven that offered escape from struggle-in-time reasserts itself as the transcendent commonweal forcing judgment and change. This is reason for hope in a time such as ours when determined secularism and dehistoricized religion conspire against the covenant in order to secure the world as it is.

To speak as we have done about the nature of the democratic experiment, about the seemingly endless fumbling toward a commonweal that eludes our designs, is to many people intolerable. It is intolerable to many on the left, on the right, and in the center (wherever that may be at any given time). Some conservatives, fearful of further change, would settle for what we have, resigning themselves to a far from best of all possible worlds. Other conservatives would throw out the accumulated rubbish of modernity and return to some true and natural order. In this approach conservatism and some species of radicalism converge, as we have already seen. "And the whole congregation of the people of Israel murmured against Moses and Aaron in the wilderness, and said to them, 'Would that we had died by the hand of the Lord in the land of Egypt, when we sat by the fleshpots and ate bread to the full; for you have brought us out into this wilderness to kill this whole assembly with hunger' " (Exod. 16). And some remembered Egypt as a time of law and order when people knew their place and what would happen next. And some, for whom the economic factor was decisive, remembered it as the kingdom of freedom beyond necessity. And some, for whom the psychodrama was everything, remembered how sweet it was to dream of liberation and resented the burden of the dream's unfolding in the wilderness. Now a murmuring people grows impatient with the pilgrimage, and the democratic experiment falters.

The commonweal lies ahead of us. At best we hail it from afar. We cannot lay down our burden until the destination is reached. But we grow impatient. We should be impatient, passionately impatient, with all that impedes our progress, with every structure of faithlessness and false security that defies the arrival of the promised future. Holy impatience reaches out to what is not yet, protests every barrier to what is to be. Then there is the unholy impatience that would call off the pilgrimage, that constructs the false consciousness of the great return or invites us to hunker down in the cave of decadence to enjoy a few last laughs over the death throes of hope.

Opposed to all this is the questioning faith, the yearning confidence, the impatient patience of those who have enlisted for the duration. They know there is no definitive measure now existing that can tell us what is just or right for all time and all situations. Justice is a fragile concept, a mutual and momentary acknowledgment by parties concerned that this is probably the best that can be done for the time being. That moment of mutual acknowledgment we call peace, which is always, until the Kingdom comes, "for the time being." And that mutual acknowledgment is love. Beyond greed and fear and dread, beyond the terms of the contract or the calculus of distributive justice, it is the recognition of the other as equal before God, as fellow heir of the promise, as fellow participant in the present pathos of the Promise's struggle toward realization.

In the cave the sophisticated smirk at the grandiose sentiments of James Russell Lowell's "Once to Every Man and Nation." It is not our style. But those on pilgrimage know he has stated the better part of the truth. "By the light of burning martyrs,/ Christ, thy bleeding feet we track,/ . . . New occasions teach new duties;/ Time makes ancient good uncouth;/ . . . Though truth's portion be the scaffold/ And upon the throne be wrong,/ Yet that scaffold sways the future,/ And, behind the dim unknown,/ Standeth God within the shadow,/ Keeping watch above his own." Not above his own, however, and on the scaffold as much as in the shadow—and, contrary to Lowell, no guarantee that it is "upward and onward."

The point is simply that "new occasions teach new duties." The just society for which we hope is elusive and our search for it keeps requiring new definitions of justice. Nowhere is this more urgent than in our thinking about international justice. If indeed the United States is to be an empire for the foreseeable future, which seems more than likely, we need to think more clearly about an imperial ethic. Our notion of the transcendent commonweal must encompass the whole of humanity, not simply the American experiment. Precisely the thrust toward universality, which is so widely deplored in the American ethos, must be reappreciated. An ancient principle in Christian ethics is that the unity of humankind corresponds to the universality of the one God. Thus the idea of America being "under God" does not imply some special privileged position, but immediately places the American experiment into a network of global accountability. It is finally from this understanding of the love and judgment of this one God, this universal commonweal, that our ever provisional understandings of justice must be constructed.

In thinking through the difficult problems of international justice, this understanding of the universality of the transcendent commonweal is utterly crucial. An imperial ethic that strives toward an ever greater degree of the mutual acknowledgment that is mandated by love and is instrumental in building a network of global accountability is something quite new in human history. It might be objected that it is so different from what has been meant by "empire" in the past that we ought to abandon the language of empire altogether. The language of empire is necessary, however, precisely because it underscores both the scandal and the responsibility implicit in the fact of the American *imperium*. It is fetching to think of the United States as but one among equals in, for example, the 138-member United Nations General Assembly. It is also a fuzzy kind of thinking that evades precisely the accountability such a picture of equality would promote. There can be no equation between the historical obligations of the United States and those of Equatorial Guinea. Nor should our understanding of mutual acknowledgment and accountability be too tightly tied to relations between nation states, which are, after all, temporary artifices under the judgment of a covenant made with the people who comprise the human family, people who may or may not be well served by existing nation states.

Justice that emerges from the mutual acknowledgment implicit in love excludes the old idea of empire that would impose one model on the whole of the human family. Because of power realities in the world today, this may not seem like a very likely prospect in any case. Yet the warning against imperial imposition is always necessary, for the kaleidoscopic character of historical change may tomorrow cluster realities in a way that makes what now seems unlikely seductively attractive. Such imperial impositions are one form of what we have called premature synthesis.

Yet another premature synthesis in the quest for international justice is to be found in perennial proposals for world government. There is no doubt we must expend much more imagination and courage in devising global patterns of mutual acknowledgment (love) leading to strctures of accountability (justice) resulting in less fragile agreement (peace). In pursuing this goal, however, we must avoid the "conundrum syndrome" that afflicts so much thinking about world government. That is, we must be free of the illusion that humankind is essentially open, sharing, kind and peace-loving or that all interests really coincide—if only we can engineer the structures appropriate to the happy reality. That is not the reality within our provisional and disjointed moment in history.

Among the more winsome of President Eisenhower's statements was his declaration that "the people of the world want peace, and someday the governments will just have to get out of the way and let them have it." This happy half-truth is also dangerously seductive in its untruth. History is indeed filled with horrendous examples of governments going to war against the desires and perceived interests of their peoples. Yet even that statement must be qualified by the observation that governments do not go to war, conflicts are not settled by duels between cabinet ministers of opposing nations. It is in the ability of governments to marshal their peoples that we encounter the troubling nexus of interests between rulers and ruled that gives the lie to General Eisenhower's charming generalization.

This is not the place to discuss the perduring, and apparently increasing, power of nationalism, but it must be noted as a crucial factor in our understanding of global justice.[5] From time to time, nationalism is declared obsolete. And in view of the universal commonweal, conflictual nationalisms (as distinct from a pluralism of distinct "peoplehoods") will one day be overcome. We must live to hasten that day, but without any guarantee that ours is that day. The history of efforts to overcome nationalism are filled with irony. Thirty years ago, for example, many saw the formation of the United Nations as such an effort. Yet, constructed as it is upon relations between nation states rather than upon relations between people, the United Nations has probably boxed history more tightly into the artifice of the nation state. In the General Assembly, where a nation of 60,000 people has a vote equal to a nation of 200 million, the system seems almost designed to parody the hope for a network of global accountability. We should not denigrate the many values served by the United Nations, not least of which is its value, despite the ironic and even ludicrous, as a kind of proleptic signal of the global commonweal to which we aspire. But neither should we, conundrum-style, think that it is, either in its present form or potentially, the transcendence of conflictual nationalism.

A further irony, which we have remarked earlier, is that those who today are most critical of American nationalism seem most enthusiastic about the militant emergence of sundry nationalisms elsewhere. Biafra, the Basques, Scotland, Ireland, Bangladesh and myriad assertions of tribal identity in other places, all claim the sympathy of many people in America and Western Europe who simultaneously declare nationalism obsolete and obscene when it comes to the greater powers. We need to clear our heads in our thinking about nationalism. Disparate peoples legitimately seek political structures that will both assert and protect their peculiar interests and identities. Such pluralism must be affirmed and nurtured, both within a given nation and globally; it is part of that mutual acknowledgment which is the prerequisite to any viable understanding of justice. Whether the present plethora of nation states is the appropriate political structure for this purpose is quite another question. There seem to be no substitutes readily at hand.

The task for the immediate future is probably not that of replacing the nation state but of complementing it with a variety of regional and transnational structures. This is a process already underway, evident, for example, in the economic regionalization of producing countries in the Third World, as well as economically and politically in the European Common Market. A much more problematic manifestation of the trend is seen in the growth of multinational corporations; problematic because it seems to be moving not to a network of accountability but to a network of nonaccountability to the people affected by corporate decision-making. More hopeful—and, unfortunately, more tenuous—is what may be the growing consciousness among Christians of the church as a universal community. In this connection, institutions such as the World Council of Churches and the Vatican, weak reeds though they be, must be seen as providentially significant in the quest for the commonweal. Of all the transnational structures, the church is ultimately crucial because it speaks most explicitly of the Kingdom which is the commonweal by which all existing structures, including the church, must be kept under judgment.

In our understanding of global justice, as in our understanding of the democratic process, the great danger is the unholy impatience that leads either to despair or to the forcing of premature syntheses. In our provisional moment pluralism must be affirmed precisely for the sake of the Kingdom, in the full knowledge that pluralism implies conflict. In a time of threatening nuclear holocaust, one cannot speak lightly about the necessity of conflict. Yet it is necessary to say with Pannenberg, "Antagonisms are indispensable for bringing present forms under criticism and for pointing to new possibilities for the reordering of the human community."[6] The great task is to learn from the necessary antagonisms while keeping in check the excessive pluralism that might make such antagonisms fatal to the human enterprise itself. This check is maintained through the mutual acknowledgment that is love, the structures of accountability that are justice, and the always fragile agreement that we call peace. Admittedly, it is not a very satisfactory arrangement. That is why we hope for the Kingdom.

Unholy impatience cannot truly love the preliminary. It thinks only the ultimate is worthy of its love, and, in a sense, it is right. But if the preliminary is the ultimate in the process of becoming, we can, in courage tempered by modesty, give ourselves religiously to the present and its tasks. Modern revolutions illustrate again and again the danger of living so exclusively for the future that one is unable to cherish or celebrate the past and present. In the name of a future "new man in a new order," the values of past and present are despised and destroyed. "He who despises the preliminary because he waits for the ultimate will not be able to recognize the ultimate in its coming. . . . To be converted to the world means to be converted to the present in the hope of fulfillment."[7]

19

The Public Piety
of a Pilgrim People

The discerning reader will have noted that from the first chapter onward we have been treating facets of a subject that today is often discussed under the rubric of "American civil religion." At the start, I stated my misgivings about the term civil *religion,* and now it is time to address that question directly. In doing so, however, my purpose is not simply to argue over definitions, such disputes are usually both tedious and sterile. To a large extent, definitions are a matter of taste, you pay your money and take your choice. On a more serious level, definitions are a matter of utility, a question of which terminology best comprehends and illuminates the subject under discussion. It is my view that the terminology of civil religion both fails to comprehend the pertinent phenomena and tends to confuse. It does this to the detriment of our understanding of the public piety relevant to the American experiment, and to the detriment of our understanding of the role of particular religion, most particularly of the Judeo-Christian gospel of the Kingdom.

The mention of the last point brings us to the primary purpose in this chapter and the next, namely underscoring the tasks of particular religion, notably of the church, in criticizing and enlivening the American experiment. Civil religion, as it is called, cannot properly be studied as a thing in itself. It is symbiotically related to, and inexplicable apart from, the explicit religious traditions that give it shape and life. Here an important caveat is in order: the public piety of Americanism has been and is now tied to explicit religion in the way I suggest; it is not *necessarily* so dependent upon explicit religion. Indeed, as we shall see, there are some who advocate the development of the American civil religion as a religion in its own right. In disagreeing with such advocacy, I would assert that the prospect of a cohesive civil religion, containing, so to speak, its own transcendent points of reference, is extremely dangerous. Fortunately, I think it also quite unlikely.

With almost weary predictability, discussion of civil religion today begins with reference to Robert Bellah's "discovery" of the subject in his 1967 *Daedalus* article, "Civil Religion in America." Martin Marty says that historians "chortled" over Bellah's naiveté in thinking he had come upon virgin territory.[1] Certainly the subject, if not the use of the term, has been among the staples of all who have thought deeply about the American experiment for almost three hundred years. Amid the chortles, however, I would interject a word of appreciation to Bellah for giving the question of civil religion both new vitality and, to some extent, new shape. It often happens that historical naiveté and a certain ignorance of the larger discussion contribute to lowering the level of cognitive inhibition. Thus a much-worn topic is addressed with fresh enthusiasm and from a new angle, much to the benefit of us all. History intellectual and other—would be a dull affair if fools did not occasionally rush in. Many of us, needless to say, have a vested interest in the acceptance of this axiom. (To Bellah's great credit, he did not rush in, make a splash, and then rush out again, but has subsequently developed his argument with considerable persuasiveness, most recently in *The Broken Covenant,* to which we will be returning.)

The subject of civil religion, by whatever name, has been around for a long time, far predating the American experiment itself. Plato and Aristotle were much preoccupied with the public piety essential to the ordering of the *polis.* Thomas Aquinas, Luther and Calvin were all, in their admittedly quite different situations and with varying degrees of lucidity, well aware of the distinctive ethic appropriate to the civil or secular sphere of behavior. Perhaps more pertinent to our discussion, Rousseau (who coined the term *civil religion*), Montesquieu, Jefferson, Weber and Durkheim are among those who fretted in a more or less systematic way about the beliefs, values, intuitions and behavior patterns that make society possible. John Dewey's "common faith" has been crucial to the American discussion of the question, and, among contemporaries, Sidney Mead, John Paul Williams, Will Herberg, Gerhard Lenski and Martin Marty have all advanced the discussion, although from divergent viewpoints. Just the spate of books and articles provoked by Bellah's essay runs into a rather lengthy bibliography.[2]

It is important to keep the history of the idea in mind, lest it be thought that civil religion is but another fad. Of course it may also be a faddish topic, especially in connection with the American bicentennial, but it is much more than that. "To the academic students of religion, civil religion was an 'ideal' topic. Even more than secular cities and godless theology, civil religion made plausible the claim that religion ought to be studied by the nonreligious. Here, God be praised, was a religion that was nonreligious, to which the denominations had no claim and which ought properly to belong to departments of religion. Civil religion sent nonprofessing gurus into spasms of ecstasy (i.e., they began to write papers on the topic)."[3]

In fact what is called civil religion requires the sustained, serious and explicit attention of the best minds both within and without the churches, both within and without the academic community professionally concerned with religion. The phenomenon of public piety may be neglected for a time, but it will not go away. Until every knee shall bow before the God of biblical revelation (which, according to best reports, is not likely to be anytime soon), we shall have to attend to the halfway house of belief and morality called civil religion. If we leave it unattended, we can be sure that others are eager to take up residence and turn it toward their own dubious, even dangerous, purposes.

One, but by no means the major, difficulty in using the term civil *religion* is that theologians and others who work out of an explicit religious tradition (the particularists, if you will) have a hard time giving serious, sustained and *sympathetic* attention to a phenomenon that they must, by definition, view as hostile. That is, if civil religion is truly a religion in its own right, it cannot help but be seen as competitor to other religions—Christianity, for example. Thus Sen. Mark Hatfield, at a famous prayer breakfast in 1973, called upon the nation to repudiate the god of the American civil religion and to repledge itself to the service of the God of biblical revelation. Many people were puzzled when, almost at the same time, Senator Hatfield led a campaign to have Congress designate a day of national repentance and prayer (Sen. Barry Goldwater and others remarked that they had no objection to the prayer part but didn't see that America had done anything for which it should repent). People were puzzled because Hatfield's call for a day of repentance and prayer seemed precisely like an exercise of that civil religion he had so roundly condemned. In fact, the Senator's intuition was sound, even if his formulation of it was confused. His two apparently contradictory actions assumed a distinction between civil religion and public piety. As a false religion, Americanism must be repudiated; as the piety of a people "under God," Americanism must be purified and revitalized.

Although he comes at it from a quite different angle, Will Herberg's critique of civil religion is similar to Hatfield's. As Herberg sees it, American civil religion is nothing other than the apotheosis of the American Way of Life. It is therefore nothing less than an idolatry which must be condemned in the prophetic tradition of Judeo-Christian religion.[4] I believe the phenomenon discussed by Bellah and others can be seen as both desirable and inevitable, but so long as the claim is made that it is a religion, it cannot help but invite the misunderstanding and hostility of those who feel they already have a religion.

The problem is compounded when we consider the sensibilities of those who view themselves as nonreligious (the secularists, or universalists, as they would have it). It is difficult to enlist their serious, sustained and sympathetic attention to a phenomenon which, when called religion, cannot help but seem sectarian. Having found their fragile liberation from whatever religions they believe they have jettisoned, they are not about to choose to become embroiled in the subject again. It is good, indeed essential, to remind the secularists that they are not so secular as they think, that they are in fact, whether they know it or not, dealing all the time with questions and dynamics that are religious in character. But we risk either rejection or the suspicion that we are simply playing word games when we tell them that they are, whether they wish to be or not, listed as members in good standing of a religion discovered by Robert Bellah in 1967. If they have to belong to a religion, they might want to consider some more venerable options. Their point, however, is that they don't want to—and they don't—belong.

Rousseau, Bellah, Mead and others who insist upon using the term *religion* to describe the operative value systems of a society have been helpful in focusing attention on the clearly religious dynamics within the social order. Maybe the use of the term *religion*—eccentric and offputting though it seems to most people—was necessary to gain attention. Attention having been gained, however, (or at least the attention of some academics having been gained) I think there are compelling reasons for replacing, or at least severely limiting, the use of civil *religion* terminology.

What we have said so far deals with one strategic reason for not calling it civil religion. Conscious as I am of the promise not to engage in tedious disputes over definitions, it is nonetheless necessary to touch briefly on the varying definitions of religion. The dispute, too simply stated, is between a functional and a substantive definition of the religious phenomenon. The first approach, the functional, is perhaps best represented by Clifford Geertz and receives strong support from Thomas Luckmann (*The Invisible Religion*) and others.[5] It is the approach used also by Andrew Greeley to demonstrate that modern man is, to cite the title of one of his recent books, *Unsecular Man.* [6] In *The Sacred Canopy* (1967), Peter Berger exhibited some ambivalence between functional and substantive definitions, but in recent years he has opted more decisively for the substantive, as is most strongly implicit in his *A Rumor of Angels.* My own bias, it will come as no surprise, is clearly toward the substantive.

To put it perhaps too bluntly, the functional definitions assume that there are social and psychic dynamics that, while converging in what is commonly identified as religion, in fact pervade the whole of life in society. So far so good. But functionalists tend also to suggest, or at least to invite the inference, that the phenomenon of religion can be explained without reference to the meaning content or truth claims affirmed by particular religions. The substantive definitions argue, on the other hand, that the phenomenon of religion is associated with categories of cognition, experience and behavior that, while they have meeting points with more generalized social reality, cannot legitimately be reduced to the categories by which we analyze other social phenomena.

In one sense, then, the functionalist approach is "reductionist," leveling the particularities of religion to conform to more general models of cognition. In another sense, the functionalist definition is "expansionist," turning everything into religion. In the first case it tends toward failure, even at the scientific level, because it does not take account of the *specifics* of religious perception, experience and behavior. In the second case this definitional approach fails because it fails to define, that is, it blurs rather than illuminates the differentiations needed if we are to speak meaningfully of what is religion as distinct from being nonreligion.

The expansionist side of the functional approach is no doubt related to the factors we discussed earlier and that have made civil religion such an attractive topic for academics dealing with religion. Not only for the academics, however. Religious people of uncertain religious commitments are pleased to discover that religion—which they feared was a residual and declining factor in an inexorably secularizing world—is really what the world is about. Just as political activists are pleased to discover that "every significant question is finally a political question," and just as psychoanalysts feel more secure in the knowledge that all history can be explained in the categories of Freudianism, so the churchly ego is reinforced by the belief that, far from going out of style, his preoccupation with religion puts him right at the center of the cosmic console. The politician invariably encounters the majority of quite sensible people who believe their anxieties about truth, beauty, love, sex and death have very little to do with politics. The psychoanalyst must come to terms with the fact that the history he so brilliantly analyzes is singularly ungrateful when it comes to paying him his fees for his troubles. And the churchman discovers to his regret that the religion he promoted is, if it is indeed a religion, a quite different religion from the one he was counting upon for income. What appeared to be his expansion turns out to be his self-liquidation.

Again, we should appreciate fully the sociological and anthropological forces that shape the religious phenomenon, including Christianity. It is neither necessary nor desirable to be as "substantivist" as, for example, Karl Barth, who would remove true Christianity from the category of religion altogether. That way, as we have noted earlier, lies another kind of reductionism; in the process of "elevating" Christianity above ordinary reality, it is relegated to the realm of subjectivity. If radical functionalism represents a reductionism of intent, this represents a reductionism of result.

Christianity is fully a part of the human story, past and present, yet it witnesses to experiences and makes claims that can be neither verified nor disproven by our rules for understanding history. The same is true of Judaism, Islam and the nonbiblical religions. They all indeed represent "social constructions of reality," but because they each treat things that are at the edge or beyond our ordinary perception of reality, we can group them together as "religious" phenomena. Because they treat these things in a communal, systematic and ordered way—each claiming to have singular insight into the nature of the Other to which it witnesses—we call each a religion. In this sense, the civil religion is not, and must not be permitted to become, a religion.

Spelling out the difference between functional and substantive when it comes to defining religion is not entirely unlike trying to draw a hard line between the dynamics of being in love and loving the beloved. "Being in love" is readily susceptible to functionalist analysis. Heartbeat, attitudinal changes, the anxieties of jealousy and separation, all these can be diagnosed and charted with wondrous precision. That is far short, however, of understanding the particular case of a person in love. Such an approach arbitrarily, and conveniently, excludes the beloved. The person in love is quite stubborn in insisting that any adequate understanding of her situation must include the beloved. She does not deny that all the generalizable psychic, physical and social indicators of "being in love" are applicable to her case. It is just that her condition is inexplicable without reference to the beloved.

Admittedly, people can be in love with being in love, just as people can be very religious about religion. In that case the putative object of the love (or the putative object of religious devotion) is somewhat incidental and, presumably, exchangeable for another. But *that* there is such an object would seem to be essential to the form of the phenomenon of being in love. Even narcissistic love has an object. The social phenomenon we call religion insists, as do lovers, that the existence of the Other is not posited in order to sustain the dynamics of religion, but that the meaning of religion is to acknowledge the existence of the Other.

The study of religion that excludes the reality to which religion claims to be a response is a science bending truth to fit convenience, it is a question of tailoring the phenomenon to fit secularism's Procrustean bed. When the candles of particularity are extinguished, not only do all religions appear gray but everything looks like a religion. That is, an exclusive focus on the social dynamics of religion easily leads to calling everything religion, for indeed these dynamics do pervade the whole of human life. Obviously, if everything is religion, nothing is religion. The "invisible religion" slides into ubiquitous religion, until everything human is religion and thus all talk about religion becomes tautological. Describing the sensations attendant upon "being in love," while excluding the existence of the beloved from consideration, may lead to a definition of loving that is indistinguishable from a pharmaceutical high or being hit by a car. The parallels between these sensations are undeniable, but as a definition of loving the approach leaves something to be desired.

In his 1967 essay, Bellah insisted that civil religion functions in a way differentiated from the denominational religions and is therefore a religion in its own right. "There actually exists alongside of and rather clearly differentiated from the churches an elaborate and well institutionalized civil religion in America. . . . This religion—or perhaps better, this religious dimension—has its own seriousness and integrity and requires the same care in understanding that any other religion does." These statements represent the fundamental problem in Bellah's argument. Yes, much better to say "this religious dimension." But if we are speaking of a religious dimension, it is not like "any other religion." Christianity, Islam, Judaism and Hinduism are not religious dimensions; they are religions.

If language is to illuminate rather than obscure, to differentiate rather than confuse, it is important to know what we mean when we speak about a business corporation as distinct from a political system, education as distinct from economics, aesthetics as distinct from medicine, and the operative values of a society as distinct from "a religion." Admittedly, all of these overlap and interact in complex and sometimes imperceptible ways within the kaleidoscopic whole we call society. But even when we speak of the "politics of medicine" or the "economics of medicine," it assumes that we know the relatively discrete realities that are interacting. The idea of "an American civil religion" emerges from a too facile confusion between "the religious" and the institution we call religion. The overarching meaning system in a society may properly be termed religious, but that does not mean it is "a religion."

A religion, in the ordinary sense of the term, has a number of characteristics which, for the sake of convenience, we will list as five.[7] (It might be objected that such a discrete approach to defining religion is ethnocentric, being applicable only to modern Western societies, but that is not much of an objection since it is a modern Western society, namely, the United States, that is under discussion. In fact, I suspect the fairly discrete institutionalization of religion is characteristic of most cultures, but that need not be argued here.) First, a religion has certain cultic aspects. People get together, usually with periodic frequency, to celebrate certain events, persons and beliefs crucial to the religion's construction of reality. Second, there are recognized leadership offices invested, formally or otherwise, with sacred authority. Third, there is some explicitly defined means of participation. There is some initiation formula, some way of knowing who belongs and who does not. Fourth, there is, at least implicitly, a statement of beliefs—and usually some way of proscribing or condemning "wrong" belief. Fifth, there is an express connection between belonging to the religion and individual and corporate behavior, that is, there is a moral code. Now—and this is crucial—in a religion all five of these characteristics are institutionalized in a coherent way. At least there is a conscious effort to knit these elements together under that religion's version of the "sacred canopy," to use Peter Berger's term.

In assessing American public piety by these criteria, I conclude that it is not properly a religion. I do not deny, however, that it could become a religion. Indeed I fear precisely that prospect. As we shall see, there are some who earnestly contend for transforming American public piety into a religion. Their arguments need to be met with equal vigor by those who care deeply about America, about the Judeo-Christian tradition and, above all, about the Kingdom to which that tradition witnesses and to which, one hopes, the American experiment is instrumental.

On the cultic aspect of a religion, people such as W. Lloyd Warner have written beautifully about the civic ceremonies which celebrate Americanism. In "An American Sacred Ceremony," for example, he tells how a whole community is bound together in its observance of Memorial Day where they experience a consecrated solidarity in the face of death, which is, it should be noted, always the final test and purpose of religion.[8] Yet Warner's Memorial Day seems far removed from anything most Americans have experienced in recent years. Perhaps this means simply that a very real civil religion is in a state of disrepair and decline.

The historian Sydney Ahlstrom recently wrote, with obvious ambivalence, about the "death of patriotic piety."[9] Touching on the cultic element, he notes, "Congress demeans the patriotic tradition by transforming the national holydays into a series of long—or lost—weekends. Given the uninspiring lead of their elders, students of all ages use American flags to patch their jeans. One senses a widespread loss of faith in the nation. Flag-waving becomes the special proclivity of militant fundamentalists, racists and the law-and-order crowd. . . . We are threatened, in short, by the snapping of those bonds of loyalty and affection essential to the health of any collective enterprise."

A civil religion in decline is one way of seeing it. Another, and I think more likely analysis, is that the liturgies of Americanism were never self-contained and integral. The signals of transcendence were borrowed from other, explicitly religious, traditions that provided a transcendent content. That is, they provided not simply an amorphous feeling of "something" transcendent, but belief about the nature of, and the experience of communion with, the transcendent. During most of American history, the churches have been a ready lender of the signals of transcendence. In the last decade or so they have become much more self-conscious and cautious about their lending policies. This does not mean they have been seized by a fit of prophetic courage over against the general culture. It does mean they have become somewhat more jealous of the symbols they can still call theirs, and somewhat more reluctant to see them debased. More than his description would suggest, I suspect Warner's Memorial Day observance depended upon the churches' easy lending policies.

This approach is supported, I believe, by the logic and consequences of recent court decisions that have increasingly excluded particularist religion from the public realm. Following a rational calculus and the logic of precedents which merely compound mistakes, and acting in indifference to the traditions and intimations of the community law is intended to serve, the Supreme Court in particular has increasingly constricted the expression of particular religious belief in our public life. Brand-name religions being forbidden, the public voice stammers and stutters in search of some nonsectarian "religion of the Republic" or else, and this more frequently, settles into a benumbed and benumbing secularism.

The cultic celebrations that were thought to belong to the civil religion will not return until the nation's credit rating is much improved. For most Americans, the signals of transcendence do not belong to America; they are discovered, nurtured and celebrated elsewhere—primarily, but not only, in particular religious traditions. Franklin, Jefferson and others thought "the sects" useful for inculcating morality, but expected their sectarian peculiarities to gradually fade away as they merged in service to the great enterprise that is the nation. But patriotic piety is not self-sustaining. Its cultic celebration will probably continue to be lost in long weekends until two quite possible developments converge; first, the moral estimate of American public purpose and practice dramatically improves, and, second, the churches reassert with greater historical earnestness the gospel of the Kingdom from which America and all human enterprises derive their religious significance. Here again, a caveat: patriotic piety is not now self-sustaining; it could become self-sustaining through national self-apotheosis. The political term for that is totalitarianism; the theological term is idolatry.

As for the second characteristic of a religion, that it has leadership offices invested with sacred authority, the question has been subjected to extensive debate, especially as it touches on the office of the presidency.[10] There is no doubt that there has frequently been, to use Bellah's phrase, "a religious dimension" in popular reverence for the presidency. To the dismay of Richard Nixon most recently, however, it is equally obvious that mainstream public piety places severe strictures upon appeals to the sacredness of office. The night the House Judiciary Committee voted impeachment, while Nixon was still president, a news commentator, well known for his hostility to Nixon, announced with tears in his eyes and quavering voice, "Now it is done, the fatal step has been taken and no one knows where it will end." Intimations of parricide! There is no evidence that many Americans are suffering from guilt qualms about having killed the king. Nor can it be said that guilt qualms are outweighed by the enormity of Nixon's crimes. Most Americans, I suspect, saw him as being guilty not of "high crimes and misdemeanors" but of low and, most inexcusably, stupid crimes. They were less offended by the secret bombing of Cambodia, with its destruction of thousands of lives, than by his cheating on his income taxes. Upon his removal from office, pundits manned the seismology stations to record the earthquake in the national psyche. Most Americans were content to observe that the whole thing at least proves the system works, and then went on to attend to business they considered more important. The presidential transition was less trauma than entertainment.

The notion of the sacredness of the presidency seems in large part the peculiar preoccupation of certain intellectuals and of media people living in Washington where they breathe air polluted by presidential power. Of course the presidency has at times possessed intimations of the sacred, and those intimations could someday be institutionalized, as in a real religion. Fortunately, that seems unlikely. If there be a sacred office in American society, it is more likely the Supreme Court. No president, no Congress, only the Court dare speak and declare its word to be "the law of the land." Only the Court is presumed to be "above politics," that is, above the opinions, deliberations and desires of a sovereign people. In the Court's pronouncements, and in writing about the Court, one encounters suggestions of self-transcendence, the notion that the transcendent is somehow institutionalized within its very being.

Fortunately for democracy, the sacredness of the oracle is diffused among nine people. More problematic, that sacredness may be increasingly jeopardized if the Court continues to move in a direction indifferent or even hostile to the beliefs, traditions and natural communities of most Americans. A severe testing of popular reverence for the Court is not to be welcomed. Under the banner of "strict constructionism," the Nixon years witnessed a shifting toward a more politically accountable Court. We may deplore some of the policy directions resulting from this shift, but we can at the same time applaud the move away from the notion that the Court is "above politics." To be above the wheeling and dealing of everyday partisan politics is of course essential. But only because the Court is then freed, in conversation with tradition as reflected in law and in conversation with the aspirations of a sovereign people, to contemplate the commonweal to which the American experiment is ultimately accountable. A Court that would be, in the most literal sense of the phrase, "above politics" would qualify as the institutionalized sacred office that might make American public piety truly a civil religion.

The third characteristic of a religion is that it has some way of defining grounds of membership. Here distinctions are somewhat more difficult and we must merely note some problems without resolving them or even pointing with any degree of certainty to a resolution. Who "belongs" to the American civil religion? Everyone who is legally an American, perhaps. Or maybe just those who espouse the "democratic faith" that is at the heart of the American civil religion, in which case non-Americans may be considered members in good standing, thus signaling the global and ecumenical character of the American civil religion that some of its proponents espouse.

Many blacks, Indian Americans and spokesmen for the rapidly growing Hispanic communities insist that the so-called American civil religion is a distinctly WASP phenomenon and has nothing to do with them. In addition, studies show that there are vast regional differences among American whites in the observance of the civil religion, with Southerners being quite devout and the West Coast almost pagan.[11] Even in the South, where Christianity most generously lends out its symbols of transcendence, most Christians would no doubt be confused or even scandalized by the suggestion that they belong to an American civil religion. That they are Americans and that they are Christians, they would readily agree. They may also be confident that the two identities fit together marvelously well. But they would almost certainly insist that what they mean by "God" is derived from the Christian part of the marriage; Americanism is a matter of being a good Christian, and only in a much more tenuous sense is Christianity a matter of being a good American. In everyday fact, unfortunately, they may see no need to make such sharp distinctions. But forced to make a choice, it is doubtful they would sign up with an American civil religion. Again, this is how things seem to be at present. If those who would transform American public piety into a coherent religion have their way, the South might be the first region in which we would witness the emergence of an American equivalent to the "German Christian" of another time and place.

Relevant to the question of who "belongs," students of comparative religion sometimes make the distinction between religions of adhesion and religions of decision. In the Roman Empire, for example, it seems that one patronized local gods much as one patronized the local cuisine. It was not necessary to fret about conflicting loyalties or belief systems, as we moderns do, because the gods adhered to the place or people where one was; offering them religious service was an essential gesture of civic good will. A similar approach is evident in Rousseau's attitude toward civil religion. Let a thousand gods blossom, so long as none of their cults interferes with the overarching devotion to the State. Christianity disrupted this comfortable doctrine with its stubborn exclusivism resulting from belief in the universality of the God of Abraham, Isaac and Jesus. Another consequence, following the Reformation, was Christianity's coming down solidly on the side of being a religion of decision. Nowhere was this development, with its resulting emphasis upon voluntarism, more evident than in North America.

To be sure, there are still ambiguities. The early Puritans resolved (perhaps by fudging) the issue of membership-by-decision with a "half-way covenant" that embraced those who had not yet demonstrated their right to "belong." Still today a debate goes on, regenerated by Karl Barth, about the legitimacy of infant baptism. But, it is important to note, these questions about the role of individual decision deal with membership in an acknowledged religion, namely the Christian church. They pose questions about whether one can belong in the fullest sense to the church without deliberate decision. The questions are a far, far way from whether one can belong to an American civil religion simply by virtue of being a citizen. If Christians, who nominally at least comprise the great majority of Americans, are uneasy about compromising membership-by-decision in what they acknowledge as a religion, they will have no truck whatsoever with membership-by-adhesion in an academically contrived civil religion which they do not acknowledge as a religion, if indeed they have ever heard of it.

Of one thing most Americans are certain: religion is a matter of personal belief. You believe *in* Methodism and, less clearly, you believe *that* what Methodism represents is right. I say "less clearly" because of course many Christians are not at all sure what their churches teach but want to be confident that they do indeed teach something in which they can have at least the implicit faith represented by institutional joining. The question of belief and its connection with membership overlaps into the fourth characteristic of a religion, the delineation of beliefs and some way of defining "wrong" beliefs. On this point Wilson Carey McWilliams has usefully noted that "belonging" in America is carefully separated from anything one may believe. Despite all the talk about an "American creed," new citizens, for example, are not asked to subscribe to any articles of faith nor, in all likelihood, even informed that a creed exists.

"American politics has eschewed any claim to control more than external behavior; the 'oaths' which it has imposed on newcomers and themselves have not been concerned with doctrinal orthodoxy—one is not required to swear by the Declaration or *The Federalist*—but with obedience to law and the rejection of force, violence, or other unlawful means.''[12]

John Wilson of Princeton writes that those who claim there is a belief system at the heart of the American civil religion are inordinately dependent upon the Declaration of Independence and the public statements of Abraham Lincoln.[13] As many surveys have indicated, a majority of Americans are ignorant of the contents of the nation's "founding documents" and many, when confronted by the provisions of the Bill of Rights, for example, reject them as subversively un-American. If, says Wilson, the presidency is really the sacred office through which the faith is proclaimed and interpreted, one would expect to find, if not many Lincolns, at least many presidents trying to do what Lincoln did. In fact, he reports, a careful search of presidential papers reveals that Lincoln stands almost alone. "The [Lincoln] legacy stands alone as a remarkable monument to a tortured soul. . . . Such transcendent reflection upon the meaning of this national experiment is absent from [his successors'] formal and informal declarations. The present incumbent [Richard Nixon] is far more typical than Lincoln in the quality and depth of religious reflection he exhibits. . . . *Ad hoc* God allusions simply do not constitute a theology; there must be some consistent exploration of relevant issues in such a way that a frame of reference oriented to the deity or to the fundamental premises of a culture . . . has a logical status or plays an effective and shaping role.''[14]

Nothing said here should be taken as denying or belittling the importance Americans place upon "belonging" in America. It is simply that neither in their own consciousness nor by a useful definition of religion is it a matter of belonging to a religion. The story is told of a frightened citizen who, rescued from a lynch mob, protested: "I didn't say I was against the Monroe Doctrine; I love the Monroe Doctrine, I would die for the Monroe Doctrine. I merely said I didn't know what it was.''[15] That, I suspect, is a fairly accurate reflection of the place of a belief system in the American civil religion.

The fifth characteristic mentioned is that of influence upon behavior, the degree to which a moral code is articulated, if not observed. As we have seen, the legal definition of belonging is limited to purely negative or proscriptive conditions. It is enough to agree not to blow the place up once one has gained admission. There is no doubt, however, that there is a positive morality attached to the American Way of Life. Generosity, sympathy for the underdog, a sense of fairness and tolerance are all generally agreed to be American virtues. Whatever religious legitimation such virtues receive, however, would seem to be derived from being a "good Christian." As we have noted, the two are indistinguishable in the minds of many Americans. Some years ago, during a debate in the United Nations General Assembly, the U.S. delegate allegedly urged the Arab and Israeli representatives to sit down and settle their differences peaceably "like Christian gentlemen." As gauche as that was, it is inconceivable that he would have urged them to settle their differences "like American gentlemen." Moral content though there be in the American Way of Life, the touchstone of morality is discovered in particularistic religion which is—increasingly, in the minds of thoughtful Americans—distinguishable from the American Way of Life.

We have now dealt at some length with the question of whether whatever we are talking about is a religion. I have argued that, for reasons strategic and conceptual, it should not be called a religion. Everyone agrees on the reality of the "whatever we are talking about"; namely, there is in American society a vague but real cluster of symbols, values, hopes and intimations of the transcendent which overarch our common life. As Emile Durkheim most brilliantly underscored, this is true of all viable societies. But perhaps it is more true of America, not least because the polyglot character of America required the articulation of commonalities that could not be taken for granted. In America "peoplehood" is not a given but an ongoing experiment in the social construction of reality.

Russell Richey and Donald Jones suggest that the "whatever we are talking about" has received at least five discrete interpretations in the current discussion of civil religion.[16] For some, such as Will Herberg, the "whatever" is best understood as "folk religion." For others, notably Sidney Mead, it is the "transcendent universal religion of the nation." For yet others, it is a question of "religious nationalism." J. Paul Williams, to whom we shall return, is in the forefront of those who see it as the "democratic faith." Finally, there are those who view it as a more ethnocentric "Protestant civic piety."

The "whatever" under discussion is, I believe, best described as American public piety. James Sellers has made a persuasive case for terming it "public ethics," but "ethics" seems both too academic and too limited to moral behavior.[17] We are dealing with a reality that is both popular and inclusive of religious dynamics and sensibilities beyond moral behavior. "Public faith" is a possibility, except it focuses on the belief system, precisely where the civil religion is weakest. Perhaps "public virtue," but it is, again, too narrowly focused on moral behavior and has, in any case, associations with the "Republican virtue" of ancient Rome that do not take into account the covenantal imagery associated with the other great model in America's historical self-understanding, namely, Israel in the wilderness. We might follow Ahlstrom in terming the phenomenon "patriotic piety," except patriotism has, at least at present, very confusing connotations and is also easily misunderstood as a subjective disposition. "Public piety" underscores the fact that we are dealing with the symbols and values that are manifest and operative in the public realm. That "piety" may strike many as weak or even pusillanimous is an admitted disadvantage. The word is perhaps partially rehabilitated by pointing out that its roots are in "duty," "reverence" and "sensibility to the sacred"—in short, it suggests all those things that the "whatever we are talking about" is all about.

Throughout this chapter we have alluded to those who would transform the American public piety into an American civil religion, in the fullest sense of the latter term. In the next chapter we will examine that proposal and suggest the appropriate response by particularist religion, notably by the churches, to its challenge.

20

American Dream, Church's Agenda

President Eisenhower is frequently quoted to the effect that our society is founded on a deeply felt religious faith, "and I don't care what faith it is." The remark is usually submitted in evidence of the utter banality of the man's mind. I hold no brief for Eisenhower's character or intellect, but suggest that, perhaps unconsciously, he reflected an understanding that is indeed at the heart of the American social experiment: it is not the business of the State overtly to define the "religious faith" upon which the experiment is founded.

At the same time, the State has a very real interest in nurturing the religious institutions from which such definitions emerge. No society, including American society, can survive without a community of values. Common assumptions, frequently unreflected, sustain the web of obligations, promise keeping and intuitions about the difference between baseness and nobility without which life in society is intolerable. Whatever the sources of this web of civility—whether divine revelation, Kantian imperatives or Skinnerian conditioning—it is both real and indispensable.

There are those who urge, however, that the American religion is too important to be left to the religious. It should not be viewed as a derivative phenomenon, shaped willy-nilly by sundry and socially irresponsible forces that are as often as not little more than, God forbid, sectarian. The state must step in to direct and nurture the faith essential to the great enterprise that is the nation. J. Paul Williams is perhaps the most forthright advocate of this viewpoint: "Americans must come to look upon the democratic ideal (not necessarily the practice of it) as the Will of God, or, if they please, of Nature. . . . Americans must be brought to the conviction that democracy is the very Law of Life. . . . The state must be brought into the picture; governmental agencies must teach the democratic idea *as religion*. . . . Primary responsibility for teaching democracy as religion must be given to the public schools."[1]

Speaking with authority in the academic community, Sidney E. Mead has moved steadily toward an endorsement of Williams' proposal. Taking off from G. K. Chesterton's observation that America is "a nation with the soul of a church," Mead has exhibited "monistic hungers and a cosmic grasp" (Marty) in his running battle against Christianity and Judaism as dysfunctional sects forever retarding the full flowering of the common religion America has in fact produced. What others call pluralism, Mead sees as a confusion of tongues, a defensive and disruptive sectarianism that can only delay the march of one people with common purpose in the company of the cloud by day and the pillar of fire by night which is the "religion of the Republic."

The approach advocated by Williams and largely supported by Mead and others is deserving of serious consideration. As the previous chapter emphasized, our disagreement with them is not because we have any less an appreciation of the religious dimensions of public life. Indeed we have previously suggested, in a way that sounds strikingly similar to Williams, that democracy should be viewed as an absolute value. An absolute value is not unlike "the Will of God." In Christian thought, however, even a so-called absolute value is never self-contained, it is contingent upon *the* absolute which is the Power of the Future. Democracy should be inculcated with religious seriousness *for the Kingdom's sake.*

The promise of the Kingdom is nurtured and proclaimed by a particular religion, Christianity. Judaism has its own theological warrants for its hope for the identical messianic age. What warrants would a presumably nonsectarian state develop for saying democracy is the will of God? What "reason" would be given "for the hope that is within us"? Theoretically at least, the state could adopt the theological warrants of Judaism and Christianity. Certainly there are many Christians who would welcome the restoration of a "Christian government ruling a Christian America." But that is hardly what enthusiasts of the Enlightenment, such as Mead, could have in mind. Or the state could inculcate democracy by the authority of Reason, with supporting evidence that it is the most utilitarian of all forms of society and government. But any number can play the game of reason, undermining the foundation of democracy as religion, as the will of God.

It would seem that the only way the state could teach democracy as religion would be by assertion of its own authority. That is, the state would have to present itself as being self-transcendent, as containing within itself the highest court of appeal. And, of course, such a state teaching democracy as religion would be the death of democracy.

Democracy is the process of keeping options open, of opening ever new options, so the present can be brought under the judgment and healing of the future. The state should inculcate and encourage the democratic process. It should even be stated in the public realm that democracy is, as Williams would have it, the will of God or of Nature. Here "God," or "Nature," or "Providence" are signals pointing toward the commonweal to which the society must always be held accountable. But the state must not attempt to fill in the content of these signal terms, that is, the state must not develop an official theology. This does not mean these terms represent an "empty transcendence," that they are without content.[2] The content of these terms is shaped and nurtured within the myriad traditions of the people, notably within the particularist religions.

The State's business, the business of public policy, is always in pursuit of the intimations of transcendence experienced by a living and believing people. It is precisely the diversity and "dysfunctionality" of the people's beliefs that keep the state modest and make democracy possible. Confronted by such dysfunctionality, the state can attempt to take matters in hand and merge the many into one, officially promoting Dewey's "common faith" or Williams' "democratic faith" or Mead's "religion of the Republic." Or the State, weary of pluralism's conversation, can declare it a hopeless cacophany and resign itself to secularism, refusing to discuss the transcendent commonweal altogether. The latter is the direction that American public life appears to be taking, at least formally. The irony, however—and this we discussed in detail earlier—is that it is impossible to eliminate the religious dimensions from public life and decision making. To choose secularism, therefore, means that essentially religious issues will be treated unreflectively, refusing to recognize them for what they are. The result is a kind of Tinker Toy common faith contrived by *ad hoc* expediency and possessing neither dignity nor coherence nor plausibility. This is, to a distressing extent, what we have at present.

The real choice, I believe, is between Williams' proposal, on the one hand, and a society of democratic pluralism publicly committed to a transcendent commonweal, on the other. Williams' proposal that the state promulgate an official theology of democracy would, I believe, be the end of democracy. The alternative, the public pursuit of the pluralistic intimations of the transcendent, requires, as we have already noted, enormous patience. It is a process that can be ended by the death of democracy but should not be until the Kingdom comes in its fulness. It requires the courage to decline all premature syntheses, including that of an official religion of the Republic.

To speak of democratic society as an ongoing conversation seems to some excessively genteel and tepid. And of course the criticism would be valid if we thought of the conversation as a group of gentlemen in their club discussing public policy over sherry. This is hardly the image appropriate to the kind of democracy America is in part and aspires to be. It assumes the contest of countervailing interests; it is brawny, rough edged and, in the eyes of many, vulgar. It involves frequent confrontation to challenge the prevailing rules by which the conversation is conducted.

Such confrontation, sometimes in the form of civil disobedience or even violence, comes from those groups who, from time to time, feel themselves excluded from the conversation. Confrontation is within the limits of the democratic conversation, however, as long as it aims not at terminating the conversation but at transforming it, usually by expanding the number of participants.

For the democratic conversation to be sustained, however, it must ordinarily be conducted through institutionalized channels. Electoral politics is one such channel. For understandable reasons, that channel is in poor repute in the post-Watergate era. Even under more usual circumstances, most Americans witness it only in the campaigning of politicians hustling for votes where it seems like a dismal level of conversation indeed, filled with bombast, image trickery and unimaginative prevarication. Yet in the halls and offices of Congress, some state legislatures and government bureaucracies, the conversation goes on. Often it is no more elevated than the discussion of trade-offs in power and patronage. As it is said in one Brooklyn clubhouse, "Ours is not to reason why. Ours is but to slice the pie." But with a frequency that may surprise the cynical, the question, "Why?" is asked. It even happens that the commonweal is invoked as politicians inquire about the kind of society for which we hope. Too often they set aside such weighty matters too soon, despairing of the resources in the public piety that might sustain real change, for they know that finally they do not generate that public piety but can at best direct it toward specific policy.

There are other institutions that participate strongly in the conversation. The courts are instrumental in defining the rules of the conversation, putatively by reference to the sacred writ of the Constitution, but frequently by philosophical judgment, in which they too often deal with questions of philosophy as though they were fixing rear-axle bearings. The universities guard one version of the American faith by distinctions between the scientific and irrational that are becoming increasingly implausible. The medical profession, notably psychiatry, delineates right and wrong in terms of sickness and health. Big business and big labor carry inestimable clout. Both are increasingly dependent upon the public policy they understandably seek to control. Neither has transcended the goal stated by Sam Gompers many years ago; when asked about the final purpose of the union movement, he promptly replied, "More!" Thus one could go on listing the participants in the conversation. For reasons of their own traditions, conceptual limitations or structural self-interest, none of these institutional participants can effectively address itself to filling in the content of the transcendent commonweal it may occasionally intuit. Who then is left?

If culture is the motor force of history, and if religion is the motor force of culture, the responsibility of the institutions of religion is magnified. Lest religious types become excessively enamored of their real or potential influence in the democratic conversation, as has happened in the past, one hastens to add that such influence is not the primary focus but a consequence of institutionalized religion's mission. The mission is one of witness and service, the result is that of societal effectiveness and influence. When this priority is reversed, we end up with the spectacle of religious leaders claiming to speak for many millions on issues of public policy when the decision makers to whom they speak know perfectly well the leaders represent little more than the opinion of a coterie of social-action bureaucrats housed in a certain ecumenical center in New York City.

This being said, the fact remains that the religious institutions are the only ones permitted and expected to define religious values *qua* religious values. In the shaping of public piety, theirs is a singular role in filling in the whys and wherefores and warrants for what otherwise remains an empty transcendence. Williams, Mead and others are right in recognizing that the operative values in our society are presently in a bad way, indeed that the process of delegitimation has gone so far as to throw into question the authority of the whole American experiment, without which authority power degenerates into mere force. But the proposal to develop a legitimating "religion of the Republic" is, whatever else might be said for it, politically unlikely. The more overt such an effort became, the more relentlessly it would be resisted by the churches, which remain the largest network of voluntary association in the society. Challenged in this way, the churches might become more jealous of their singular social role to which they have too often been indifferent in the past. Apart from such resistance, which could irretrievably divide the society, it seems unlikely that the courts, the university and other institutions could collaborate in articulating officially the faith essential to a civil religion in the full sense of the latter term.

The churches, including of course the synagogues and other institutions of religion, will remain the socially legitimated centers for the articulation and celebration of the religious faith which is the source of America's public piety. Although I am not sanguine, I am not as pessimistic as some about the churches' fulfilling this role more energetically and creatively than they are at present. The churches have long since come to an accommodation between Christian "covenant theology" and the imperatives of the Enlightenment; an accommodation resulting most notably in the now secure acceptance of toleration and pluralism. The "halfway covenant" devised to serve a Christian society has been extended to the whole of the American experiment, which is no longer certain it is a *Christian* experiment in even the most tenuous sense of the term. Indeed, for their own sake as well as the society's, the churches no longer yearn for a "Christian America," except, of course, in the sense that most Americans be Christians.

Pluralism, tolerance and voluntarism have all been more firmly secured by the breaking of the WASP religious hegemony. This is in part the result of the emerging influence of the immigrant churches of the last century, such as the Lutheran and, most notably, the Roman Catholic. Also Jewish communal life has in recent years moved dramatically toward a more explicitly religious identification, combined with the keenest vested interest in the strengthening of religious pluralism. A growing number of Jewish thinkers are beginning to believe it may have been a mistake to think Jews were safest in a secular milieu. A completely secularized society is one in which there are no ultimate sanctions against evil, including the evil of anti-Semitism.

When speaking of the legitimating power of the churches, one is well aware of the prophecies of secularization that have dominated religious thinking in recent years. One notes that J. Paul Williams is in the company of Rousseau, Franklin, Jefferson and a host of others in asserting that the "sects" are fast disappearing. There is every reason but the evidence on the side of that argument. We are surrounded by signs of religious revival, forcing us to rethink most of our assumptions about the link between modernization and secularization. It may be that modern, technological society, with all its painful differentiations of persons and roles, greatly increases the need for a place in which people "can get it all together." That place, among others, is religion. And, despite flirtations with Eastern mysteries and the "new polytheism," I suspect the Judeo-Christian tradition is so firmly established that that place will be, with varying degrees of centeredness, in the churches.

Writing on "The Birth of New American Myths," Robert Bellah suggests that the Eastern mysteries might complement, or even replace, the Judeo-Christian tradition.[3] Of course that is quite possible. In a typically functionalist manner, however, Bellah fails to consider what the content, the cognitive substance, of such religions would mean for the American experiment. In both its contractual and covenantal themes, the American experiment is inextricably tied to Western notions of rationality and historical purposefulness. The religious, ontological, if you will, legitimation of these notions is derived from the Judeo-Christian tradition. This tradition affirms in a unique way that our notion of reason's power to explore the order (and disorder) of the universe and our notion of history as linear and purposefully moving toward a *telos* are not illusions but reflections of ultimate reality. These notions cannot be sustained by Eastern religions which assume the illusory character of what we call reality. The American experiment may be in need of new religious myths, but not just any religious myths will do.[4]

The continued strength of institutional religion is not necessarily good news for the revitalization of public piety. There might be a withdrawal on the part of the churches from the culture-forming tasks. Such a withdrawal has marked revivalistic "evangelical" Christianity at least since Billy Sunday. Conversely, there may be abject abdication to prevailing cultural or counter-cultural moods. In this connection, Will Herberg's railings against the worship of the Great American Way of Life will remain pertinent. Another formula for disaster is contained in a recent article in one of the country's leading liberal Protestant journals, where it is argued that the only future for the institutional church lies in its "embracing every manifestation of higher consciousness [in order to] adopt and adapt the search for alternative life styles."

The church needs rather an imaginative reappropriation of its own tradition, a theological recovery of nerve, a new confidence in the distinctiveness of its own truth claims, a new courage to live in dialectic with the larger culture, an unembarrassed readiness to affirm the scandal of its particularity. Only such a church can "save its own soul." Only such a church can contribute significantly to renewing and reshaping the public piety.

While resisting both secularism and the establishment of a civil religion, the churches must note, analyze and expose the religious dynamics at work within our public life. One very honorable model was the churches' role in the civil rights struggle of the fifties and part of the sixties. The churches theologically legitimated the civil-religious assumptions that, within ten years, dismantled a century of legal Jim Crowism and restarted the nation on the way toward racial equality. It is a course that will not, I think, be turned back, although, with equal certainty, it has not advanced fast enough.

Similarly, the churches were crucial in exposing and discrediting the civil-religious assumptions designed to legitimate America's disastrous venture in Indochina. In the case of civil rights, the churches' role was one of positive legitimation; in the case of Vietnam, of negative delegitimation. While only a minority of religious leadership was actively opposing the war, religious legitimations were, for the most part, effectively withdrawn in a way perhaps unprecedented in American history. To be sure, Cardinal Spellman one Christmas assured U.S. soldiers they were fighting Christ's battle. More important, the Cardinal and his aides were immediately on the defensive and strove, unsuccessfully, to make the remark "inoperative," as they used to say in the Nixon era.

Identifying the nation's war with divine purpose would, during wars past, have been considered by most Americans to be unexceptionable, perhaps even mandatory. Billy Graham, consciously or otherwise, signaled his support of the war by his close and uncritical association with those in charge of it. But he consistently declared his neutrality on the moral issues involved, if indeed, he implied, there were moral issues involved. ("I am a New Testament evangelist, not an Old Testament prophet.") Such a declaration of neutrality by such a bellwether of public piety was, to say the least, extraordinary. In addition, Mr. Graham's public statements show that he well knew his "neutrality" was most virulently under attack not from those who wanted him to endorse the war effort but from those who wanted him to condemn it. Some church bodies did formally condemn the war. More important, supporters of the war in most churches considered it a victory if they could obtain their church's silence on the war.

Even in these two efforts—civil rights and the Vietnam war—there are those who say the churches were more influenced by than influential upon the general culture. The churches, it is alleged, simply jumped on moving bandwagons to demonstrate their relevance. Obviously, there is no easy answer to the question of who influences whom. Religious leadership is as agile in jumping bandwagons as is any other group. But any effort to belittle the role of the churches in these two instances of shaping public piety is, I believe, a gross distortion of history. Only those familiar with these movements can know the courage and tenaciousness with which a minority of American religion pressed the issues before they were joined by mass movements. Without romanticizing the role of organized religion, both the civil rights movement and the antiwar movement are inexplicable without the sanctioning power of institutional religion—in the first case a positive sanction, in the second a negative.

This is not to say that religion was the only or even most important factor. The Brown decision of 1954, the person of Martin King, the student rebellion, President Johnson's mendacity and a host of other factors make up the story. But in every telling of the story, we get to that point where people did not feel uncomfortable when they declared in public that a policy was moral or immoral. It would not have been possible to make the explicitly moral argument part of the everyday, taken-for-granted discourse without reinforcement from those religious institutions that are widely perceived as the specialists in morality. No doubt the moral argument frequently degenerates into moralism and self-righteousness. No doubt the theologically literate are uncomfortable with the idea of the churches as society's custodian of morality. That, however, is one of the inevitable burdens and embarrassments of being a religion. In any case, whether the churches' role in civil rights and Vietnam demonstrate the "residual" or "emerging" power of religion depends as much upon the strategy and confidence of religious leadership as it does upon any allegedly inexorable tides of secularization.

Curiously, it was also during the sixties that American religion seemed to be happily and mindlessly jettisoning its distinctive heritage and celebrating its loss of confidence as a sign of renewal. The phenomenon reached bizarre proportions in solemn reports about the death of God, but that was merely one of many successes perpetrated by religious leaders eager to persuade the general culture that traditional religion was finished. Here one speaks more specifically of what is called mainline Protestantism, the approved curator of public piety. Among Roman Catholics, something genuinely new and shaking had happened. John XXIII and Vatican II raised questions long forbidden and encouraged thinking about what had been previously unthinkable. But what occasioned the shaking of the foundations among mainline Protestants? Certainly there was no new intellectual breakthrough that compelled the abandonment of religious affirmation. There was little or nothing in "religionless Christianity" (which, as it was vulgarized, should not be blamed on Dietrich Bonhoeffer), or in "secular Christianity," or in "the death of God" that went beyond David Strauss, Feuerbach and Nietzsche.

Perhaps the loss of religious nerve was in part a delayed reaction to the superficiality of the religious boom of the 1950s. So much soothing invited some shocking. In book publishing—and therefore to some extent in the marketing of ideas—there is usually a gap of several years. Those who in 1961 were writing their blasts of the complacency of the Eisenhower era could not anticipate that a few years later America would feel itself gripped by crisis. Others no doubt saw the beginning of radical change and mistook it for the coming of the Kingdom. Two contradictory perceptions of reality emerged, but they led to a similar result.

Some saw the "secular city" replacing religion as the sign and instrument of the Kingdom's coming. Others, caring more about institutional religion, saw the religious boom of the 1950s and its social clout in the early years of the civil rights movement and assumed religion was strong enough to withstand some candor. Thus we were blessed with a spate of books under the generic title "Everything You Never Believed About Christianity But Were Afraid To Say So." Nineteenth-century unbelief could come out of the closet, so to speak. There was no more reason to be weighed down by "the baggage" accumulated over the centuries. Institutional religion seemed strong enough to make it on its own, reinforced by its demonstrated social utility, without the props of inherited hypocrisies. (As late as 1967, Clergy and Laity Concerned about Vietnam, then numbering about thirty-thousand people in loose association, seriously considered reconstituting itself as a denomination, bound by the creed and koinonia of "the Movement.")

Then too, there is something of the suicidal in all of us, and among Christians this is frequently confused with bearing the cross, the central symbol of life through death. There was much talk during those years of

the need for the institution to die. There emerged a theological legitimation for what sociologist Anton Zijderveld described as "the anti-institu-
tional mood" in his book *The Abstract Society*.⁵ To be sure, there were
welcome instances of a willingness to take instituional risks, as in
ministry in the inner city or in speaking out for unpopular causes. But,
more often than not, there was a determined effort to be liberated from
institutions, a belief that institutions were *qua* institutions false, alienating
and antithetical to the gospel of freedom.

Perhaps we will never have a satisfying explanation of the passion for
self-liquidation by which American religion, especially the more cultural
potent sectors of Protestantism, was seized in the 1960s. Nor can we
unequivocally condemn what happened. It may be that, in some way we
do not understand, the loss of religious nerve was symbiotically related
to the assertion of social concern. Some students of the subject suggest
there is indeed a trade-off between religious confidence and social concern. This is the argument at least strongly implied in the work of Dean
Kelley *(Why Conservative Churches Are Growing)* to which we referred
earlier. The historical evidence suggests such a trade-off is not necessary.
There are numerous instances, in America and elsewhere, where intense
religious and institutional revival was accompanied by renewed potency
in the formation of culture. If we are concerned both for the vitality of
religious particularism and for the shaping of public piety, such evidence
is reinforced by our hope and determination.

If our hopes are to be realized, the institutional life of the church must
be invested with theological respectability. This does not mean we should
"theologize" existing ecclesial polities, attributing to them a degree of
absoluteness. Nor does it mean the church should hold back on controversial issues in order not to alienate its constituency. It does mean it is not
only respectable but necessary to be concerned about the health of the
religious institution as such. It does mean a new degree of accountability
in conversation with the actual membership of the believing community
which is, after all, the church.

In discussing the threat of an established civil religion, Herbert Richardson underscores the importance of "institutionalized ecclesiastical religion."⁶ "If Christian groups are only voluntary associations within a
state, then they leave unchallenged the pretense of the state to possess
the authority to order all society. . . . The church affirms, rather, that it
has been established by God and invested with a general competence with
respect to the highest ends of all life. For this reason it rejects the notion
that the state possesses a general authority, and questions not merely the
decrees of the state, but its *right* to decree. This is how the existence of
the church limits the state's claims for itself."

Richardson may be only slightly alarmist in seeing parallels between the "German Christianity" nurtured by the Third Reich and proposals that the U.S. government should sponsor an official civil religion. But he is certainly correct in arguing that the check on this possibility must be firmly institutionalized. "It is *institutionalized ecclesiastical religion* that is the real limitation on the state's claim to a general sovereignty over society, not mere individual beliefs. The Nazi state tolerated, even encouraged, 'freedom of religion.' It allowed every individual to believe what he wished as long as that belief did not seek an institutional expression that might interfere with the state's ordering of time and space. In fact, in modern states it is frequently suggested that such individualistic religious beliefs are superior to institutional religion, that somehow it is only the unperceptive who express their beliefs through loyalty to a church."

Richardson and others have noted that the Nazis, while countering Christian belief with their own mythology, concentrated their efforts on weakening institutional loyalty to the church. In education, publishing, youth work and myriad other fields the state restricted the church's activities, while all the time insisting the church was perfectly free to pursue its "purely spiritual" work. The same of course is now in large part true of those societies under the domination of the Russian empire. It is not panic mongering but prudence that observes that these specters cannot be entirely exorcised from our own thinking about our society. We dare not be complacent when, for example, and as is presently the case, the Internal Revenue Service presumes to define what is "religious activity" and therefore tax exempt.[7]

The oddity of the American situation is that, if the state ever does seek to impose an official civil religion, it will discover that presumably devout Christians have already dismantled the institutional resistance to such a step. Confusing the crucifix with the phoenix, and both with anti-institutionalism, these Christians will have the "church in diaspora" they so fervently seek. In their own version of the great return, the faithful few will be most literally encaved. In the catacombs once again, they will gather not to plan the conquest of an empire but to celebrate their chosenness. Meanwhile America will be left with a heritage of transcendence, but it will be an empty transcendence. Empty transcendence is a vacuum inviting content, and if it is not filled by particularist religion it will in all likelihood be filled by the modern state. Ideas of independence are not enough to resist this development. Institutions that lay claim to sovereignty, institutions of independence, are required. "The alternative to civil religion," Richardson writes, "is not mere Christian belief or faith in transcendence, but *ecclesiastical Christianity*. . . . Mere beliefs and faith in transcendence can be absorbed into a civil cult. There is nothing the church (or any one else) believes that cannot be woven into the state's mythology."

Richardson and other champions of particularism are not, I believe, appreciative enough of the positive need for public piety and of the church's role in sustaining it. Nor, apparently, do they recognize the possibility of the American experiment's revelatory and instrumental role in the coming of God's Kingdom.[8]

There are some urgent items for an agenda if the churches are to play their part in revitalizing and redirecting American public piety. The following list is far from exhaustive, but it is a partial response to the reasonable question, Where do we go from here?

The first item, and in many ways the most problematic, is theological Reconstruction. Of course it is not enough to decide it would be strategically advantageous to have a revival of religious nerve. Confidence is not something that can be picked up or set aside at convenience. It depends upon a renewed sense of security in the distinctiveness of Christian (and Jewish) existence and belief. That depends, in turn, upon a sustained, intelligent and passionate assertion of religious truth claims about human nature, history, the victory of life over death, and the struggle's final vindication in the coming of the Kingdom.

Prospects for such a theological reconstruction are uncertain at best. The religious literature that is still widely viewed as "advanced" and "exciting" is, for the most part, still floundering in antisocial subjectivity or else obsequiously accommodating to cultural moods, whether those moods be conservative, counter-cultural or revolutionary. Theologians such as Wolfhart Pannenberg, Karl Rahner and Jürgen Moltmann are frequently dismissed as being excessively "Germanic," as though, in distributing his gifts, the Spirit practices affirmative action along national lines. Perhaps we are still to a large extent dependent upon the Europeans because great theology emerges from great catastrophe, and Americans of this century have not experienced that. (If, on the other hand, that is the price to be paid, one might just as soon forego great American theology for a time.) Others say the people I have cited are preoccupied with system building, when everybody knows that Barth and Tillich were the last of the system builders. Now the celebration of the intellectually frivolous and irresponsible is endemic, further corroding the internal life of the churches and, in the larger community of reasonable discourse, confirming every reason given for not taking theology seriously.

My hope and very restrained expectation is that we will soon see signs of a major reaction against the theological abdication from which we have suffered in recent years. And this in part because the various dogmas and moods of the culture to which the churches have been accommodating are themselves increasingly discredited; in part because soon a great many people must become sated with the frivolities and fads of the neophiliacs (admittedly, I may underestimate people's appetite for that sort of thing); and in part because the sheer intellectual weight of the theological tradition cannot be forever denied.

An urgent concern is that the reaction not be reactionary. What we have learned about dialogue with the larger culture and about overcoming the prejudices so much part of past denominational securities must be assiduously nurtured. A more productive dialogue between church and culture, however, will be marked by a livelier dialectic. The church will not be inhibited in asserting that it has something to teach, as well as much to learn. While "the world may set the church's agenda," as it was commonly said until recently, the church will not be afraid to challenge what reigning culture brokers say the world is about. While ever open to the promise that God is indeed "doing a new thing" (Isa. 43), the church will be increasingly doubtful that the media are handling God's press relations. A legitimating "theology of" whatever movement, cause or idea made its debut last year will be immediately suspected of being the bought endorsement it most probably is (bought not for money but, much more insidiously, for the plaudits that come to the "relevant").

Without such a theological renaissance—the confidence that Thomas Aquinas is at least as likely a source of truth as Erik Erikson, and that the Eucharistic altar is at least as close to the sacred as the baths of the Esalen Institute—the churches will not have much to contribute to the shaping of public piety. Of course theological renewals cannot be ordered to schedule. We can, however, wait and work for them with holy impatience.

There are a number of public policy debates now going on which are closely related to public piety. Perhaps as the churches try to relate to them with intellectual rigor, we will be forced to recognize our theological weakness. Recognition could be a step toward remedy. Or, as some prefer to say, the reflective application to practice may produce a new orthopraxis (not bad jargon is the next best thing to no jargon).

There is, for example, the debate about the nature of human life as it is posed by the issues of abortion, "the right to die" and a veritable revolution in medical technology. Regardless of how one feels about the policy conclusions emerging from the 1973 Supreme Court decision on abortion, most churches are guilty of criminal neglect in not publicly challenging the intellectual and moral disaster that is the reasoning of the majority opinion. The decision is fraught with questions of ultimate concern treated as questions of mere technique and individual convenience. Similarly, questions being raised about reproduction and the definition of death pose issues of historic proportions. The operative public absent from debates over national security, especially as they touch on the ethics of changing nuclear policy. On these and related issues, there are of course the pacifist voices such as the Friends Service Committee and the Fellowship of Reconciliation. There are also the few Maoists, Che Guevaraists and sundry pop Marxists comforting one another in perpetual emergency committees and drawing salaries as second- or third-echelon bureaucrats in church-related social justice departments. And, of course, there are the professional blessers of the hardware of death, including, sad to say, most of the military chaplaincy and too many religious leaders who believe patriotism and militarism essentially conjoined.

The operative values in our society now are, as a result of the Vietnam experience, more strongly antimilitary. As a basic bias, this may be healthy enough. It is unfortunately combined, however, with a popular weariness with the discussion of war and peace, and a growing cynicism about the possibility of changing anything that really matters. The result may be that, just as public sentiment has become largely antimilitary, the militarists may capitalize on popular weariness and cynicism to exercise an increasingly free hand. A further irony is that, unless it is undertaken thoughtfully, increasing cuts in military spending, necessary though they be, may force greater dependence upon relatively "economical" nuclear weaponry. At present the churches are for all practical purposes absent from the debate over, for example, "destruction" and "deterrence" in U.S. nuclear policy and the meaning of "security" in a world such as ours.

Yet another issue in which the public piety and the churches as institutions have enormous stakes is related to social policy in the broadest sense. We have witnessed in this century a sharply rising awareness of the society's responsibility for meeting human needs. Problems that used to be attributed to individual laziness, the will of God or just bad luck have become the object of social policy. We can applaud this development, in which the churches played no little part. Accompanying this growing sense of society's responsibility, however, was a more ambiguous development, namely that programs reflecting the society's responsibility should be implemented primarily, if not exclusively, through the agencies of the state. This process escalated rapidly during the years of the New Deal and, with variations, continues to this day. There was a brand of conservatism that opposed the welfare state, as it was called, but the mainstream of liberal opinion, together with whatever radicalisms were around, was solidly supportive. Only in recent years have those who care deeply about the plight of the poor begun to reexamine the linkage between social responsibility and state implementation. In education this concern surfaced, for instance, in protest against the centralized control of the schools in New York City exercised by the teachers union, headed by Albert Shanker, now president of the nation-wide American Federation of Teachers. In antipoverty programs, the desire for decentralization was expressed in the much and unfairly derided provisions for "maximum feasible participation of the poor."

What is at stake in this question touches upon the very heart of American pluralism. A serious challenge is raised to the existence of what might be called intermediate structures, that is, all those structures that stand between the individual in his private life and the monster institutions of the society such as corporations, big unions and, above all, the state. In the field of welfare services, where many intermediate structures have been church-related, the churches have shown themselves to be excessively, and, one suspects, unreflectively, acquiescent in surrendering control—and in many cases whole structures—to the state.

One is mindful of Richardson's cautions about the importance of *institutionalized* diversity within the society. There are alternative ways of exercising responsibilities that indeed belong to the whole society, other than state implementation. While the state necessarily has the sole power of taxation, there is no necessity about its having the sole or even primary role in meeting the human needs for which such taxes are raised. Other approaches must be explored before the self-aggrandizing bureaucracy of government, reinforced by the fast increasing unionization of the fast increasing numbers of state employees, precludes alternatives. This issue should be sharply and urgently debated, first of all, for the sake of those for whom such programs are designed, notably the aged, children without homes and with special problems, drug addicts, newly released convicts and many, many others. Then for the sake of the myriad "natural communities" in American society which are weakened when the programs of caring are subsumed under the impersonal aegis of the state and could be strengthened by what has come to be called "community control."

With the broadest possible domestic and international consequences, a great debate is now under way regarding the ethics of equality. John Rawls' *A Theory of Justice,* which we discussed in a previous chapter, may well turn out to be the most important book on public ethics to have appeared in many years. Among intellectual journals and social theorists generally, sides are being taken and long-neglected value questions are being explored in the liveliest fashion. The voices of theologians and religious thinkers have been absent from the public debate to date. Rawls' contribution is that he raises so lucidly the ethical and religious assumptions in the conflict between a variety of capitalisms and socialisms, offering rigorously consistent arguments that emerge from the culturally dominant doctrines of man and the universe. The ethical theory advanced by Rawls and others has the most direct bearing both upon values of our society, and consequently of other societies, are being rapidly transformed, for better or for worse. Some choices, once made, may well be irreversible, or at least as irreversible as anything can be in history.

It is not that Christians are unaware of these issues. It is that few seem to have anything distinctively Christian to say about them. There are notable exceptions, but the general pattern is that scientists of all sorts come to bio-ethics centers eager for moral guidance from the religious traditions, only to be met by theologians and ethicists eager to be acknowledged as secular intellectuals.

On another issue: It is long past time for the churches to work at lifting the mantle of public piety from the public school system as it presently exists. The religious issues should be surfaced in, for example, the school's role in teaching, as the National Educational Association puts it, "moral and spiritual values." Whatever majority Protestantism perceived as the social needs for the public school mythology in the days of Horace Mann and John Dewey, those needs are largely irrelevant to the latter part of the twentieth century. Indeed, that mythology is dangerous; it is weakening familial and communal institutions and perpetuating no longer credible definitions of "religion" that are at the base of outmoded notions of the separation of church and state.

This does not mean an attack upon public schools although it will certainly and deliberately be misinterpreted that way in some quarters. When the issue of greater educational pluralism—through voucher payments to parents, for example—is raised, a vigorous reaction may be expected especially from an increasingly bureaucratized educational establishment. The churches can begin to address this whole issue by a thoughtful challenge to the definition of religion as it has evolved, in a confusedly zigzagged way, through years of Supreme Court decisions. In doing so, we must refuse to view the question of educational diversity as "a Catholic issue." While in this and other instances each part of the religious community has its own tradition of focused concerns, these are all issues confronting our common life. They are *our* issues, as Christians and as Americans.

The public piety is also in a state of confusion regarding matters of war and peace and the meaning of national security. The bifurcation between "doves" and "hawks," painfully pertinent to a contorted moment in our national life, must now be transcended. Christian realism must be reconstructed, for it cannot continue living on the sediment of Reinhold Niebuhr's contribution, nor can it be simply reasserted in the form that, much to Niebuhr's final regret, was misappropriated to give moral carte blanche to the present generation of war criminals still in high places.

Outside a small circle of specialists who seem determined to make the subject as arcane as possible, the voice of institutional religion has been domestic social policy and, perhaps more significantly, upon the "redistribution" of the world's wealth, or poverty, as the case may be.

This brief listing of issues concludes with the last-mentioned question of world poverty. On a par with the prevention of nuclear holocaust is the ethic that should guide American power in a hungry world. History and history's Lord are judging us on this question in a most singular way. On no issue even approaching its import is the public piety in such sorry disarray. The criteria of Matthew 25 are still in force, giving sufficient reason to tremble before the judgment that is to come. Meanwhile, foreign assistance is slashed, trade inequities multiply, multinational corporations are given a free hand and millions look forward to an early and wretched death, while most Americans sit by either in indifference or in a sense of impotence. The indifference the churches can challenge directly, the sense of impotence we can join with others in trying to overcome. Of course world development is a complicated subject, that is to say the obvious. We dare not, however, neglect compassion by pleading complexity. Compassion need not be patronizing, we need make no apologies for it; it is the recognition of human solidarity under judgment. Combined with justice, which is hope active in love, it is a beginning toward answers. It may be that there are fewer answers than we would like to think. But, in terms of the moral health of our society, compassion and a sense of justice *are* answers. If the churches do not take the lead in cultivating these answers, I fear no one will.

While we have argued that there probably is not now and should not be in the future an "American civil religion," the civil-religion debate has exposed anew a rich lode for religious reflection and action. Although discovered again only recently, thoughtful men and women know that the deposits are as old as society itself. One hopes they will not be hastily stripmined and then abandoned. There are pits and passages that have been intricately wrought by many who have been here before us. Theologians, ethicists, politicians, social scientists and religious leaders must go exploring together, stubbornly calling into question one another's angle of vision.

As Christians and as Americans we seek God's word and will in a time and place not necessarily of our choosing but certainly of our trial. It is probably not the definitive time and place, surely not the best time and place, but it is our time and place, and his with us. It is a time of many times. A time for dancing, even if it be to the songs of Zion in a foreign land; a time for walking together, and in solitude; a time for marching in momentary triumphs, and in defiance of impending defeats; a time for crawling through hopes shattered and dreams betrayed; and then a time for falling to the final enemy—but not before, through our tears, we glimpse the New Jerusalem and hail it from afar, knowing it is all time toward home.

Notes

CHAPTER 1

1. Frank Kermode, *The Sense of an Ending: Studies in the Theory of Fiction* (Oxford University Press, 1967), p. 23.
2. Peter F. Drucker, *The Age of Discontinuity* (Harper & Row, 1968). Viewed in terms of the larger discussion of contemporary American society, it might be observed that Drucker's analysis, contra his title, underscores continuities.
3. Sydney E. Ahlstrom, *A Religious History of the American People* (Yale University Press, 1972), p. 1094.
4. Sydney Ahlstrom, "The Radical Turn in Theology and Ethics," *The Annals,* January 1970.
5. Ahlstrom himself does end up on a more hopeful note, suggesting that current confusions may in fact lead to a "vindicating of the idealism" that has so marked the American experience (*Religious History*, p. 1096).
6. Perhaps the most impressive statement of "liberation theology" is Custavo Gutierrez, *A Theology of Liberation* (Orbus, 1973). See also, "Liberation Theology and the Captivities of Jesus" by Richard John Neuhaus in *Worldview,* June 1973.
7. For a more thorough discussion of the crypto-liberal attitude toward revolutionism, see "The Thorough Revolutionary" by Richard John Neuhaus in *Movement and Revolution* (Doubleday, 1970).
8. A detailed development of this critique of Charles Reich is in "Dreaming Ahead" by Janet Welt Smith in *Worldview,* August 1973.
9. Peter Berger elaborates this point in his essay in *Movement and Revolution.*
10. Peter Schrag, *The End of the American Future* (Simon & Schuster, 1974).
11. Elisabeth Kübler-Ross, *On Death and Dying* (London: Tavistock, 1970).

CHAPTER 2

1. David Halberstam, *The Best and the Brightest* (Random House, 1969).
2. Daniel Patrick Moynihan, "Peace: Some thoughts on the 1960's and 1970's," *The Public Interest,* Summer 1973.
3. For this idea of a "usable" past and its relation to a "usable" future, I am indebted to Martin E. Marty, *The Search for a Usable Future* (Harper & Row, 1969).

CHAPTER 3

1. Lowell Streiker and Gerald Strober, *Religion and the New Majority* (Association, 1972).
2. Michael Novak, *The Rise of the Unmeltable Ethnics* (Macmillan, 1972).
3. Dean Kelley, *Why Conservative Churches Are Growing* (Harper & Row, 1972).
4. Richard M. Scammon and Ben J. Wattenberg, *The Real Majority* (Coward, 1970).
5. Novak and I carried on an exchange on this subject in the December 1972 and January 1973 issues of *Worldview*. One of the chief difficulties in his argument is related to the definition of *ethnic*. In addition, it seems to me to be unhelpful to pretend that the divisions of the past can be uncritically celebrated, as though the center will hold as long as you pay it no mind. It is also a mistake to underestimate what is perhaps the most universally cherished value among "ethnics," namely the value of becoming "American." This point has been well made by Andrew Greeley in a study of patriotism among Catholic ethnics (*Worldview*, February 1973). Novak is no doubt right in saying that American public piety has frequently been portrayed in a narrow way that reinforces the "WASP hegemony" against which he so passionately battles. The hope which I share with Novak is that the American experiment will be enriched as the "Kowalczyks" and the "Smiths" really begin to collaborate with a more mutual sensitivity in restating the many meanings of America. It is that hoped-for collaboration, rather than a celebration of a cacophany of ethnic chauvinisms, that makes the "ethnic renaissance" so promising.
6. That the author is Senior Editor of the last-named magazine no doubt has something to do with the bias implicit in that "even."
7. The concept of "status politics" and its connection with anti-intellectualism is developed by Hofstadter and others in *The New American Right,* edited by Daniel Bell (Criterion Books, 1955).
8. Kevin Phillips, *The Emerging Republican Majority* (Arlington House, 1969).
9. *The New York Times,* April 23, 1972.
10. For a further treatment of this exclusion of "ideological resources" see my *In Defense of People* (Macmillan, 1971) especially Chapter Five, "In the Absence of a Vision—Survival."
11. The McGovern defeat resulted, I believe, from a combination of incompetence and massive bad luck, beginning with McGovern's betrayal by his first running mate, Sen. Thomas Eagleton. But the effort itself was aimed in the right direction.
12. Jeffrey Hadden, *The Gathering Storm in the Churches* (Doubleday, 1969).
13. Rodney Stark and Charles Y. Glock, *American Piety: The Nature of Religious Commitment* (University of California Press, 1968).
14. *In Defense of People.*
15. Sociologist Greeley, himself a priest, has published extensively on this subject. For an introduction to his approach and findings, see *New Horizons for the Priesthood* (Sheed and Ward, 1970).

CHAPTER 4

1. Peter Berger et al., *The Homeless Mind* (Random House, 1973).
2. Ibid., p. 202.
3. *In Defense of People* (Macmillan, 1971).
4. For an elaboration of this point, see Peter Berger, *Pyramids of Sacrifice* (Basic Books, 1975).

5. "The end of ideology" is, of course, a phrase associated with Daniel Bell and his 1960 book of that title. I am aware that Professor Bell would take issue with this depiction of his argument (see his lengthy discussion of what he meant by "the end of ideology" in *The Coming of Post-Industrial Society* [Basic Books, 1973]. Professor Bell's original intentions and reconsiderations aside, however, his argument was generally and, I think, understandably received in the terms I suggest.
6. Sidney E. Mead, *The Lively Experiment* (Harper & Row, 1963).

CHAPTER 5

1. Quoted in Robert Handy, *A Christian America* (Oxford University Press, 1971).
2. Ibid.
3. Quoted in Sydney Ahlstrom, *A Religious History of the American People* (Yale University Press, 1972), p. 147.
4. Martin E. Marty, *Righteous Empire* (Dial, 1970).
5. See John Murray Cuddihy, *The Ordeal of Civility* (Basic Books, 1974), especially Chapter 22, "Jews, Blacks, and the Cold War at the Top."
6. I am indebted to Elliott Wright for suggesting some of the distinctions to be made in "styles of doomsaying."
7. *Commentary* magazine, which has become increasingly reactive in recent years, has been especially vigorous in expanding the concept of "anti-Americanism" in order to criticize almost everything of which it disapproves. It is, as I suggest, an overexpansion.
8. Helmut Schoeck, *Envy* (Harcourt, Brace & World, 1969).

CHAPTER 6

1. Frances Fitzgerald, *Fire in the Lake* (Atlantic, Little, Brown, 1972).
2. The transcript of Mr. Kissinger's Senate confirmation hearings as Secretary of State are especially illuminating on this score.
3. Novak, *The Rise of the Unmeltable Ethnics* (Macmillan, 1972), p. 20.
4. For this observation I am indebted to Prof. Wilson Carey McWilliams.
5. For a discussion of the connections—or lack of connections—between crowding and social ills, see William Whyte, *The Last Landscape* (Doubleday, 1968).
6. Quoted in John Brooke, *King George III* (McGraw-Hill, 1972), p. 167.
7. Quoted in Richard Hofstadter, *The American Political Tradition* (Knopf, 1973), p. 212.
8. In Noam Chomsky, *American Power and the New Mandarins* (Pantheon, 1969), p. 289.
9. In Richard Barnet, *Intervention and Revolution* (World, 1968), p. 79.
10. Ibid., p. 13.
11. J. Hector St. John de Crèvecoeur, *Letters from an American Farmer* (Signet Classics, 1963), p. 64.

CHAPTER 7

1. Daniel Bell, *The Coming of Post-Industrial Society* (Basic Books, 1973), p. 480.
2. See the author's "The War, the Churches and Civil Religion," *The Annals*, January 1970.

3. The best survey and bibliography of Pannenberg's work is E. Frank Tupper, *The Theology of Wolfhart Pannenberg* (Westminster, 1973). The most readable introduction to Pannenberg's own writing is *Theology and the Kingdom of God* (Westminster, 1969), edited by Richard John Neuhaus.

4. William Stringfellow, *An Ethic for Christians and Other Aliens in a Strange Land* (World, 1973). See, for example, p. 114 for the summary conclusion that intimations of Jerusalem in the American experiment are "the essence of the doctrine of the Antichrist."

5. Jacques Ellul, *The Meaning of the City* (Eerdmans, 1970), p. 37.

6. In Theodore Roszak, *The Making of a Counter Culture* (Anchor, 1969), p. 118.

7. Two-kingdoms thinking has its counterpart in other religious traditions. The heart of the idea is always a determined dichotomy between the sacred and the secular and the ethic relevant to each. Apologists for any tradition are inclined to view its ethical failures as "distortions" of, for example, "true" Lutheranism, or "true" Roman Catholicism or "true" Methodism. Such reasoning, however, fails to take seriously that each tradition is an *historical* phenomenon and its "essence" cannot be separated from its empirical form.

8. R. V. Sampson, *The Discovery of Peace* (Pantheon, 1973), p. 200.

9. See, for example, the essays by Martin J. Buss and Kendrick Grobel in *Theology as History* (Harper & Row, 1967), edited by James Robinson and John Cobb.

10. Quoted in a letter to the author from Abraham Joshua Heschel.

11. See Gutierrez, *A Theology of Liberation* (Orbis, 1973), especially pp. 153–167.

12. Roland Bainton, *Here I Stand* (Abingdon, 1950), p. 303.

13. For a fuller explication of the eschatological significance of the Christ event, see Wolfhart Pannenberg, *Jesus-God and Man* (Westminster, 1968).

CHAPTER 8

1. Augustine, *Confessions,* xi, 14.

2. Alfred North Whitehead, *The Concept of Nature* (Cambridge University Press), p. 73.

3. Pannenberg, *Theology and the Kingdom of God,* p. 62.

4. There is, of course, no reason in principle why God could not be addressed as "Mother" and referred to with female pronouns. Christianity, however, is not a bundle of principles but a timed gathering of historical particularities. Among such particularities is the masculine world and conceptual framework which shaped Jesus' thought. The images used by Jesus can be supplemented but cannot be supplanted. Our inability to abandon masculine imagery is, therefore, not a question of sexism but of Christology.

5. See, for example, "A View from Another Country" by John W. Holmes in *The Foreign Affairs Kaleidoscope,* Special Studies No. 214, Council on Religion and International Affairs, 1974.

6. Nathan Scott, *Three American Moralists* (Notre Dame, 1974), pp. 22, 37.

7. A. D. Lindsay, *The Modern Democratic State* (Oxford University Press, 1962), Vol. I, p. 163.

8. Hofstadter, *American Political Tradition,* p. 25.

9. Robert Benne and Philip Hefner, *Defining America* (Fortress, 1973). The phrase "thwarting the future" is theirs.

10. See Peter Berger, *Rumor of Angels* (Doubleday, 1969).

CHAPTER 9

1. Philippe Jullian, *D'Annunzio* (Viking, 1971). And Martin Green, *The von Richthofen Sisters* (Basic Books, 1973). The latter is especially instructive on the connection between cultural decadence and political authoritarianism.
2. Michael Harrington, *Fragments of the Century* (Saturday Review, 1972).
3. Oswald Spengler, *The Decline of the West* (Knopf, 1926), p. 187ff.
4. Robert Heilbroner, *An Inquiry Into the Human Prospect* (Norton, 1973).
5. See "The Thorough Revolutionary," *Movement and Revolution* (Doubleday, 1970).

CHAPTER 10

1. Walter Rauschenbusch, *The Righteousness of the Kingdom* (Abingdon, 1968), p. 282.
2. Ibid., p. 284.
3. Ibid., p. 28.
4. Ibid., p. 279.
5. Ibid., p. 188.
6. Ibid., p. 132.
7. Norman Cohn, *The Pursuit of the Millennium* (Oxford, 1970), p. 187ff.
8. Ibid., p. 234.
9. Mircea Eliade, *Cosmos and History-The Myth of the Eternal Return* (Harper, 1959) and *The Sacred and the Profane* (Harper, 1959), especially Chapter II.
10. Bryan Wilson, *Magic and the Millennium* (Harper & Row, 1973).

CHAPTER 11

1. Quoted in William Leiss, *The Domination of Nature* (George Braziller, 1972), p. 23.
2. Leiss, ibid., pp. 49–50.
3. Ibid., Chapter 2. It should be noted that this connection between holiness and the ordering of nature is strongly present in the thought of many Christian theologians, particularly in Thomas Aquinas.
4. Ibid., p. 68.
5. Ibid., p. 71.
6. For an explication of this tendency of Marxists to engage in radical revisionism for the sake of maintaining Marxist orthodoxy, see the author's "The Pilgrimage of Michael Harrington," *Worldview*, May 1974.

CHAPTER 12

1. Ernest Lee Tuveson, *Redeemer Nation* (University of Chicago Press, 1968).
2. Ibid., p. 87.
3. Ibid., p. 85.
4. See Tuveson on Adams, pp. 20ff.

5. In "Profile of a Theologian," *Theology and the Kingdom of God* (Westminster, 1969).
6. See Max Stackhouse's introduction to Rauschenbusch, *The Righteousness of the Kingdom,* (Abingdon, 1968).

CHAPTER 13

1. Ludwig Ott, *Fundamentals of Catholic Dogma* (Herder, 1955), pp. 35ff.
2. Abraham Joshua Heschel, *Man Is Not Alone* (Farrar Straus, 1951), pp. 5–6.
3. Pannenberg, *Theology as History* (Harper & Row, 1967), p. 28.
4. Jaroslav Pelikan, *The Spirit of Eastern Christendom* (Chicago, 1974), pp. 14–16.
5. Van Harvey, *The Historian and the Believer* (Macmillan, 1966).
6. Ibid., p. 64.
7. Ibid., p. 158.
8. Ibid., p. 282.
9. Ibid., p. 104.
10. Robert L. Wilken, *The Myth of Christian Beginnings* (Doubleday, 1971).
11. Ibid., p. 61.
12. Ibid., p. 205.
13. Ibid., p. 206.

CHAPTER 14

1. Tuveson, *Redeemer Nation,* pp. 102–103.
2. John Rawls, *A Theory of Justice* (Harvard, 1971).
3. Ibid., p. 303.
4. Ibid., p. 302.
5. Ibid., p. 28.
6. Ibid., 28–29.
7. Ibid., p. 121.
8. Ibid., p. 121.
9. Ibid., p. 167.
10. Ibid., p. 168.
11. Ibid., p. 176.
12. Ibid., p. 143.
13. Schoeck, *Envy* (Harcourt, Brace & World, 1969).
14. Rawls, p. 583.
15. Ibid., p. 439.
16. Ibid., p. 441.
17. There are many other problems with Rawls' thesis. Walter Kaufmann, for example, argues persuasively that one cannot endorse distributive justice without also endorsing retributive justice, with all its nasty overtones (Kaufmann, *Without Guilt and Justice* [Wyden, 1973]). Much of Rawls' theorizing would also seem to be irrelevant in that it is conceptually limited to a type of self-contained society that probably exists nowhere in the world and certainly cannot accommodate the facts of global diversity. It is therefore of little use in precisely the area in which we need most urgently to be thinking about distributive justice, namely in the distribution of wealth in a hungry world.
18. Rawls, p. 536.
19. Ibid., p. 211.
20. Ibid., p. 211.

21. Ibid., p. 421.
22. Ibid., p. 423.
23. Ibid., p. 587.

CHAPTER 15

1. Quoted in John Sisk, "The Fear of Affluence," *Commentary,* June 1974.
2. Karl Popper, *The Logic of Scientific Discovery* (Hutchinson, 1959), p. 111.
3. Quoted in Michael Sharratt, "Popper on Knowledge," *Clergy Review,* June 1974.
4. See Pannenberg, *Theology and the Kingdom of God* Chapter III.

CHAPTER 16

1. Robert Handy, *A Christian America* (Oxford, 1971).
2. Hofstadter, *Anti-Intellectualism in American Life* (Knopf, 1963), p. 408.
3. H. L. Mencken, "On Being an American," *Prejudices: Third Series* (Knopf, 1922).
4. Quoted in Sandy Vogelgesang, *The Long Dark Night of the Soul* (Harper & Row, 1974), p. 56.
5. Richard E. Morgan, *The Supreme Court and Religion* (Free Press, 1972).

CHAPTER 17

1. For details of "the prisoners' dilemma," see Rawls, *A Theory of Justice,* p. 269.
2. Pannenberg, *Theology and the Kingdom of God* (Westminster, 1969), p. 108.
3. Quoted in Tuveson, *Redeemer Nation* (University of Chicago Press, 1968), p. 75.
4. Pannenberg, *Theology and the Kingdom of God,* p. 110.
5. Ibid., p. 111.
6. For an argument in favor of America's autarkic possibilities, see Peter Passell and Leonard Ross, *The Retreat from Riches* (Viking, 1972).
7. For example, B. Bruce-Biggs, "Against the Neo-Malthusians," *Commentary,* July 1974.

CHAPTER 18

1. Pannenberg, *Theology and the Kingdom of God,* p. 123.
2. An almost classic statement on the relation between law and ethics is H. L. A. Hart, *The Concept of Law* (Oxford, 1961). For more recent discussions, see Harold J. Berman, *The Interaction of Law and Religion* (Abingdon, 1974), or *Religion and Morality,* edited by Gene Outka and John P. Reeder (Anchor, 1973).
3. *The Chicago Declaration,* edited by Ronald J. Sider (Creation House, 1974).
4. Eugene Genovese, *Roll, Jordan, Roll: The World the Slaves Made* (Pantheon, 1974).
5. Boyd C. Shafer, *Faces of Nationalism* (Harcourt Brace, 1972), offers a thoughtful survey of the varieties and strengths of modern nationalisms.
6. Pannenberg, *Theology and the Kingdom of God,* p. 125.
7. Ibid., p. 126.

CHAPTER 19

1. Martin E. Marty, "A Nation of Behavers," unpublished paper delivered at American Academy of Religion, Chicago, 1973.
2. *American Civil Religion,* edited by Russell E. Richey and Donald G. Jones (Harper, 1974), offers the best summary of the discussion to date.
3. Ibid., p. 5–6.
4. Will Herberg, *Protestant, Catholic, Jew: An Essay in American Religious Sociology* (Anchor, 1960).
5. Clifford Geertz, "Religion as a Culture System," in *The Religious Situation 1968,* edited by Donald R. Cutler (Beacon, 1968), and Thomas Luckmann, *The Invisible Religion* (Macmillan, 1967).
6. Andrew Greeley, *Unsecular Man* (Schocken, 1972).
7. The five-part distinction is adapted from John F. Wilson, "The Status of 'Civil Religion' in America," in *The Religion of the Republic,* edited by Elwyn A. Smith (Fortress, 1971).
8. W. Lloyd Warner, "An American Sacred Ceremony," in *American Life: Dream and Reality* (University of Chicago Press, 1953).
9. Sydney Ahlstrom, "Requiem for Patriotic Piety," *Worldview,* August 1972.
10. Among more recent discussions of the sacral character of the presidency is Michael Novak, *Choosing Our King* (Macmillan, 1973).
11. Studies by Richard B. Dierenfeld *(Religion in American Public Schools),* cited by Martin E. Marty, op. cit.
12. Wilson Carey McWilliams, *The Idea of Fraternity in America* (University of California Press, 1973), p. 108.
13. See John F. Wilson, "A Historian's Approach to Civil Religion" in Richey and Jones, *American Civil Religion.*
14. Ibid., p. 121–122.
15. Quoted in Marty paper, op. cit.
16. Richey and Jones, pp. 18ff.
17. James Sellers, *Public Ethics* (Harper & Row, 1970).

CHAPTER 20

1. Quoted in Richey and Jones, p. 84.
2. Robert Bellah, *The Broken Covenant* (Seabury, 1975), p. 258. Bellah offers a more positive assessment of the viability of "empty transcendence."
3. Ibid., see especially the final chapter.
4. For a discussion of the distinctive ways in which various religions construct reality and their implications for personal and social life, see John B. Cobb, *The Structure of Christian Existence* (Westminster, 1967).
5. Anton C. Zijderveld, *The Abstract Society* (Doubleday, 1970).
6. Herbert Richardson, "Civil Religion in Theological Perspective," in Richey and Jones.
7. Frank Patton, "Religion by Government Permission," *Worldview,* November 1974.
8. There are elements of a more positive appraisal of these possibilities in Richardson's earlier *Toward An American Theology* (Harper & Row, 1967).

Name Index

229